Steven Primrose-Smith was born in Darwen, near Blackburn, in 1970. He managed to escape in 1996 and has since lived in Austria, Spain and the Isle of Man. He now lives somewhere between the latter and the Costa del Sol. From the Open University, he has a BA(Hons) in English Language and Philosophy and a BSc(Hons) in Mathematics. He also has an MA in Philosophy from University of Wales, Trinity Saint David. His first book, *No Place Like Home, Thank God*, describing his three-year, 22,000 mile bicycle ride around Europe, is an Amazon Bestseller.

Also by Steven Primrose-Smith

FICTION

GEORGE PEARLY IS A MISERABLE OLD SOD

NON-FICTION

NO PLACE LIKE HOME, THANK GOD

HUNGRY FOR MILES

CYCLING ACROSS EUROPE ON £1 A DAY

Steven Primrose-Smith

Rosebery Publications

First published in 2015 by Rosebery Publications
1 Perwick Rise, Port St Mary, Isle of Man

Copyright © 2015 Steven Primrose-Smith
All rights reserved.
steven@primrose-smith.com

ISBN-13: 978-1519327260
ISBN-10: 1519327269

Except in the United States of America,
this book is sold subject to the condition
that it shall not, by way of trade or otherwise,
be lent, re-sold, hired out, or otherwise circulated
without the publisher's prior consent in any form
of binding or cover other than that in which it is
published and without a similar condition including
this condition being imposed on the subsequent purchaser.

Names have been changed where appropriate.

More information and photographs can be found at
www.RideAndSeek2015.com.

To Ken,
wherever you are.

Table of Contents

Author's Note..9

Acknowledgements..11

Chapter 1: Sorry? You're Doing What?........................13

Chapter 2: Let's Get Ready to Trundle.........................21

Chapter 3: The Leaving of Liverpool............................33

Chapter 4: The King of Pain..45

Chapter 5: A Smack in the Face....................................75

Chapter 6: Days of Easy Gorging................................100

Chapter 7: Coasting to France.....................................124

Chapter 8: Lost in the Ker-Zone..................................136

Chapter 9: Naked in the Cemetery.............................162

Chapter 10: Farmers with Guns..................................175

Chapter 11: The End of France....................................191

Chapter 12: The Way of St James................................203

Chapter 13: The Valley of Fruit...................................242

Chapter 14: Led Astray by Teens.................................265

Chapter 15: Filling a Void...296

Appendix 1: Gear..305

Appendix 2: Costs...308

Author's Note

Some readers want loads of juicy technical details about the bike and the gear that was carried; others want none of that boring rubbish. To try to please both parties I've omitted this information from the text but included an appendix listing everything I took with me.

I've also taken a similar approach regarding how we spent our budget. Listing every supermarket transaction in the text would have been unbearably dull, but if you want to see what we each spent, that too is provided in an appendix. I have also kept a running total of what I alone spent at the end of each chapter.

You will notice this book contains no photos. I could have added them but their inclusion would have made this book more expensive for you. I figured you'd prefer to keep the cash in your pocket and view the photos on the project's website. It contains far more images than could ever have been included within these pages. If you want to see them, they are freely available at www.RideAndSeek2015.com. I hope you enjoy them.

Cheers,
Steven

Acknowledgements

Many people helped us on our way, either before we set off or while on the road. Thank you to Richard at *Bikestyle* in Douglas, King of Crisps Geraint, the folks at *Ty'r Acrau* farm, lovely Raminta Urbonaviciene, John Davis at *Glynteg Farm*, my wonderful nurse Melanie in Swansea, *Wheelies* and *Schmoos* also in Swansea, our hosts at *Bevene Fawr Farm*, Rob and Cath at *Gelli Farm*, everyone at *Seabank Farm* and *Gilslake Farm*, John at *Ivy Cottage*, Eric at *Eastbury Farm* and Sandra at *The Butcher's Arms*, Campbell and Catherine Orr in Ilfracombe, Maureen and Dave "Goody Bag" Simmonds, *The Bike Shop* in Tiverton, *Lynstone Campsite*, Neil and family in Trevone, everyone at *Penmarlan Caravan and Camping Park* including Mark, Jackie and Mark, the folks at *Higher Roslin Farm*, Steve at *Highwinds*, all at *Eweleaze Farm*, Susie and Mark near La Rochelle, and Anne and James in Viseu.

Thank you to everyone who donated to *Action Against Hunger* on behalf of our ride. Your valuable contributions are helping those people for whom living on one pound a day is not a choice.

Finally, I'd like to thank everyone who followed us on *Facebook*, on our *Ride And Seek 2015* page. Frequent lack of power meant we were unable to post as often as we would've liked but your words of encouragement helped us when bellies were empty, legs were aching and arses were tender. Thank you.

Chapter 1: Sorry? You're Doing What?

I first met Ken on a mountainside in southern Spain. Something immediately struck me as odd about him, perhaps because he was sitting on the ground eating huge handfuls of grass.

It was late spring and I was out walking with my mate Boz. The day was hot and we spied a crumbling *cortijo* ahead, a perfect place to shelter from the sun while we ate our lunch. As we turned into its shade, we spotted a lonely figure sprawled on the ground. Ken was the man Sarah Palin imagines when she thinks of Jesus Christ: tall, white, blue-eyed, bearded and with brown hair past his shoulders. All that was missing were the stigmata and the automatic weapon.

He had taken us by surprise. Generationally speaking, the Spanish have only recently freed themselves from having to lug basketloads of fish up and over these mountain passes. They have no desire to wander them now for pleasure. It was rare to see anyone else walking in those hills. If you did see an elderly Spanish gent roaming this area, perhaps no one had told him the Civil War was over.

My first thought was danger. Despite Ken's saintly appearance, his grass-eating seemed to suggest he was, well, some kind of nutter. But Boz was there to protect me. He might have only come up to my knees, and I'd never seen him have a fight, but he always gave the impression that if something kicked off he'd have your back. Besides, I'm a lover, not a fighter. Or a coward as we're usually known.

"Are you alright?" I asked Ken.

He realised we were there for the first time and then uttered a really quite beautiful response.

"Oh hello," he said. "I'm just gorging myself on this wild rocket."

Focussed on the laboratory-made bread and processed ham in our rucksacks, we hadn't noticed the entire hillside was covered in this free-for-the-taking, small, green leaf. I pulled up a piece and tasted it. It was deliciously peppery.

Ken asked if he could walk with us. He may not actually have been eating grass but there were other aspects of his appearance that might still have placed him in the Nutter category. But there was something about him that fascinated me, not least because he had an annual income of just £1,000 and it was on this meagre sum that he lived.

He spent his summers wild-camping on various beaches on the south coast of England and had decided to enjoy this particular winter in Spain. He would occasionally help out a farmer near the secluded beach he'd selected as his temporary home but in return would only receive his lunch. He didn't need to be paid. With a dinner inside him and a free pitch on the beach, he rarely needed money, except to fly him and his bike from one place to the next. Ken was the most relaxed man I ever met. He made *Scooby-Doo*'s Shaggy seem dangerously over-stressed.

Not everything was perfect in Ken's life though. With his long hair, sun-bleached clothes and tattered trainers he looked every inch the typical hippy, and yet although his lifestyle meant he frequently brushed up against the hippy community, he struggled to make friends with them. He didn't do drugs, hardly drank and wasn't into the New Age spiritual bollocks and positive energy, man, that usually went with the territory. He was lacking meaningful human company. He had fewer friends than Katie Hopkins.

Although Spain's parched countryside offered limited

resources, he knew his nuts, berries and mushrooms and foraged frequently in the UK, availing himself of nature's free larder. As we walked, he'd occasionally point out something edible that we'd taken to be just another weed.

We agreed to meet him at a particular spot the next weekend for another walk.

"We'll see you there at nine," I said.

"Hmm," he replied, looking uncomfortable. "I don't have a watch." He thought for a moment. "No problem. I'll just go there when it gets light and wait."

Imagine that! A life without clocks, a world where time has no meaning.

After our second walk Boz and I took Ken to a local restaurant in the little village of Maro. It was a tiny place but, this being Spain, it was bright and loud, full of people and a blaring telly nobody was watching. I suddenly felt like we'd done something cruel, as though we'd taken a puppy and thrown it on to a motorway. Ken was visibly uneasy with the din, the scraping chairs, the screaming kids, the raucous TV quiz host, living as he did his peaceful, outdoor life. He may have been rewarded with a free dinner, a pint or two and a conversation but I felt he would've preferred to be on the beach in his own world and not in our noisy, crap-filled one.

Spring had already sprung. Not long afterwards, Ken moved on to his next location. He gave me his email address but he only checked his account every six months and we lost contact. The last I heard, he was living in a cave on the island of La Gomera.

Although Ken was gone, he and his lifestyle were often in my thoughts, especially when I looked at my dwindling bank account. The three-year cycling adventure that had taken me all over Europe (see my book *No Place Like Home, Thank God* if you're interested) had devastated my funds.

Could I live like Ken? Would I be happy? I'd no idea, but

these were the questions that floated through my brain whenever I visited my online bank account and stared at its tiny, barely positive numbers.

If the idea of foraging holds any appeal there's a book you really should read. It's called *The Wild Life: A Year of Living on Wild Food* by John Lewis-Stempel. For a full calendar year the author attempts to survive purely on the food he's caught, killed or collected himself. Under his own rules he's not allowed to spend any money on anything to eat or drink.

Lewis-Stempel has an advantage that most of us don't: He has farmland on which he can legally shoot rabbits and birds. You might think the book's premise sounds dull. After all, it's about a bloke taking potshots at pigeons and describing how he renders his own fat for frying. But it's not dull at all. It's wonderfully inspiring and, after reading it, Ken popped back into my head.

So here we had one man spending no money on food and drink and surviving for an entire year and another, Ken, who foraged here and there and had a daily budget of around £3, using which he also managed to move from country to country. And then there was me, aching to do another long distance bike ride and with very limited funds. An idea was beginning to form.

There's a charitable challenge you may have heard of called *Live Below The Line*. In fact, you may have taken part. Tens of thousands do so each year and the number is growing. The idea is that, for five days, from a particular Monday at the end of April to the following Friday, you can only spend £5 in total on all your food and drink.

The purpose of the challenge is twofold: You get sponsored and raise funds for your chosen organisation. But you also get a little taster of the challenges of living on the same tiny amount as a very large percentage of the world's poorest people, those who live below the poverty line.

The downside is that during the week's event *Facebook* fills with yet more photos of people's dinners, except instead of the boastful restaurant feasts that normally get posted, now all the meals look insipidly vegan and sit sadly on a little saucer to make them look bigger than they actually are.

The challenge isn't perfect – it has some strange rules – but as a way to expand your consciousness about a genuine world problem, it's a great concept. And if you're a bit of a chubber like me, it's a good way to lose a bit of weight too.

Importantly, under the rules of the *Live Below The Line* challenge, your daily pound only covers food and drink. So you can drive to work in your petrol-powered car, pop out at lunchtime and buy yourself a sexy, purple cardigan and visit the cinema in the evening (but no popcorn, mind). None of these things is included in your weekly fund. You also get to store in your double-door fridge the minuscule weekly ration of cheese you decided to buy and bake it in your beautiful oven, both of which use electricity that would have to be included in your weekly budget were you really living below the poverty line. Except you wouldn't have a fridge or an oven or a car and you'd probably be working too hard to find time to go to the cinema.

And then my idea finally crystallized. How about a bike ride that lived below the line? It would have a daily budget of one pound but, to make it more of a challenge, the one pound would have to cover all day-to-day costs. As well as food and drink, it would pay for the fuel to cook the food, accommodation along the way, all bike consumables like tyres and inner tubes (but not structural repairs, as these costs should be spread across the lifetime of the bike) and any toiletries we purchased en route. It would also have to cover any visits to the cinema and all the sexy, purple cardigans, but

I doubted I'd require either of those.

So what, you might say? Others have made trips – long ones too – entirely for free, for no pounds at all a day. And there's you, Steven, with your massive one pound, you fat, greedy sod. You might tell me Tom Allen managed a three-week trip from Penzance to Edinburgh with no money at all. Or you could say George Mahood set off from Land's End with nothing but his pair of Union Jack underpants and made it to John o'Groats. Hell, Paul Smith, better known as the *Twitchhiker*, got around the world for free. Surely, Steven, if you have a *whole pound* to spend each and every day then you'll probably end up getting drunk every night on champagne and snorting cocaine off prostitutes' arses.

The reality is that unless you have money, or unless you are going to forage *absolutely all* your calories, then you are going to have to resort to blagging. Or begging. Or stealing. Paul Smith tweeted his way to a whole planetload of free flights in a huge blagfest. It's just a pity he didn't seem to enjoy anywhere once he arrived.

And, in the long run, or even the medium run, blagging isn't sustainable. Twitter eventually gets bored of stumping up for your holiday. You need a constant supply of willing victims, er, donors to pay for every snack or meal. Your existence would be reduced to a demoralising series of begging sessions, or you'd simply be taking advantage of the generosity of others. But if, on the other hand, you could move from A to B for very little, without the need of anyone else's constant financial help, then your travel becomes sustainable. It becomes possible to keep moving indefinitely. Perhaps not sensationally, like the *Twitchhiker*, but genuinely, like Ken.

But surely cycling and foraging must have been attempted before? A scour of the internet turned up a single, credible attempt. Vin Cox, the man who once held the Round-The-

World record by circumnavigating the globe by bicycle in a wearying 163 days, is a keen forager. He tried to cycle from his home in the south-west of England to Scotland, surviving purely by foraging. On Day Two he was so hungry he had to buy some biscuits. Later on, after scooping up some tasty-looking roadkill, Cox fell sick and wisely abandoned the project entirely. So if a seasoned hunter-gatherer like Vin Cox couldn't do an entirely foraged trip – even one that lasted just a few days – then an idiot like me with no foraging knowledge whatsoever would really need that pound coin to fall back on, especially because of the length of the route I'd decided.

And what was my route? My thinking went something like this: What meal is tasty, provides protein and is based around a creature stupid and ugly enough that I wouldn't feel bad about killing it? That's easy. Fish! Where are the fish? In the sea. Where should I cycle? By the sea. Where was my bike currently living? The Isle of Man. Where is a nice place to spend winter? Near my girlfriend, Nina, on the south coast of Spain. And the route was born. I would cycle from the Isle of Man to Gibraltar, the Rock being where the fish-filled Atlantic ends and the depleted Mediterranean begins, and hug the coast of England, Wales, France, Spain and Portugal, a distance of approximately 3,700 miles. To conserve calories I'd limit my daily cycling distance to 37 miles so the trip would last a nice, round 100 days and be filled with millions of delicious, little fishes.

That was it. I had my plan and I decided to announce it to family and friends and, occasionally, to strangers. My mum's reaction was entirely predictable: I was going to die. Obviously. According to her crystal ball I've been going to die on every bike ride I've ever started. She didn't know from which link of the food chain my death would pounce, whether from a poisonous mushroom or some toxic berry or a manky roadkill badger but sure as salmonella-tainted eggs are eggs, it'd kill me. So I had that to look forward to.

With everyone else, I was met with one of three reactions. The one I wasn't expecting was a kind of blank stare. I could see some sort of computation going on behind the eyes but all that processing didn't amount to a statement or a question. I didn't know how to take that and so I didn't push it.

Everyone else was split down the middle. Half of people, and this was mostly but not exclusively men, said how they'd absolutely love to do something like this – oh, the freedom and the fishing! – but, y'know, there's the wife to think about, and the kids, and the job. And couldn't alcohol be exempted from the budget? And they weren't that keen on the camping, to be honest. Nor the cycling. The rest said how they couldn't imagine anything worse. So I didn't appear to be selling the whole thing particularly well, which was a problem because I'd decided it would be more enjoyable if other people came along with me.

Soon I'd begin the hunt for my team. Received wisdom on the subject says you should only ever go on a long distance trip like mine with people you know well and can still get along with when the going gets tough. I didn't have that luxury. I'd take anyone who wanted to come.

So, my plan was finalised. It'd last 100 days, cost £100 and would be completed with a small bunch of complete and utter strangers. What could possibly go wrong?

Chapter 2: Let's Get Ready to Trundle

It was three months before the start of what I had named *Ride and Seek* and it was time to get busy. I posted my plans on a couple of internet cycling forums and on several *Facebook* groups and sat back to wait for the inevitable tsunami of interested cycle-foragers.

I was already certain of two part-time cyclists. My brother planned to do the first week with me, and my mate Mark had agreed to do his home county of Devon and neighbouring Cornwall. Ideally, there'd be four or five of us in total. If dozens were interested, we could split up into smaller teams. As it turned out, dozens weren't interested but I was encouraged by a steady trickle.

What was unexpected and, if I'm being honest, slightly disturbing was the negativity my idea had generated in the cycle forums, although I'm sure it was well-intentioned. But here, have a read of a few edited highlights from *CycleChat* and *CTC*'s site:

"The concept of foraging and fishing to provide fuel for many miles of cycling a day appears flawed to me. You can consume a huge amount of calories through hot, arduous cycling in Spain. I am struggling to see how you can fuel yourself adequately to make sensible progress possible."

"There are loads of bits of coast where you will struggle to fish. I think you will do better begging."

"I would think you will need to find three thousand

calories a day minimum. You will be pushed to achieve that by foraging, and too much fish will reduce your immunity to cuts and scrapes."

"I feel that you might be stretching this a bit too far or it's not well planned. £1 is more tokenism than anything else. If it's a foraging challenge, why not set up camp in the wild for a couple of months and do it properly? If the inclination is an adventure bike journey to see people, places and culture and achieve considerable distance on the cheap than make it at least £10 a day. That will certainly avoid illness and create a cohesive group to enjoy the ride with. The way you describe it thus far, it's best not to bring along others and put them at risk."

"One thing that hasn't been talked about much is how you intend to deal with frayed nerves when the going gets tough. Many adventures I've read about take a bad turn when people disagree about a course of action. A harrowing example is the Donner Party."

The Donner Party? Bloody hell! They ended up eating each other. Mmm, I thought, I should take a bigger pan.

But was I being irresponsible and putting others at risk? I didn't think so. I mean, we – whoever we turned out to be – were all adults. No one could be forced to follow the rules of the trip if things got too nasty. I really had no intention of scattering Europe's western coast with a series of shallow graves as we buried riders where they fell. Besides, I wasn't taking a shovel. I would only have my handy, collapsible, toilet-making spadelet – my sanitary trowel as I like to call it. It would take me ages to dig a grave with that thing.

In parallel with this Nile of negativity, I had a real-life chance to see just what one pound a day could buy. The official *Live Below The Line* week was upon us and I'd decided to try their five quid challenge. If I couldn't manage this happily, or at least tolerably, while stationary then the bike ride was a non-starter.

I went out and bought some pasta, a bag of flour, six eggs, a couple of potatoes, an onion, a bag of sugar, a small carton of tomato purée and three tiny tins of tuna. Being in Spain at the time, I also pilfered a handful of lemons from my girlfriend's tree. I even stretched to a one euro packet of bacon containing five small rashers of pig that turned out to be approximately two microns thick.

Over the course of the week, I baked a couple of loaves and smeared my bread or toast with a basic but surprisingly tasty home-made lemon marmalade. That covered most breakfasts and a few snacks between meals. Lunch was a fried egg butty or bacon on toast. Dinners clearly had to be the showpiece meal. Over those five evenings I sat down to a couple of pasta dishes, a jacket potato with tuna, a Spanish potato tortilla and, to celebrate the coming of Friday and the end of the ordeal, a potato and foraged rosemary pizza. I know the pizza sounds rather dull but it was inspired by one I'd once eaten in Rome and had been truly delicious, whereas mine was, as you correctly guessed, bloody rubbish.

I survived. I often felt hungry but when you start any kind of diet you spend all your time thinking about food and that alone will make your belly rumble. But then I calculated how many calories I'd consumed and it was only between 1,300 and 1,800 a day. I weighed myself and discovered that in five days I'd lost over five pounds (2.5 kg). This wasn't good.

I did some more number-crunching. I entered the details of the ride into an online calorie counting site and it calculated the journey alone would burn around 300,000 calories and that equates to 88 pounds (40 kg) of human blubber. And if I maintained my *Live Below The Line* calorific intake and weight loss, I'd shed a pound a day for 100 days. I'd probably start the ride weighing close to sixteen stone (100 kg). Subtract the other numbers and – oh dear God! – I'd finish the ride weighing approximately a stone and half (10 kg). Maybe the cycling forum critics were right.

I'd been working on a set of rules for the trip. For example, we couldn't ask for anything except water, since water is almost free. We couldn't dumpster dive or beg. We weren't allowed to steal, although fruit hanging over a garden wall was fair game, but definitely no leaping into farmers' fields and helping ourselves. We couldn't work for money or sell our organs or fluids.

"What happens if people give you things?" my mum asked.

"They won't," I replied solidly. "This is western Europe we're talking about."

On my European tour, people didn't start to get generous until I was well into the eastern, poorer countries. Nothing more than water had ever been spontaneously given in the west. But, just in case, I added a rule to say we were allowed to accept food if offered but couldn't put ourselves in a position to make that likely to happen, such as sitting outside a supermarket with a sign around our necks saying we had fourteen starving children to feed.

I had a list of eleven people who'd been in touch to say they wanted to come along. That said, most of them had a reason why they might not be able to make it. One had a house to sell. Another was waiting for news about a job. With eleven people plus me, my brother and Mark, we'd have to split into teams. But at this point, it was still possible I'd be doing this thing alone.

Then came the 15th of May, the deadline for a definite

decision, and suddenly a lot of people stopped responding to my emails. With time to think of the reality of the ride, their initial enthusiasm had waned, even the ones without a ready-made excuse. Maybe they'd made the same calculations as I had.

But, fortunately for me, not everyone had opted out. Three on my list had confirmed their interest. We would be a team of four – the perfect number – small enough to wild-camp without splitting up over several locations and large enough to divide up and forage for different things. Perfect.

Less perfect were the planned extensions to my almost non-existent foraging knowledge. It was now the month before my final *Open University* exams and I was revising for two courses at once. If I buggered them up, I couldn't afford to take any more courses and would have to abandon six years' on and off study. The revision had to take priority.

I did learn the occasional foraging nugget. Did you know you shouldn't eat city pigeons because they carry chlamydia? Maybe other members of the animal kingdom carried different sexually transmitted diseases. Perhaps there's a clue in their names. Thrush and crabs don't take much guessing. But this was information I needed to know. It would be unconvincing to return home to Nina after feasting on a diet of sparrows, starlings and sea bass to discover I had gonorrhoea, syphilis and genital warts.

To be honest, the roadkill options seemed unlikely to tempt me, but just in case we achieved those levels of hunger, it was important to know just what we could eat. I watched a *YouTube* video about an amiable old duffer with a chest freezer full of creatures he'd scooped from the road. He claimed none of it had ever made him ill. The first badger he'd eaten had already turned green before he'd scraped it from the tarmac, which seems like a bold way to begin a new hobby. The secret is in the cooking apparently. You just have to boil it for long enough. Only once in his life had food made him sick and that was at a friend's buffet. It makes you wonder just how dodgy those prawn vol-au-vents had to be to bring down a man who could happily stomach a mouldy mammal.

Another *YouTube* video offered more useful advice should we lack the old fella's iron constitution. The mantra was simple: "Fleas are good. Flies are bad." Yes, if the animal was fresh enough that its fleas hadn't flown then it was a goer. If the flies had arrived, it was better to flee.

At this point in time, while alternating deathly boring revision with the viewing of grim *YouTube* films, I was still in Spain. In a few days, I'd be leaving to return to the Isle of Man and my *OU* exams. Before then, Mark, who'd join us in Devon, was having a birthday party. He had good reason to celebrate. After suffering and recovering from brain cancer a few years ago, he'd convinced himself he'd never get to his 53rd birthday, and here he was, alive and kicking and going a bit mad.

After a pub crawl involving several hundred beers, we went back to Mark's house. Knowing my lack of passion for all things spiritual, his missus Julie decided she'd do a tarot card reading to predict the success of my bike challenge. I had to pose a question.

"Alright then. Will I succeed and will I finish alone?"

Then either she picked four cards or I did – like I said, there'd been a lot of beer – and I got a strength card, a tower and the ten and knight of tentacles. Somehow these cards were assigned to my past, present and future in an entirely bollocks-filled way and a prediction resulted. I was hoping the tentacle reference indicated something about how deliciously octopus-based my summer diet would be, but it turned out Julie had actually said pentacles. What the hell is a pentacle anyway?

"The cards have spoken," she announced. They hadn't. I would've noticed. "Your project will be successful. You have your family and friends behind you." That wasn't true either. "Your idea is a strong one. If all others let you down, you will still finish the route on your own."

What a rubbish woolly prediction! So basically I'd finish it, alone or not. That was no good. I wanted to be told I wouldn't make it as far as the English Channel. I wanted to defeat the cards. This meant that if I worked my nipples off to get to the end, whether with the others or not, Julie could still smugly say, "Ah, yes, that's what the cards predicted!"

Anyway, the birthday party continued and Mark turned up the jukebox in his living room to an ear-bleedingly loud level at four in the morning and accompanied each track with his own take on badly-timed bongo-drumming. The next day his neighbour came around and went absolutely and justifiably mental at him. I've never before seen a man so angry. His face went puce, he ground his teeth and his outburst contained the word 'fuck' quite a lot. Had there not been an iron gate between them I reckon Mark's birthday would've been his last. Why couldn't Julie have predicted that?

On the morning of the 27th of May I said goodbye to Nina at Málaga coach station and took a bus to the airport. We'd spent the previous evening on a massive tapas run around the city centre.

Maybe you think this an odd relationship, with my disappearing for months on end, and it was. But Nina said she didn't mind my trips and, besides, she liked her space.

"I don't do much for you," she'd said. "So I wanted to do this."

She had organised a lovely hotel for our final night

together. After an evening of laughter and *boquerones*, it was great to leave Spain on a high. I was already looking forward to seeing her again at the end of September. And I think she was looking forward to seeing a more svelte Steven. I hadn't told her I'd only actually weigh a stone and half.

Since no one else within the team lived on the Isle of Man – not much of a surprise really – the official start point had moved to just across the water in Liverpool on the 16th June.

Once we got around the dinner table on the first evening in Manxland, it turned out my brother, Dave, had double-booked. The weekend after we were due to set off he'd agreed to act as a back-up driver for his wife's attempt at the Isle of Man's quaint-sounding Parish Walk. It's actually a foot-blistering 85 mile yomp that must be completed within 24 hours. Apparently, at the award ceremony a few days later, most of the recipients are usually on crutches. So, with the clash in Dave's diary, he'd first thought to reduce his participation in the ride to just two days before abandoning the idea altogether.

To make matters worse, it then turned out he hadn't actually booked our ferry tickets to Liverpool as he'd told me he had – and I was planning to leave at a time when the Isle of Man is crawling with tens of thousands of *TT* motorcycle enthusiasts and the ferries are rammed. A speedy online shopping spree got me one of the last tickets available and avoided an embarrassing email to the rest of the team to tell them to start without me. Silly sod.

My bike – the trusty, rusty steed that'd completed 22,000 miles around Europe and finished completed knackered – needed a lot of fixing. It'd been sitting in my parents' garage for the last two years. Just to give myself plenty of time, and the bike mechanic no excuses, I dropped off my machine – sorry, folks, I have no name for it – with loads of time to spare. It was, after all, a new, geographically closer bike shop I'd never used before. With well over two weeks for them to fix it up and give it a decent service I could concentrate on my final revision without worry. I also ordered lots of bits and pieces I needed for the trip – a new stove, a dinky miniature back-up fishing rod, a solar panel, adventure sandals. Everything was falling into place. Nothing could go wrong.

The exams came and went. My studies with the *Open University* were now finally over. This made me sad. I love the *OU*. I'd planned to keep doing degrees until the only ones remaining were those actually useful for getting a job, like law and accountancy and other tedious stuff like that. Unfortunately, UK government arsery meant even the *OU*'s cheaper courses were now way above what I could afford to spend. School was out, forever.

I'd called up the bike shop a couple of times and been fobbed off. It was *TT* week, they said. They were busy but I didn't need to worry. It'd be ready in time.

I spent my now studyless free time buying the remaining equipment I needed and watching as many foraging videos as possible.

"Do you know how to skin a rabbit?" Dave asked me.

"I don't really want to have to skin a rabbit."

"No, but if you do, do you know how?"

"I've read how to do it. It sounds easy enough."

"I can get you a rabbit."

Apparently fluffy bunnies make a regular appearance on the airport runway where he's a fireman and occasionally responsible for clearing away animals and birds that might, in their cute cartoon way, inadvertently bring down an airliner.

"Ah right," I said, and forgot about it.

Two days later, sitting at the dinner table, Dave appeared and dropped a suspiciously warm sack into my lap.

"There you go!" he said. "I didn't enjoy doing that. The

shot didn't kill it properly. I had to stamp on its head."

Lovely.

My dad, who is in all respects a gentle, old soul, has a strange penchant for getting up to his elbows in the blood and entrails of dead creatures. He never seems happier than when sawing the head off a pollack he's just caught.

"I'll show you what to do," he said enthusiastically while grabbing a large knife. And he did. And it was pretty much what I'd expected, except there was something unbearably macabre about removing the skin and fur of something that was still tepid.

From that point I took over, jointed the little thing and cooked it in honey and mustard. The rabbit was tasty, but it had died for me, not some anonymous consumer as it would've done in the supermarket fridge, and that made me fairly certain the only creatures I'd bring myself to slaughter would be fish. Although nothing that looked like Nemo.

Five days before my ferry was due to leave, I got a phone call from the bike shop.

"Ah, good. Is it ready?" I asked.

"What? No, we haven't started yet. Like I said, we've been busy. You need a new head set."

"Yes, I know. I told you that when I brought it in."

"And a new front wheel."

"And you've got those, right?"

"Well, we need to order the parts."

"From off the island?" I asked, panicked.

"Yeah."

I was leaving on a Monday morning. Between now and then there was a weekend and this Friday happened to be a public holiday.

"So can you definitely get the bits?"

"We can try," he said casually. I nearly fainted. They'd had the bike for two weeks and hadn't even looked at it. The start of the whole project was now in jeopardy.

I had to do something quickly. I phoned up *Bikestyle* in Douglas. I usually get my service done there but this time had opted for the closer place, and asked – nay, begged – for their help. They could manage something if I got my bike to them as quickly as possible. I called back the useless bike shop.

"I need to pick up my bike right now," I said urgently.

"It's at the mechanic's."

"Alright, where does he live? I'll get it from there."

"Sorry, that's not possible."

"What?"

"No one is allowed to visit the mechanic's."

"Sorry?" Clearly the man with the spanner was an illegal immigrant, chained to a wall in a filthy workshop and paid in old potatoes. "Is there nothing I can do to get my bike right now?"

Then he said something odd for a Manxman.

"Listen, even if you were the Queen, I couldn't let you go there."

Mmm, suspicious. Perhaps it wasn't an illegal immigrant. Maybe he had Diana at the workbench.

I was eventually allowed to pick up my bike from the shop the following morning, I hoofed it to *BikeStyle*, and Richard, their technical guy, whose knowledgeable words flowed like a calm, confidence-inspiring honey, said he'd do his best to sort it. Two hours later, I got a phone call to say my bike was ready. That was a speedy service by any standard. The trip could begin!

Monday came and the ferry, heaving with leather-clad motorcyclists, arrived in Liverpool. In a few minutes I'd meet my team. There was Dave, a 35 year-old from the West Country, Hungarian chef Sabby, also 35, and Joe, a 21 year-old who'd just finished university.

I was excited, and a little nervous. I mean, what if one of them was a complete dick? Or two of them? Or even all three? One hundred alcohol-free days travelling thousands of miles with three utter tools suddenly didn't seem so appealing. Perhaps the internet's negativity had been entirely justified. Maybe this trip had been badly thought out. In a few minutes I suspected I was about to find out.

Chapter 3: The Leaving of Liverpool

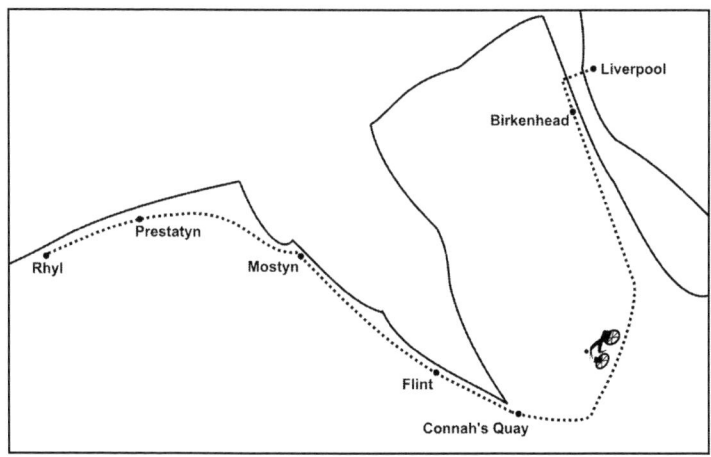

I pushed the loaded bicycle through Liverpool's busy pedestrian shopping centre. Since Liverpool is the gateway to the Isle of Man, I've been there often, and there's always something about the place that makes me feel uncomfortable.

One reason is the disparity in the way the younger men and women look. The females are generally slim and pretty with an over-complicated hairdo, like they're on the way to a wedding or something. Admittedly, they've usually gone overboard on the foundation. In Liverpool, apparently, the *Orange* shop just sells make-up. But the blokes are scary. They look like a different species, wandering around in vests with open sores and missing fingers. Those women seem to be going to a lot of unnecessary effort to attract them. These fellas would be interested if the lasses rolled out of bed, threw on a dress made of *Lidl*'s carrier bags and brushed their teeth with dog turds. I suspect the women are hunting for footballers.

The other problem with Liverpool is that they won't stop banging on about *The Beatles*. I mean, *The Beatles* were alright, but they were no *JLS*, were they? John Lennon wasn't bad. His heart was in the right place. That place, once he'd made a few quid, being anywhere that wasn't Liverpool. But if there's a God then I'm convinced He's reclaiming *The Beatles* in order of talent. John – the best one first – and then George. It'll be Ringo next, and then Paul in about 6,000 years. Sorry, but he's committed too many crimes against music.

As you walk around town, you can sense the council offices are filled with people in brainstorming sessions trying to think up one more way to milk *The Beatles*' huge, wobbly udder. Not long ago, there was an exhibition on the river front called *When Elvis Met The Beatles*. In reality, their paths only crossed once and for about twenty minutes when they sat around in an embarrassed silence staring at each other.

The plan was to dump the bike at the hotel I'd booked for the night and then, after meeting the crew, hit the town for a knees-up. But most of the crew found me first.

"Hey, Steven!"

How did Sabby recognize me, I wondered? I assumed it was the cycling shorts, the panniers and my full set of fingers. Hungarian Sabby was slim, about six foot tall with short, dark hair and spoke with accented but otherwise perfect English.

"I thought I'd get started on the beard," he said with a smile.

We'd all swapped emails in the last few weeks and the consensus was that we'd ditch shaving equipment and each spend our time on the road trying to grow a beard as jihadist as possible. Young Joe was the only one not convinced it was going to work out for him. He'd only ever grown tufts before. But here was Sabby with the beginnings of a fine bush.

We arranged to meet at the train station a little later after I'd sorted myself out. Continuing to the hotel, I bumped into Joe.

"Good luck finding the room," he said.

Joe had decided to share with me after brother Dave dropped out. He'd already checked in and was wandering back into town to meet the other Dave, the one who'd be cycling with us. Joe too was slim and around six foot with blonde-brown hair on top of a boyish, hair-free face.

I was shown to my room at *The Feathers Hotel*. I followed the receptionist down scores of maze-like tunnels, turning left and right and pushing through unseen doors, each corridor seemingly narrower than the last. It felt like I was going to turn a corner and see the Minotaur.

I dumped my gear and found the team sitting in the evening sunshine on the steps of Liverpool Lime Street station. And it was here I met our final team member for the first time, and it seemed I'd accidentally recruited Gandalf's younger brother.

Dave is one of those people who you meet for five minutes and then say, "Ah, he's a character, isn't he?" He sat there with a smile that flooded his face and, if I'm being honest, a rather ridiculous piece of jaw fluff. It was only a goatee, but a goatee that hung several inches from his chin and which you could stroke like a small puppy. And, we'd later discover, he did. His first words were lost on me but his West Country accent made whatever they were sound joyous. It was hard to talk to him that evening without thinking, "Is it possible he's just a tiny bit mad?"

We moved from the steps to find a source of food. As Sabby had his bike with him we needed somewhere in town where we could eat outside and keep an eye on it. This was

Liverpool after all.

We found a Wetherspoon's in the town centre with a small, outside fenced area and sat down. Joe, Sabby and I each ordered the standard meal-and-a-pint deal. Dave was more of an expert. The waitress came out with an armful of plates.

"Steak and kidney pie?" she asked.

"That's mine," said Dave.

"And a sausage, egg and chips?" she said looking at Joe, Sabby and me in turn.

"That's mine as well," Dave said, grinning. "What?" he protested. "It's a two-meal deal."

He finished both his platefuls before we were halfway through ours.

We soon learned that Dave was no stranger to gorging. In fact, one of his pastimes was to enter eating competitions. Although he'd been unsuccessful in his local pub's nettle-eating event – he'd only managed to eat 25 feet of nettles in an hour – he'd fared better at garlic-eating, stuffing down 33 cloves in a minute. Afterwards, he discovered the world record was only 34.

Joe and Sabby were a little more guarded with their information, perhaps not wanting to give too much away too early or, more likely, being unable to top Dave's tales of gastronomic excess.

Joe though had just submitted the final dissertation for his physical geography degree and, while awaiting the result, was using this trip as a sort of Last Summer of Freedom before he submitted to the horrors of wage-slavery.

Sabby was a chef who travelled to where the work took him. He was also connected to the *Debrecen Bike Maffia*, an organisation that sounds like a misspelt, teenage organised-crime syndicate, but which in reality distributes food and other necessities by bicycle to the needy back in Hungary.

He'd brought a communal gift from home, a bottle of fiery apple brandy – *pálinka* – and he passed it around for a quick slurp each.

Liverpool was sozzled, and sitting outside on the street made us a target. Four young women stumbled out of Wetherspoon's, complaining they'd been kicked out.

"It's 'cos we was cleanin' the toilet mirrors," one of them slurred scousely at me.

"Yeah," said another, leaning heavily on the fence between us. "We're nurses. They were disgust – hic! – disgustin'. We know our health 'n' safety."

"Do you think maybe you were thrown out because you're just a little bit drunk?" I asked.

She shrugged and smiled.

"We're not drunk," she said as she slid down the fence.

They were impressively inebriated for half past eight. I ordered a round of drinks. This was our last chance for the next three months to enjoy the loveliness that is beer. Alcoholically, the nurses were some way ahead of us but I felt sure that, if we put in the effort, we could catch them up.

A three-way fight broke out just up the street. The rest of the town ignored it like it was a perfectly normal thing to happen here, which it may well be. Then a tall, middle-aged bloke marched out of Wetherspoon's and stood by our table.

"Merry Christmas!" he said.

"Err, merry Christmas," we replied.

"I'm pissed an' I've just done loads of coke," he said proudly before saluting us. "Merry Christmas!" he repeated.

Off he strolled wishing seasonal greetings, albeit the wrong season, to everyone in his path.

We finished our second pints and sat there. Several people came up to us to beg for change. I waited for someone to get the next round. Nobody did.

"My back wheel collapsed today," said Dave happily.

"Isn't that something you should've checked before you set off?" I asked.

"Probably."

I kept waiting. No more beer was forthcoming. This was it, our final night's party. Oh well.

Here we were, the big day, the 16th of June.

If you want to go from Liverpool to Wales – and we did – then your first mission is to cross the Mersey to reach the sticky-out, knobby bit of Merseyside known as The Wirral. There are three ways you can do this. You can add miles to your trip while cycling through urban hell to Runcorn and crossing the water there. Or you can take the famous ferry 'cross the Mersey. Finally, you can use one of the tunnels beneath the river. Given we only had our daily pound coin, the ferry was a needless extravagance, and no one wanted to cycle via Runcorn. Luckily, the tunnel was free, but bicycles were only allowed through before six in the morning or after eight at night. I'd seen a video of someone cycling through and, even at these lower volume times of day, the traffic made it look an unpleasant thing to do.

We'd arranged to meet at half past five in the morning outside the tunnel's entrance. I'd located this dark hole on Google Maps. It was easy to find. Nothing could go wrong.

Joe and I cycled from the hotel through town, back past Wetherspoon's. We passed a couple having an early morning argument and then found Sabby already on his way. Dave was nowhere to be seen. A few minutes later, I checked my map.

"It's just around this corner," I said confidently. "There!" We all looked at the entrance, confused.

"There's a No Entry sign," said Joe.

"Yes," I replied less confidently this time.

Apparently, we'd located the exit to the tunnel. The

entrance must be somewhere close. We asked a passing security guard. He gave us a complicated series of instructions.

"It's about ten minutes away," he added.

The entrance, inexplicably, wasn't anywhere near the exit. It was already twenty to six.

We raced around town and found the entrance. But – buggeration! – there was a sign saying the tunnel was closed for maintenance until half past six. A traffic policemen popped out of the on-site office.

"Can we get through on bikes?" I asked.

"No," he replied. "Even we can't get through. You'll have to wait until it opens at half past six."

"But at half six we're not allowed through."

"Ah yes, you're right."

"Will we be allowed through at half past six?"

"Why?"

"Eh? Because it's been closed until then."

"No."

Brilliant. And where the hell was Dave? We thought perhaps he was waiting at the tunnel's exit but Joe managed to get him on his phone and he was lost in the centre of town, wheeling around and around like a confused wizard. It was close to six. Even if the tunnel had been open we wouldn't have been able to get across in time together.

"I'll go and find him," said Joe helpfully.

It looked like we'd have to travel via Runcorn after all, adding twenty ugly miles to our first day. I waited for Dave and Joe to return, feeling annoyed at the lack of glory on this, our first day.

"Hello!" said Dave, rolling up to me with a huge grin.

I found it difficult to muster a smile. It was ten past six. This was my first chance to see Dave's bike. Joe's and Sabby's were high-spec'ed touring bicycles with a sensible amount of luggage. Dave's was made of girders and was carrying more bags than a bin van. They were piled on top of each other in a gravity-defying structure. A woollen teddy bear his mum had knitted was strapped to the front. I noticed his ground mat on the back of his bike.

"Is that fastened on?"

"No."

"What? It's just balancing there?"

"Yeah."

No possibility for mishap there then. The policeman emerged from his office again.

"Right, lads, you can go through if you like," he said. "The tunnel won't open to cars for twenty minutes. You've got it to yourselves."

Ah, an auspicious stroke of luck to begin our challenge. We wouldn't even have to fight the tunnel's traffic. We disappeared beneath the Mersey and popped out ten minutes later in sunny Birkenhead.

I'd expected this area of the north-west to be an industrial wasteland but we quickly found the Wirral Circular Cycle Path and it took us on a pretty trail past attractive houses and through Eastham Country Park. We emerged near a beach looking back towards Liverpool. A supermarket trolley had been casually discarded on the sand as a bit of improvised urban art.

We leapt across the Wirral, taking a right turn near Connah's Quay into Wales. With the sun continuing to shine and the gentle breeze, this was perfect cycling weather.

There are still many British cycle paths that make you scratch your head at the sheer idiocy of their design. We followed a track that shadowed a dual carriageway. It suddenly turned, crossing the busy road on to the central reservation. Oh, we thought, the cycle path obviously continues on the opposite side of the dual carriageway. But no, the cycle path stopped, right there, in the middle of the central reservation. Bonkers.

By the rules of *Ride and Seek* we were allowed to bring a small amount of food with us. I'd allowed this to prevent a torrential downpour from jeopardising the whole expedition early on. Terrible weather could've hampered our first attempts at fishing and foraging, and even reaching a supermarket. By the rules of *Live Below The Line*, however, this was cheating. Don't worry though. The cost of this food will be taken into account. I needn't have worried about the weather. It was gorgeous, and it was on porridge we'd brought with us that we dined when we stopped for a rest at Flint Castle.

For Dave, though, the weather was too good. The sun turned his pasty legs a vivid scarlet almost instantly. It didn't help that while pushing his bike in and out of the castle's grounds he repeatedly smashed his own calves with its pedals, breaking the skin each time. It was as though he'd never pushed a bike before. Day One and his legs looked a bloody mess.

We set off again and, short on water, performed our first survival task when we popped into the graveyard of St Mary and St Peter Church in Bagillt and filled up from the tap there. At the same time Joe introduced me to hawthorn leaves from bushes growing in the grounds, which despite being known as "bread and cheese" didn't taste of either, or of anything much at all. He also took a minute while refastening his panniers to bungee himself in the nuts. The resulting squeal of pain told me it was the sort of thing you only do once.

It was still early afternoon when we reached Mostyn, today's target, and with such beautiful weather we decided to continue and get a little ahead of ourselves. We came across some sand dunes and went to have a look for fishing possibilities. The tide was way out but that didn't matter because on the way to the beach we were distracted by a forest of prickly beasts that Joe identified as sea holly. It was just as well one of us had done some homework.

In the UK, the rules are that you can forage freely but you must have the landowner's permission to dig anything up. The prized part of the cool blue-green sea holly is its root. We assumed the sand dunes to be public land and with such a vast quantity of specimens figured it'd be fine to take a root or two.

After a tour through the trailer parks of Prestatyn, or maybe they were static caravans – what's the difference? – we stopped around sixish to cook our first evening meal. With his chef status, Sabby nominated himself as team cook. On the promenade's concrete wall he set up an impromptu kitchen *The Hairy Bikers* would've been proud of. Fuelled by his petrol stove that sounded only marginally quieter than a rocket launch he knocked up a rice and lentil dish with a sauce containing the sea holly roots we'd collectively cleaned, peeled and chopped. They taste like a cross between a parsnip and a Brazil nut and, to be honest, with their tough, inner root they really aren't worth the effort.

While we tucked into our dinner, a tractor rolled across the wet sand and got itself stuck, its wheels spinning uselessly. Every attempt to escape exacerbated the situation. It was nice to have something to watch while we ate – a sort of outdoor TV dinner – even if this was the worst action film ever. I hope they got it sorted before the tide came in.

Dinner was done. It hadn't been enough but it'd have to do for now. We packed away the portable kitchen and set off in search of a place to stay. Outside of countries where it's legal – like Sweden and Norway – I'd never wild-camped before and I was a little wary of where we'd end up. I imagined a night of disturbed sleep, lying with one eye open and listening for the rozzers.

We cycled through Rhyl along its windy seafront and then, realising the lack of opportunity by the water, we headed inland. The route took us up large hills, past a forest with ground so steep that a camping pitch would've been impossible. We cycled around and around for close to two hours getting sweatier and sweatier at a time when we all just wanted to stop and sleep. We were beginning to lose the light. Maybe this just wasn't going to work.

We ended high on a hill next to a farm. There just wasn't enough public land. Perhaps there was another approach.

"Let me try something," I said.

I walked to the farm building and knocked on its door. No one answered. There was another building opposite. I gave that one a try too. After a few minutes, and preceded by a happily yapping dog, a cheerful old fella came to the door. I told him what we were doing and asked if he knew where the farmer was.

"Ah, he's new an' he's never here. He's bought a kennel about an hour away. He'll be there."

"Do you reckon it'd be alright to camp in his field?"

"Aye, sneak in. What's the worst that can happen?"

"I could be arrested."

"Aye," he chuckled.

"If I am, will you be my character witness?"

"Aye," he said, smiling and closing the door.

Yes, we finally had somewhere to stay.

After setting up the tents we decided to make some tea and more porridge – the starving skinflint's best friend – and I returned to the old fella's front door to ask if he could fill our water bottles. It took him an equally long time to answer. I suspect he'd fallen back asleep and I'd woken him again. He seemed markedly less cheerful this time but directed me to an outside tap.

We were in our tents not long after nine. It had been a much longer day than planned – 57 miles instead of 31 – and with little foraging, but we were ahead of schedule. Now that our route would hug the coast, we could take some time to fish, if the tide ever came in. I was sure I'd sleep well in the knowledge that no rozzer would nab me tonight. The journey had begun!

Days Completed: 1
Ride and Seek: **Total spend £0.00, per day £0.00**
Live below the Line: **Total spend £3.80, per day £3.80**

Chapter 4: The King of Pain

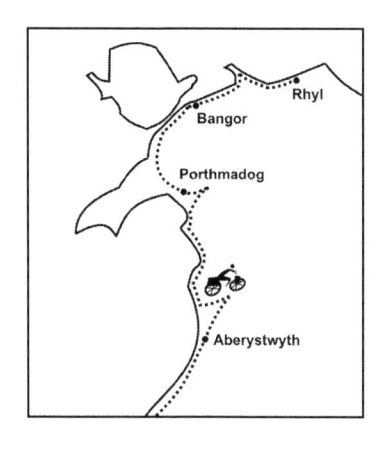

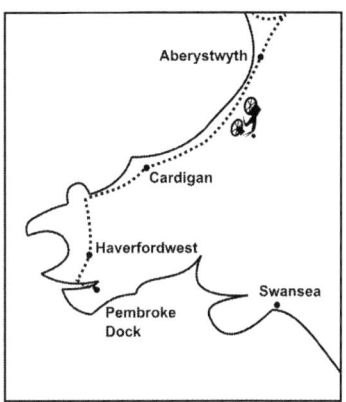

No, of course I didn't sleep well. I was in a tent, for pity's sake. During a gale. But at least I was warm and dry. That's the best you can hope for when you're camping.

We got up and had some more porridge and a little coffee. I say "a little coffee" because all I'd foolishly brought with me was a tiny, red plastic beaker from an ancient cooking kit. Everyone else had adult-sized cups rather than something you'd find in a doll's house.

The reason for carrying such a beaker was its light weight. When touring like this, every gram matters. Unless you're Dave. He'd brought along not one, but two builder's mugs. In fact, all his dining kit was heavy and ceramic. His preferred eating vessel was a bright yellow *Winnie the Pooh* bowl starring the grinning face of Tigger.

We finished our porridge and Dave came over to talk to me. I had to interrupt him.

"You've got some oats in your beard, Dave."

"Have I?" he replied with surprise, stroking his face.

You could've made a small meal from what resided in his fur.

I perused the map of today's route.

"We pass *Butterfly World* this afternoon," I said.

"I wonder how many calories are in a butterfly," asked Dave.

"It's not meant to be a foraging opportunity."

He looked disappointed and continued removing chunks from his face. Then he farted.

"More tea, vicar!" he said, grinning maniacally.

We packed up the tents and rolled down the hill back to the coast under a threatening, grey sky. It was cold for June. Everyone was wrapped up. Approaching Colwyn Bay, the bike path skirted the low sea wall beyond which lay huge boulders. The tide was in. We were suddenly warmed by the prospect of fish for lunch.

No one on the team was an experienced fisherman. I'd been into coarse fishing when I was twelve but my overriding memory of those miserable few months was sitting by Cocker's Lodge, a large pond in Oswaldtwistle beside a disused chemical plant, and catching nothing. And I mean nothing at all. My keepnet never kept anything. I'd assumed I was doing something wrong. Then we went on holiday by a river in the wilderness of Canada. Within ten minutes of arriving I half-heartedly plopped my bait into the water and immediately pulled out a fish. It wasn't my technique that was at fault. It was bloody Cocker's Lodge and its chemical soup. Its fish had probably mutated long ago and simply walked out of the place.

This patch of Welsh coast was a stupid place to fish. We balanced precariously on slippery rocks, casting our hooks into shallow, seaweed-strewn waves and the only result was that Joe got his spinner caught fast on the bottom and had to sacrifice it to Neptune. We gave up, determined to find a better spot later.

And we did. Five minutes down the path, we found a place that guaranteed success because someone else was also fishing there and he, we assumed, unlike us, knew what he was doing.

We quickly set up our gear again. The other fisherman had two rods leaning against the sea wall with their lines disappearing out to sea. Two rods! That's a proper fisherman. Rain started to fall. He went to sit inside his van and read a newspaper. It's exciting stuff, this fishing lark.

As Joe had previously lost his tackle, he had to tie on some new equipment. He foolishly asked me for advice on how best to do this.

"Well," I said, trying to sound like I knew what I was doing and then failing. "My dad taught me this a couple of days ago."

With the spinner and weight already attached to the leader I demonstrated a technique that involved looping the line eight or so times around the swivel and then fastening it off. (Don't worry if terms like 'leader' and 'swivel' mean nothing to you. You're better off not knowing.) I demonstrated it on my own line.

Joe crouched down to tie on his own lure. He then stood up, thrust his shoulders back and prepared to cast, probably imagining the fishy bounty he was soon to reel in. He swung the rod over his head and proudly aimed it seawards. The newly attached gear removed itself from his line, arced through the sky and plopped uselessly into the ocean. Fish 0, Lost Tackle 2.

We stayed for another half an hour and caught nothing. The only consolation was that Mr Two Rods did no better and so maybe it wasn't our fault, as though not knowing anything isn't a handicap. It looked like it would be fish-free pasta again for dinner.

We got soaked in Llandudno. The rain poured down and we struggled to find our way out in the direction we wanted. Sabby took out his mobile to find a map and exhibited the full power of his colloquial English.

"Argh! My phone's gone full retard," he said. "It says we're in a river."

"Maybe that's the weather forecast."

It was certainly wet enough. Today had been miserable, weather-wise and fishing-wise. Fortunately, we were still living from the food we'd brought with us, the odd cereal bar here and there to keep us going. We'd yet to discover how far our pound would stretch in the supermarket.

We'd cycled little more than 30 miles but it was getting to that time again and we decided that, rather than hunt pointlessly for a wild-camping spot, we'd see if another farmer would help us, or at least have the good grace to be miles away from his farm and have a neighbour friendly enough to tell us.

We found a beautiful house surrounded by fields with immaculate lawns and a view across the Menai Strait to Beaumaris Castle. We amassed outside its front gate. I waited to see who was going to ask if we could stay here. No one moved.

"Oh, I see. I'm doing this again, am I?" I said.

Although I'd got this trip together, I'd long ago said that once we started I wasn't going to be the leader. There'd be no leader. We'd work as a team. But obviously no one else wanted to be the cheeky bastard and so, if we wanted somewhere to sleep tonight, it fell to me to do the dirty work. In many ways it made sense for me to do it. Dave and Joe seemed quite shy and sending Sabby might not have been a wise idea in a country growing less and less tolerant of immigrants. Who knew who lived inside this house? It might be Nick Griffin.

I strolled up the driveway and knocked on the front door but I could already see the occupants inside, a couple in their thirties, sitting sedately at the dinner table in their conservatory, and they could see me. This felt a bit awkward. The man put down his napkin and walked to the door. At least he wasn't dressed in a Nazi uniform.

I'd had some business cards printed that included details of our mission translated into French, Spanish and Portuguese. Maybe somewhere down the road they would help. At the last minute I'd decided to add a Welsh translation – I have a Welsh aunt – and I think that's what swung it here. Geraint, a man with a permanent half-smirk on his face, was the Welshest man I've ever met.

Unfortunately, none of the fields around the house was his but as a keen cyclist himself – he and his wife had done Land's End to John o'Groats a while back – we were welcome to camp in his garden.

"Just don't shit in my rose bushes," he added with a grin.

We set up our tents on his lovely lawn and Geraint came out for a chat.

"Here, have some crisps," he said, placing four large bags on the grass before turning to go. "They're from my company. It's not really foraging, I know." Then he thought for a moment. "If you do want to forage, you can take what you want off that gooseberry bush. We can't stand 'em."

While the rest of us gathered sour, green berries, Sabby set up his kitchen on the lawn. He was cooking pasta in a tomato sauce when Geraint's smiling face reappeared.

"Do you fancy coming inside for some shepherd's pie? There's not much but you're welcome to it."

Did we fancy shepherd's pie? Well, yes, of course we did. Sabby looked a little put out that we were choosing someone else's grub over his, but c'mon!

And there wasn't just pie. There were cheesy vegetables, spuds and, to maintain the theme of our ride, a crumble made with blackberries that Geraint and his wife had foraged last year. They'd been frozen; they weren't rotten or anything.

His crisp company – *Jones o Gymru* – celebrated all things Welsh although there were only four different flavours for now, fairly standard ones using local ingredients, like Welsh potatoes, Welsh sea salt and Welsh rain. I asked if there were plans to provide *really* Welsh flavours, like laverbread or leek, or maybe even daffodil, but alas there weren't.

I hadn't expected this generosity, not in western Europe and especially not in the UK. Surely it wouldn't happen again. We'd just got lucky with a nice fellow cyclist and his surplus of pie and crisps. Tomorrow we'd return to meat-free dinners containing gnarly old roots.

"Good morning," said Geraint brightly, with his customary smirk and carrying a pot of coffee as he approached our circle of tents. This really didn't feel like the roughing-it I'd been anticipating.

Last night's would-be pasta dinner became today's breakfast and then, after getting Dave to remove the *fusilli* from his beard, we packed up. We left Geraint's place with one final act of kindness, a letter written in Welsh to present to the staff of his café in Porthmadog. If we could get there before it closed at two, then they'd give us lunch. Was Geraint the nicest man in the world?

We cycled through Bangor, past the bridge to Anglesey and into some woods along a pretty cycle track. The smell hit us immediately. Garlic! A quick search and we found the source – ramsons or wild garlic – with its long, green leaves on a single stem.

You have to be careful when tracking down ramsons. They look very similar to lily-of-the-valley, a plant easily poisonous enough to kill you. According to legend, lily-of-the-valley sprung forth from Mary's tears at her lad's crucifixion. Fortunately, Mary's tears weren't garlic-flavoured and neither is lily-of-the-valley and so we knew we were safe.

Ramsons, like lily-of-the-valley unfortunately, grow in huge carpets and so once you've located it you've probably found enough for a decent meal, or a damn good poisoning. We stuffed several plastic bags full of them.

Moving along the track, we were hit by another fragrance, the sweetly cloying aroma of elderflowers, hanging in large, dense, white-flowered bunches. I had a plan, a slightly decadent one, and it involved this perfumed blossom. I collected a few handfuls and placed them inside an old five-litre plastic bottle that Geraint had given me for this very purpose. The next stage of my experiment would have to come later.

Dave had a plan of his own. Perhaps seduced by the inescapable sexiness of your typical Alabama redneck, he was a fan of chewing tobacco, but a reluctant one. He was hoping this trip would help him kick the habit and had decided upon a less addictive replacement leaf to free him from his addiction. He'd taken to chewing nettles instead. At least now he wasn't getting stung for tobacco.

Our foraging success continued, and it wasn't all food. Joe found a steel nut on the floor and pocketed it as an ideal improvised fishing weight. Given how much we were leaving on the sea bed, we'd need a steady supply of new tackle. And later that day, our finds became a little more sartorial.

"I wish I'd brought a hat with me," Sabby had complained yesterday.

And what should he find a little further up the cycle path but a baseball cap in pristine condition and not full of nits or head lice eggs or anything. Probably. He scooped it up and, with more pride than was warranted, placed it on his head.

As if to celebrate Sabby's good luck, a gaggle of schoolchildren cycled past, whooping and bell-ringing, accompanied by two grinning teachers. At least I think they were teachers. Maybe it was a bunch of kids trying to outrun a couple of paedos. Perhaps we should've paid closer attention but, I'm sorry, we were too busy looking for food.

We kept moving, the sky the colour of a steel elephant. Near Caernarfon, we came across a curious structure, especially for a residential area: a two-storey metal platform protruding into the Menai Strait. We'd been wary on our two previous fishing attempts. In both cases, the sea had been shallow and the bottom covered with easily snaggable seaweed. But this platform stood in some very deep water. Not only that but the water flowed past rapidly. This appealed to my lazy mind. It meant rather than spinning – repeatedly casting out and reeling in – I could simply drop my tackle into the water and let the current give my pretend plastic fishy the illusion of movement. Never work harder than you need to.

We wheeled our bikes on to the platform and I took out my telescopic rod. As planned I dropped my spinner into the drink. This water really was zipping by. Maybe it was moving too quickly. How could a hungry, little fish impale itself upon my hook at that speed? I wondered how many more unsuccessful fishing attempts we'd suffer before we'd just chuck the rods and reels into the water and abandon the idea entirely. And then, miraculously, I felt something tugging on my line.

"I've got one!" I shrieked a little too effeminately. "I've got a fish!"

I reeled in and remembered my dad's advice. The reel, apparently, wasn't much good. It couldn't take a lot of weight. Land the fish as soon as it's out of the water, he'd said. Luckily, the dual-decked nature of our platform meant Joe on the lower level could grab my fish as it came past his face. It was a barely legal pollack but certainly big enough to eat, especially if you're hungry and already sick of porridge.

Sabby took it upon himself to dispatch the fish and fillet it immediately. He'd never killed a fish before – none of us had – and his choice of murder weapon was a curious one, a large hatchet.

"What do I do?" he asked.

"Hit it on the head with the back of the axe."

He nervously plopped the fish on to the floor of the metal platform in preparation for its execution. But because life wants to endure, the fish made a bid for freedom and attempted to flip and flop itself towards the platform's edge. Sensing the removal of fish from his evening meal, Sabby swung wildly with the axe, missing twice with a comedy metallic clang before finally connecting the blade with the upper body of our little fish, removing its head along with a good inch of edible body flesh.

"Classy," I said.

Sabby looked thoughtful. He'd taken a life. He was a killer now.

I dropped my tackle back into the water and immediately hooked another pollack of the same size. The new, lethal Sabby dispatched this one much more professionally. He was become Death, the destroyer of fish.

This was going to be a doddle. If we kept this up, we'd have a bucketload within half an hour. And this seemed to be the direction we were heading when Dave extracted his first victim, another pocket-sized pollack. It was how I'd dreamed this trip would be, reeling in fish after fish. To make things better, the sun appeared through the clouds as though the man upstairs was suggesting a pleasant evening seafood barbecue rather than huddling under canvas slurping a heart-warming fishy stew.

Who would be next to catch? And who'd be the first to land a monster? Well, as it turned out, no one. Despite staying there for another two hours, no one caught anything else.

We drew up a fishy league table. I was winning with two points and Dave held second place with his single fish. Joe and Sabby had yet to score, which was a little unfair on Sabby because the rod he'd ordered online hadn't actually arrived in time for the trip and so he'd spent the afternoon just standing around with his hatchet in hand waiting to kill something. To make it fairer we'd allowed him special budgetary permission to buy a rod at the first fishing shop we came to.

We would probably have stopped fishing earlier but, inexplicably, Dave discovered he had a puncture in his front tyre. This was a puncture he didn't have when he'd rolled his bike on to this perfectly smooth platform half an hour earlier. He couldn't fix it or even inflate any of the six spare inner tubes he'd brought with him. It turned out his bicycle pump didn't work but it took him a long time to realise this.

Sabby opened up his own toolkit, a set of gleaming instruments that would've looked more at home in a surgery. He took out a shiny, silver pump and fixed Dave's problem in seconds.

There would be no more fishing today. Skipping the Llyn Peninsula, we were heading directly to Porthmadog. We cycled down an utterly gorgeous cycle track, once the route of an old railway line, and then back on to roads over gentle hills before Dave suffered another puncture, this time in his back tyre.

While Sabby worked his magic once again, I snoozed in the sun on the roadside grass. I quickly got bored, decided to read something and discovered I'd somehow managed to kill my *Kindle*. On previous trips, it'd lived a gentle existence in my handlebar bag and survived tens of thousands of bumpy miles. This time I'd relegated it to a back pannier where, in the space of 100 miles, I'd squeezed the life out of it.

We continued towards Porthmadog but were three hours too late for our appointment. Obviously, it was true there's no such thing as a free lunch. But as we passed Geraint's café, we could see his smiley face through the window, talking to his staff, and he waved us over. The food had all been packed away but he kindly gave us a piece of cake and some more crisps, the official racing food of the *Weight Watchers* cycling team.

Three days in and it was already taken for granted I'd be negotiating every field. I'd become The Fixer. At a farm called *Ty'r Acrau*, I located Nosferatu, a vampiric farmhand who crept around the shadows of the site's huge barns. With a withered finger, he pointed to a field containing the farmer, who nonchalantly directed me to a comfortable-looking bit of flat ground. I hadn't expected it to be this easy.

Despite the evening sun, the air temperature was low enough for breath to be visible. Sabby quickly floured the fish and fried them, chopping six little fillets into twelve tiny pieces and adding three each to the rice, raisins and ramsons medley he'd already placed in our bowls. There's something about camping that makes all food taste better but this meal really was delicious, especially the postage stamp-sized flake of pollack. We looked forward to future fish-filled evenings when we'd catch barracudas rather than sticklebacks.

After a cup of tea and a nip of pálinka we crawled into our tents while it was still light and wrapped up warm to guard against the freezing air, the farm machinery a gentle hum as the farmer in a distant field continued to work into the night.

As we packed away in the morning, the farmer came over and asked if we needed some water. We followed him to the sink in his milking shed.

"Looks like a nice day," I said, filling up a bottle.

"'Snot gonna last," he replied pessimistically. "There were two drops on my iPad this morning, so there's a fair bit o' rain coming."

I assume he was using a weather app rather than just leaving his tablet outside and seeing how much precipitation it collected.

"Says it's gonna rain for a week," he continued.

What? No! Before we set off, a heatwave had been predicted. The only gorgeous day we'd experienced so far had been our first. And now, only three days later, torrential rain was forecast. That said, this was Wales. Maybe here a single full day of sunshine constitutes a heatwave.

We set off and cycled through Harlech, past its rather grand castle. In town there's a hill and, still very blobby at this stage, I was bringing up the rear. Reaching the top, I found Sabby with his arm in the sewer, the heavy, metal drain cover sitting on the tarmac.

"What are you doing?" I asked, fearing he'd had enough and was attempting to hide.

He removed his arm and presented us with a little, fat thrush. How it'd got inside the drain was a mystery. It was too fat to have fallen through the grid and couldn't have grown to that size down there. Sabby carefully placed it on a roadside wall. It sat there, not moving. Dave eyed it hungrily but no one suggested a method of preparation.

We carried on down the coast, through the seaside resort of Barmouth, today looking a bit sad and windswept. I was hungry. The energy from my breakfast porridge was waning and I suddenly craved the sugary doughnuts and ice cream selfishly offered by each seafront café. I was determined to put all such thoughts out of my mind and move on quickly, which is more than was possible for the two trains stranded here in 2014 when a storm smashed the seawall and buggered the rail line. It was two weeks before the carriages were loaded on to trucks and driven the 74 miles to Chester. Presumably they'd let the passengers off before then.

As we approached Tywyn, we discovered that someone had built a new bridge especially for cyclists and pedestrians, the Tonfanau Bridge. It looked very shiny and expensive. The project apparently cost £400,000 and, at a length of 50 metres, is the world's longest Vierendeel truss bowstring footbridge. I've no idea what any of those words mean.

We got speaking to a couple of fishermen. They told us this area was great for bass. I love sea bass. I wanted sea bass. I wanted *lots of* sea bass.

"Be here an hour before high tide and you can't go wrong," he said.

"What time's high tide?"

"About eleven tonight."

Ah. But that was possible. We had nowhere particular to go. Beneath the bridge there appeared to be a secret passage to rough grasslands and, beyond that, the beach and sea. We wheeled our bikes through and realised this would be a great place for our first truly wild camp. It was miles from any houses, no one else was about and, since we'd got there by stealthy means, no one else would turn up later. We'd have the place to ourselves.

First, though, we needed provisions. We cycled into Tywyn to look for water. There were no public toilets, not even at the railway station, and so I tried the sports centre. The staff were great.

"No, don't have tap water," a young fella in a tracksuit said. "Follow me."

He opened up the gym especially for us.

"There you go," he added, pointing at a mineral water dispenser the size of a bass drum.

Nice. But if they're not refilling that huge canister with tap water every time it's empty, the council will never be able to afford another Vierendeel truss bowstring footbridge.

We also spent our first money of the trip, blowing far too much on a packet of bacon, two tubes of tomato purée and a couple of bulbs of garlic. The supermarket, even a small, village one like this, was a difficult place to be. My eyes were drawn to shelves of pointless crap, things I wouldn't normally buy but which today, only four days since we'd started, had a powerful allure. *Mr Kipling's Mini Battenbergs* had never seemed so tempting.

Back to the beach, the place was still deserted. Despite the earlier forecast, the sun was out. For an hour we curled up like cats beneath its warmth. But no loving owner was going to dish us up a tin of *Whiskas*. If we wanted more variety in tonight's dinner, we'd have to go a-searching.

Nearby was a huge rock pool and we decided to supplement our sea bass with a little seafood. We trawled the pool looking for life, but despite the water's crystal clarity nothing animal lived here, not a prawn, crab nor limpet. A river ran through it. Maybe its freshwater explained the lack of sea life. Or maybe something else in the river water was killing it off.

Like fertiliser. There was, after all, tons of seaweed around here, including sea lettuce, laver and the lovely-sounding gutweed.

It was today that we first noticed Dave's tendency to forage to excess. Rather than collect a couple of meals' worth of bladderwrack – that's the brown-green seaweed with ugly, little blisters on it – he gathered a giant carrier bag of the stuff. I don't suppose it really mattered. His bike was already so heavy that carrying yet another sack would be, relatively speaking, like adding a tin of biscuits to a Sherman tank.

Fifty metres from the beach was a natural bowl in the grassland that provided shelter from the increasing wind.

This would be our kitchen and bedroom for the evening. It would also be our games room. Surely Dave had a pool table strapped somewhere on his bike.

Evening approached and Sabby was almost salivating over the prospect of the fish feast that'd be arriving shortly. He was planning on firing up the kitchen for our bass-travaganza close to midnight.

"Rather than start cooking in the dark, wouldn't it make more sense to make some dinner now?" I said.

I was hungry. I didn't want to wait until midnight, especially as there were no guarantees.

"What will we do with all the fish we catch?" he asked.

"Take it with us. Use it tomorrow. Besides, what if we don't catch anything?"

Sabby laughed. As though that were a possibility! We'd got off the mark now. At least two of us knew how to fish. And, besides, via insider information, we knew this spot had rich pickings. But he agreed with my caution and made pasta with a tomato, bacon and bladderwrack sauce. It's just as well the seaweed was chopped finely. It's a bit bloody chewy. God knows what Dave was planning to do with three tons of it. Nobody else wanted to eat it again.

We sat around, feeling the joy of an almost full stomach. The pálinka was passed around for the final time, its once friendly, now empty bottle introducing a note of melancholy. Dave thought back to happier times when his belly was bursting and told us of yet another eating competition he'd won. The aim had been to munch through as many bowls of super-hot chilli as possible. Each bowl held 300 grams.

"How many did you eat?" I asked.

"Twelve."

"Twelve? But that's nearly four kilograms of chilli, for God's sake!"

"Yep."

He shifted uncomfortably and then farted.

"More tea, vicar!" he said, laughing like it was the first time he'd said it.

The fishing hour was upon us and suddenly our quiet stretch of beach filled up with people: lone fishermen, couples walking hand-in-hand, men walking dogs. We'd planned to set up the tents immediately after dinner but now felt we should wait until the intruders buggered off. The tents could wait. We had fish to catch.

We ran excitedly to the shoreline, expanding our rods to their full size as we went, and cast out into the surf. One minute later, the likely success of tonight's expedition had already been determined.

"I'm stuck," I said.

"Me too," said Joe.

Twenty metres down the beach we could see Dave wrestling with his rod, his hook caught fast on the bottom.

A little way out to sea, five or six small boats bobbed about. Each contained a fisherman or two. One of them reeled in a fish. We tugged our lines free and moved both up and down the coast, but it was the same everywhere. The sea floor was a forest of weed. Our fishing advisers hadn't told us that if we wanted to catch bass we'd need a boat. Despite what we'd led ourselves to believe, we hadn't become overnight fish whisperers who could charm our dinner out of the sea. We were just a bunch of bassholes.

We gave up around quarter past ten and returned to the spot we'd decided to sleep. There were still a few people milling about.

"They'll go soon," I said, lying in the grass, "although it'll probably be dark by then"

"Are you going to put your tent up now?" asked Joe.

"No, I'll wait a little while."

Suddenly a single fat droplet of rain splashed on my forehead.

"It's raining!" cried Dave. "It's raining!"

The clouds burst. With the speed we moved, you'd have thought it was pouring boiling oil. All four of us scrambled to construct our nylon homes as quickly as possible. It didn't matter if anyone saw us now. They'd all be running for whichever secret passage they'd taken to get here.

Once inside my tent, I realised the drawback of setting up too quickly. It wouldn't be the first time a speedy erection would result in an embarrassing failure. In my haste to build the tent with as few pegs as possible, the outer sheet was touching the inner one, a guarantee of subsequent dampness. But it was raining too hard to do anything about it now. I lay back on my sleeping bag and realised I'd also built my tent on top of a massive hump. I'm an idiot.

It stopped raining in the early hours but my tent was soaked inside and out. The small mountain beneath my ground mat hadn't help me sleep. My back felt like I could've got down on all fours and made a serviceable washing basin.

With wet gear, no fish and a continuing grey sky, a certain gloom hung over the camp. We decided to set off early. It had already started spitting when we took refuge in a bus shelter and cooked up our porridge. Sabby also found a few remaining bits of sea holly root in his panniers and cooked them up for us in beef stock. I drank the savoury liquid but tipped away the woody, little lumps. They hadn't improved by hanging around his bag for three days. Am I making this foraging lark sound like fun? I didn't think so.

Look at a map of Aberdovey, sitting on the estuary of the river Dyfi, and imagine you want to travel south to, say, Ynyslas just across the water. You can almost touch it. But unfortunately it's twenty miles by road, which is an annoyance in a nice, dry car but a complete pain in the arse on a bicycle on a wet Saturday afternoon.

And boy, it can rain in Wales, can't it? Snowdonia, the area we'd steered around these last few days, exceeds 3,000 mm a year on average. That's five times what London gets. Today it felt like we were getting a sizeable portion of that average and most of it was running down my neck. I don't know why I hadn't anticipated this weather. I can count the number of times I've visited Wales without rain on one water-wrinkled finger.

We'd come to a decision. Joe had a refuge in Aberystwyth. He still had access to the house he'd rented while at university there. Tonight we'd hide there and give ourselves the chance to dry our soggy gear. It might even provide enough time to allow my newly webbed feet to return to normal.

We still had many miles to go to reach it, east along the river Dyfi to Machynlleth and then west along the opposite bank. We stopped to look at a waterfall in the hamlet of Furnace but, to be honest, all I could see today were waterfalls.

There was one thought keeping us all going. With each passing day, and each mile southwards, our chance of good weather increased.

"Just wait until we get to France, Dave," I said. "It'll all be alright then."

I have to admit I found it very difficult to ride anywhere near Dave. For one, his bike made various clanking sounds as it rolled and there was an annoying ticking noise as the strap from one of his panniers rubbed perpetually on his spokes. On top of that, Dave rode his heavy bike like a man fighting a bull, all physically-exhausting, heaving shoulders. It looked knackering. But, worse still, he always seemed to be in too high a gear for the gradient and every leg-straining revolution of his pedals appeared to require more energy than any human could possibly muster. Whenever I ended up cycling behind him, I became instantly out of breath on his behalf.

On the edge of Aberystwyth is a steep slope called Penglais Hill. To the town's students it's simply known as The Hill. The university campus sits on top and, with a lot of the student accommodation in town, it provides a frequent if unwelcome struggle as the hungover climb skyward for lectures.

Today we approached the hill from the opposite side. As was customary now, young Joe was the first to reach the summit. I'd assumed he was very fit but he confessed the real reason for always being first to the top. He was a kayaker, and to allow him the independence to paddle up and down Wales without a car, he'd modified his gears to enable him to tow a boat. His current load was nothing compared to a kayak and he danced merrily to the top of each slope. Sabby was usually in second place. Oddly though, today he was occasionally slipping behind me and even Dave's unaerodynamic, two-wheeled breezeblock.

We wheeled down The Hill into Aberystwyth and its centre. All I could smell was fast food. The porridge, pasta and rice-based diet had finely attuned my sense of smell. A meaty waft of hamburger grease nearly overcame me, and when I turned a corner to be confronted with a *KFC* I almost fell off my bike.

We brought our gear into the backyard of Joe's terraced house and, with the rain now stopped, hung out our sodden tents on his washing line. My leather sandals, the only footwear I had with me, were sodden and slippery. Their texture was how I imagine Dale Winton's skin to feel.

We took turns at showering, our first for five days. I didn't feel like I needed one. I'd been showering all day.

We finally connected Sabby with a fishing tackle shop and he got himself geared up as permitted, excited to join the fishing team and hopefully jump to the top of our fishy leader board, especially given how poorly we'd all performed so far.

Sabby wanted to get started right away. We all went down to the shore. The sea seemed tantalisingly close but between us and the water was a field of slippery rocks. They went on for miles and took ages to traverse. Dave got to the sea first. With his first cast he got snagged and lost more tackle. We were hopeless.

Instead we had a look in the rock pools for tasty morsels but found nothing to eat but limpets. I'd watched a *YouTube* video on how to prepare them, but they definitely fall into the category of "starvation food". They're famously as chewy as a power ball.

"I do want to try limpets," said Joe, "in case they're better than everyone's been saying."

"Me too," I replied. "Maybe there's a Limpet Illuminati laughing at their cunning for convincing the world they're rubbish."

But neither of us were hungry enough this evening to knock the little shells from the rocks and prise out the *Pirelli McNuggets*.

Joe's brother lived just around the corner and in the evening he invited us over for something to eat. He was leaving Wales shortly to work in Slovakia as a missionary. I didn't know missionaries still existed. I thought we probably had too much religion already. He served up a beef stew and, before diving in, took me by surprise by saying grace. I didn't know anyone still did that either.

This evening and the dinner at Geraint's felt a bit cheaty but none of it had been prearranged or asked for, and offers of food were allowed under the *Ride and Seek* rules. However, with *Live Below The Line*, you aren't allowed to accept any meals and so I devised a way to account for any freebies so we could try to reach the end successfully under both sets of regulations.

Joe's house had been a welcome bolthole from the dismal weather, but we'd cut today short to stop here and had now fallen behind schedule. We'd need to make up the difference soon. No one wanted this experiment to go on any longer than the planned 100 days. Besides, Joe had already booked a flight back from Gibraltar and had to be there on time. Kayak gears or not, he wouldn't want to cycle back home again.

The elderflower project I'd started three days ago could now move on to Stage Two. To be honest, I'd forgotten about it and the whole thing would probably have been better with fresher flowers but I decided to work with what I had.

I took my five litre plastic bottle, added a sachet of yeast I'd brought with me for this purpose as well as half a bag of sugar, and half-filled it with water. I re-fastened the cap and gave the whole thing a big shake. I was making wine.

I'll be honest. I'd never made wine before. I'd made plenty of ginger beer and figured if I replaced the ginger and lemon in the recipe with elderflowers I had foolproof way to generate cheap if not entirely delicious booze. We were only talking small quantities – a couple of bottles in total – but enough for our Wales Completion Party. Yes, this stuff wasn't going to be laid down for a year to improve. We'd be sampling it in a week or so. Besides, there was no point in aiming too highly for flavour; the flowers had already started to go a bit manky.

Ahead of his new missionary position, Joe's brother was cleaning out his cupboards and he gave us some bread, more oats and, best of all, a pack of plump sausages, which made a welcome change that morning from the daily tedium of porridge.

Joe said his final goodbye to his student digs. I strapped my wine factory to the top of my front pannier rack, whose fitting was the only completed task by the crap bike shop on the Isle of Man during the seventeen years they had my bike. It was the first time I'd had a front rack and it took a while to get accustomed to the heavier steering. I had my light sleeping bag in one front pannier but a much heavier sack of food – my pasta, flour and sugar – in the other. This, I'd later learn, was a Bad Idea. Adding the vat of wine to the top really didn't help either.

The weather had brightened up and so rather than leave Aberystwyth immediately, and with Sabby desperate to play with his new rod, we figured we could catch our lunch. We spent some time fishing from the lighthouse jetty but, with its walls that sloped outwards as they plunged into the sea, both Dave and Sabby lost tackle without being compensated with a meal. I merely lost two hours of my life. Fishing, or uselessly-pointing-a-stick-at-some-water as it should be called, was beginning to annoy me.

Before leaving town, we hit our first big British supermarket, *Morrisons*. As I spend most of my time between Spain, where supermarkets tend to be small, and the Isle of Man, where supermarkets expect at least one of your kidneys for a dozen eggs, I was blown away by how cheap their budget lines were.

Joe, with his recent experience of thrifty studenthood, knew all the bargains. During his degree, his weekly food budget had been around ten pounds and so he was close to living below the line for the entire three years of university. Well, that is until you factor in the cost of alcohol. But here at *Morrisons*, nutritious, calorific peanut butter was only 62p. In Spain it'd cost three or four times that amount. We bought a jar as well as – deep joy – more porridge oats and some strawberry jam. These may not be the components of the most mind-blowingly spectacular meal but we could hardly baulk at well over 7,000 calories for only £1.62.

This cost-effectiveness does highlight something truly awful about Britain though. In a country where a pot of jam can be had for less than 30p, a large loaf for 41p, and £1 can buy you two and a half kilograms of spaghetti – that's 25 portions! – there are still 1,000,000 people a year who need to use food banks. Something has gone seriously wrong. I don't know how David Cameron sleeps at night, although I suspect it's in a coffin.

We continued down the coast on the A487. After a relatively flat start to Wales, the hills were here. Joe would once again reach the top first with me in second place, but Dave and Sabby spent a long time pushing. This was hardly surprising with Dave's bike, constructed as it was from an alloy of lead and limestone and dangerously overloaded, but Sabby had been climbing the earlier Welsh bumps with relative ease. Now he was struggling.

The traffic started to thicken and we craved quieter roads. We looked at the map and, foolishly as it turned out, decided to try some smaller lanes closer to the coast. The lanes twisted and turned, rarely going in the direction we wanted, and the hills got shorter but steeper. A rapid downhill would be followed by an uphill that reduced me to pushing too. There was a look of anguish on Sabby's face.

Our progress slowed to that of an earthworm. Repeatedly pushing my heavy bike skywards had my girlie arms aching. It would take us months to reach today's destination at this pace.

Food was on our mind. Sabby was thinking ahead and planning dinner. Near Pontgarreg we passed a farmhouse selling duck eggs via an honesty box. They clearly didn't have much faith in the trustworthiness required for such a scheme. A human figure stood unsubtly behind the living room curtain watching our every move. One pound bought us six large eggs and a huge dollop of suspicion.

At the first opportunity we slipped back on to the A487 and had to suffer the traffic if we wanted to move in a vaguely forward direction, which we definitely did.

Our target had been Dinas Cross, farther than the usual daily 37 miles because of yesterday's interrupted ride, but evening was here, it was getting colder and everyone was tired. We decided to get as far as Cardigan and, to match its name, find somewhere warm and fluffy to stay.

We reached the edge of town. It was pleasantly reassuring to think that, kind farmer willing, I'd be lying snugly inside my tent within a few minutes. And then there was an explosion.

Dave's horror show of a bike had suffered its third puncture. To make matters worse, there was a large hole in his back tyre, the sort that only appears in the oldest and most knackered of rubber wheels. He hadn't given his bike even the briefest of inspections before leaving home. I'd have had more confidence in his bike if it were made of talcum powder.

Fortunately Dave had brought a spare, foldable tyre with him. Less fortunate was that it was the wrong size, too narrow for his inner tubes. I wandered off in an attempt to keep warm and to prevent me from throwing something at Dave's head. By the time I returned, former bike mechanic Sabby had found a solution and we were ready to continue. And that's when it started to rain.

At the first farm with an empty field, I threw my bike against its dry stone wall and hurried to the farmhouse. The portly farmer had no problem with us sleeping in his field.

"Just stay clear of the dogs though," he said. "They'll eat you."

The rain was coming down harder now. We climbed into

our tents and waited for it to stop in anticipation of dinner. But it didn't and it clearly wasn't going to. We needed a contingency plan. Sabby quickly boiled up some water in the entrance of his larger tent and we each ran there, ducking for cover, to apply the heated liquid to the boring oats in our bowls. Still, tonight, anything was better than nothing. And anything else would have been better than porridge.

We hadn't caught up any of the miles we'd needed to. In fact, we were further behind. We were slowing down, and I was hungry. Emergency porridge wasn't enough. It was only eight o'clock but, with the rain pouring and the crew each retired to his home, I sat bored, *Kindle*-less, amusing myself by flicking slugs off the tent's inner lining.

Tonight's storm hadn't been expected. I checked on *AccuWeather* and there'd only been a 4% chance of rain this evening. It rained all night. Well done, *AccuWeather*.

The next morning, over breakfast, we learned the reason for Sabby's earlier distress. His knee was acting up, and it wasn't the first time. Although in his mind he was Sabby the Chef, he'd had to give up professional catering as a result of a recurring knee problem that flared up because of twelve-hour shifts standing in the kitchen. He decided to take it easy for a day or two.

As we packed up, the farmer came out to say hello. He asked me where I was from. I mentioned Blackburn.

"Ah, I was up near there on the moors rally driving."

He didn't look like a rally driver.

"When was that?"

"Around the time of the murders."

"Eh?"

"The Ian Brady thing."

Geographically, he was a bit off. Ilkley Moor is over in Yorkshire, quite a way from my home town, but I don't suppose he's the only person who associates the word Blackburn with horror.

We cycled into Cardigan and to *Tesco*. I stayed outside with the bikes. A large, middle-aged woman sat beside me on a bench.

"Looks like it's brightening up," she said.

"Yeah, I'm a bit sick of this rain."

"There won't be any rain for a couple of days."

"How do you know that?"

"I can feel it in my knee."

"Eh?"

"Yes, my knee tells me when it's going to rain."

Wow, a water-divining patella!

"Really?" I asked.

"Oh yes. When rain's coming it gives me gyp. It's worse in thunderstorms. It's painful enough to make me cry."

She was being serious and I didn't want to appear flippant, but I had to ask.

"Have you ever considered, y'know, living somewhere a bit drier?"

"Nah. I lived in the Midlands and it was too dry. It got my chest."

What an amazing woman! She was a human version of those little weather houses, where the plastic woman comes out when it's dry and the man when it's wet. I wondered if other ailments provided information for this one-woman weather station, perhaps an infected ear that announced the arrival of snow, or tornado-predicting haemorrhoids.

The lads emerged from the supermarket. They had restocked on essentials, and bought salted peanuts to refuel us on the road and sultanas to improve the morning porridge. It'd take more than that.

We headed to Fishguard and down a quiet lane to its lovely little harbour in Lower Town. The sun shone happily.

That woman's knee was proving to be more reliable than *AccuWeather*.

It'd been several days since we'd pulled a fish from the sea and we were losing our earlier confidence. An old fella gave Sabby some tips on how to catch pollack close to the harbour wall using bread as bait. All I could think of was the smaller lunch we'd be having as Sabby tore chunks from the communal sandwich loaf. This was the first time, and far from the last, our restricted diet would mine a peevishness I'd previously been unaware of.

As we left the harbour fishless, a Dutch woman wanted to pick up my bike to see how heavy it was. She tried, failed and rolled her eyes at me as though I'd purposely filled my panniers with rubble just to annoy her.

We moved to the longer jetty in Fishguard itself. As we arrived, a bloke was packing up.

"I've been at this all morning," he said.

"Caught anything?"

"Nope, nothing."

That wasn't what we wanted to hear but we had to give it a go. I searched my tackle box to try something new but everything – spinners, hooks, swivels – had started to rust. If I caught another fish, I wouldn't have to hit it on the head to kill it. I could just wait for it to die of tetanus.

My tackle had suffered another casualty. The vibrations of daily cycling had shaken loose the nut fastening the handle to my reel. Without a nut I could still use it but I had to be careful and constantly hold it in place. Without the handle it'd be useless. Even *with* the handle, I was useless enough.

Suddenly a yell of joy erupted. Dave had liberated another fish from its salty confines. It was no bigger than the others had been but perhaps we were now on a roll.

We weren't on a roll.

On the way to Milford Haven, cycling through a heavily wooded area, we were once again overcome by the powerful aroma of garlic. We found its source and filled several bags with ramsons. Our second foraging success of the afternoon was less conventional when Dave found an orange in a lay-by. Its citric juiciness added a welcome new flavour to our restricted diet. We put out of our minds the idea that you're not supposed to eat stuff you've found on the floor.

Oranges were not the only fruit. Turning east towards the rather negative-sounding town of Neyland, we cycled down a lovely cycle path lined with bushes full of tiny wild strawberries. We simply picked and ate. It would've taken a month to collect enough for a pie.

We crossed the toll bridge – free to us – over the river Cleddau to Pembroke Dock and started searching for a place to put our tents. The first house I visited didn't own the fields around it but gave us directions to one that did. Although we followed those directions to the letter, we arrived at entirely the wrong house.

I knocked on the front door. Through the window I could spy a blonde-haired woman in a dressing gown. Perhaps this was a bad time.

"No, this isn't the farm," she said in an eastern European accent.

"Ah, alright then. Sorry to have bothered you."

I turned to leave.

"But you can camp in the garden if you like."

"Can we? Wow, thank you."

"And there's an outside toilet here if you need it."

With the short, well-maintained lawn and bathroom facilities, it was as good as a campsite.

I checked on the condition of my wine factory. The plastic container was starting to harden. It was full of carbon dioxide. Fermentation had begun. I quickly unscrewed and rescrewed the lid to release the pressure. Soon we'd have wine.

Once our host had got dressed – it seemed only appropriate – she came out for a chat. Raminta was from Lithuania and was really rather lovely.

Sabby sat on the floor, preparing his portable kitchen. The occasional flash of pain would cross his face. As well as bike technician and chef he had also sold herbs via Ebay and knew the powers they supposedly possessed. He brewed up a yarrow and lavender tea from plants he'd foraged today hoping to cure his knee. Had it been ready, I would've had more faith in the curative powers of my wine.

Raminta gave me a short tour of her greenhouse and allowed me to forage some lettuce and a little dill. She'd moved to Wales quite recently when her daughter started studying psychology at Swansea University. Raminta was a dentist and said it was a while before the locals accepted "the foreigner". They might just have been saying that though. Only an idiot would purposely piss off a woman with access to dental gas and a hand-drill.

Sabby drank his herb tea and then Dave, Joe, Raminta and I sat and watched him prepare what turned out to be a fabulous dinner. Using some of yesterday's duck eggs, he made a huge, industrial *frittata*. Technically, it was a poor man's version, with flour to add calories and bulk, but with an interesting collection of other ingredients: loads of chopped ramsons, Raminta's dill, foraged rosemary and even Dave's little fish. We each got what seemed like a giant slab of its omelettey goodness and, when soaked in the soy sauce Sabby had brought with him, it tasted like a slice of heaven. He christened it "Ramsons in the Hole". We'd been on the road for a week now and it was the first evening meal to completely fill the void within.

Raminta rounded off dinner with a mug of coffee, a

wonderful heat source on a chilly evening. We thanked her for her generosity and she said goodnight.

"She's nice," I said.

But Sabby changed the mood.

"I can't go on."

"What?"

"My knee. It feels like someone is sticking a knitting needle in it."

It had been keeping him awake at night. The broad smile that had covered his face during the first few days of the trip had been worn away by discomfort. His knee was horribly swollen and looked like a large piece of unstable jelly.

"I really want to do this but I can't go on," he repeated.

He was close to tears.

Days Completed: 7
Ride and Seek: **Total spend £2.24, per day £0.32**
Live below the Line: **Total spend £6.88, per day £0.98**

Chapter 5: A Smack in the Face

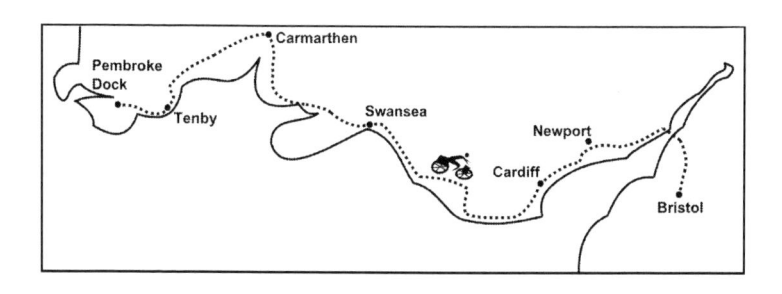

After Sabby's announcement the mood was low. He would stay with us until one of his friends could collect him. But Sabby's departure would be a blow. He'd taken control of our kitchen and delivered some tasty stuff, especially given the restrictions placed upon him. And besides, we were supposed to be a team of four. I'd seen us as the Four Bikemen of the Apocalypse, riding boldly into town, except there was no War, Death or Pestilence and all four of us were Famine.

My sleep had been interrupted in the night by my wine-making chores. I didn't want an explosion in my face. To reduce maintenance over the coming hours, I'd removed the cap, squeezed in the sides of the plastic bottle and resealed it. As the murky brew grew in strength and produced more carbon dioxide, its plastic walls would snap out again.

"It's cracked again," I said to Joe.

"Is that a good sign?"

"As long as it's still cracking, that's good. When it stops cracking and you hear the sound of straining plastic, you probably want to move away."

In the south-west corner of Wales, we now headed eastwards towards Tenby, home to the official Most Beautiful Beach in Europe, as voted in the *Tenby Gazette*'s Most

Beautiful Beach in Europe competition. Only joking. It really did win. Tenby is gorgeous, a lovely walled town and long, tidy beaches fringed with a clear, pale blue sea.

The town was gently humming with tourists. It would've been extremely pleasant to stop for an ice cream or a pint but all thoughts of such pleasures had to be excised from the brain.

We decided to take advantage of the sunny weather to fish from the harbour. We had an audience. My body tends to behave differently when someone is watching. I was once doing a river walk in Spain. I'd climbed to the river's source in the cool morning air and then walked down beside it, skipping merrily from rock to rock. Alone for hours, I'd gambolled without incident. As soon as I passed a party of picnickers, something went wrong with my legs and I ended up face first in the water.

Anticipating a similar incident today, I made a prophesy.

"With all these people about, I bet the first time I cast with this silly bloody reel, I lose the handle," I'd half-joked.

Joe smiled. I cast my line into the sea and then went to reel it in. There was a space where a handle should've been. Joe was now laughing.

"It's down there," he said.

Sitting on the seabed, visible through three metres of crystal clear water, was my black handle. I looked around to see who'd witnessed my embarrassing failure and caught the eye of a sniggering woman. Sometimes I'm Mr Bean.

Without a reel, my rod was useless. Luckily, shortly before setting off, I'd bought a five quid pen rod, a thin, telescopic one that collapses literally to the size of a ballpoint pen. I expanded it, fastened on the accompanying toy reel – at least it felt like a toy – and tried to fish again, desperately avoiding further amusement to any onlookers by accidentally launching the whole lot into the sea.

After half an hour, Joe finally placed himself on our fishy leader board by pulling in a tiny, brightly-coloured fish that we couldn't identify from my *Collins Gem* Book of Fish and was too small to eat in any case. It looked tropically poisonous and was swiftly thrown back into the ocean. That was as good as it got today. I'd really expected fishing to be more fun than this.

The cycle path out of Tenby to Saundersfoot went through a couple of old, dark and dank railway tunnels. Emerging, blinking into the bright afternoon sun, we met Route 4 of the *Sustrans National Cycle Network*. By its very nature, a long distance cycle path will appeal to a lot of people travelling with heavy bags, and so the maxim "the flatter, the better" should've been very much in the mind of the cycle route's designer. It wasn't. The path hunted out steepness wherever it could be found. We climbed a long 16% hill and then, nonsensically, an even steeper 14% one. The afternoon continued with one hellish ascent after another. This was doing no favours for Sabby's ailing knee. Later, the route followed the A40, took a five mile inland detour and then returned to the A-road about ten metres further along.

"And we're trying to survive on one pound a day," I said, finishing my spiel to this evening's farmer.

He reached into his pocket and extracted a coin. It'd never occurred to me that we could've also got our hosts to stump up for our daily allowance.

"No, no," I said. "I'm not after your money. I just wondered if we could camp in one of your fields."

"Ah right. Aye, no problem. Just go down the road and through the first gate on your right."

We talked a bit more. I asked him his name so I could acknowledge him within these pages.

"You're writing a book?" asked John. "I'm going to write a

book."

"Yeah, what about?"

Now I need to tread carefully here because, as I have since discovered, his chosen topic has already ended in one libel case, but it involved local corruption at the highest level.

"My wife doesn't want me to write it," he said, "but I will. I'm going to blow the lid off Carmarthen."

I thanked him for the field and turned to leave.

"Ah," he said, remembering something.

"Yes?"

"There are a few bullocks in that field." He paused. "You'll probably be alright though. They'll just be a bit inquisitive."

We cycled up the road and let ourselves through the barred gate. Twenty or so baby bulls immediately surrounded us and stared. Joe placed his bike against a tree and started to set up his tent. One of the bullocks moved in and licked his *Brooks* leather saddle.

"No," he yelled. "It might be your mum!"

The cows crowded us. I ran at them, flapping my arms, to chase them away so the others could set up without being trampled. Eventually our tented village was complete. The bullocks got bored and wandered off to the far end of the field to discuss whatever it is that interests bullocks. Heifers probably.

Sabby cooked up a huge pot of rice mixed with sultanas and the spring onion-like stalks of yesterday's ramsons. Hard boiled eggs were added and the whole lot dressed with olive oil, soy sauce and chilli. We were going to miss him.

We'd enjoyed very little small talk in the week we'd been together. Tonight we chatted over our food and a few delicious cups – in my case, thimblefuls – of elderflower tea.

I realised for the first time that the others' motivations for this trip were different from mine. Although my resources were scarce, theirs were non-existent. It was the challenge that made me want to complete it, to see if I could live like Ken, and to see if it would be enjoyable on such a budget. But Dave, Joe and Sabby were seriously strapped for cash. The money wasn't there for any other type of journey. This explained why no one wanted to put a hand in his pocket around the pub table in Liverpool.

I woke up at half past six to the sound of serious snorting. It was very close. I stuck my head out of the tent and was face to face with twenty bullocks in a line, staring right at me. They'd formed a plan, and one involving our removal from their field. The herd were just waiting for the command to charge from its leader. At the risk of waking everyone I shouted at them but they stood their ground, impassive. I, or a floating head as they saw me, was clearly no threat. I needed something bigger to scare them away. I had an idea. I slapped the inside of my tent, its grey exterior shaking and flashing in the morning twilight. They were spooked and jumped back. Another slap of the fabric sent them scurrying away to rethink their attack. I'd won the Battle of the Little Bighorns.

In the morning Dave was feeling playful.
"I've got a dog beard," he said to me.
"What are you on about?"
"I've got a dog beard," he repeated.
He leaned forward, stroking his chin.
"Eh?"
"Go on," he said. "Stroke me. Stroke my dog beard."

I gently, and reluctantly, touched his fur. As soon as I made contact, he leapt forward towards my face, barking loudly like a rabid dog. I jumped back nervously. He laughed loudly at his trick.

"What the hell was that?" I asked.

"I learned it off a tramp."

Joe had seen what happened.

"If a tramp had done that to me, I think I would've just killed him as a gut reaction."

Dave was still guffawing, the silly sod.

Today our target was Swansea and, unknown to me, it was going to end badly.

Near Llanelli, the cycle path took us along the seashore. A huge beach stretched ahead of us, the sea barely visible miles away.

Maybe the reason we'd caught so few fish was down to our spinners. With live bait instead, perhaps we'd have better results. I leant my bike against a rock and walked out on to the beach. It was covered with thousands of lugworm casts, the thin snake of sand removed when the worm digs its hole, like a waiter had got clumsy with a huge bowlful of unappetising grey spaghetti.

I'd seen a video explaining how best to dig for worms. The juicy creature lives several inches below the surface, halfway between its cast and a small vent about a foot away. The video had suggested using a shovel. Two scoops and the worm would be exposed, ready to be dropped into a *Tupperware* box, or eaten fresh from the beach if your foraging isn't going as well as hoped.

Unfortunately, the only available digging implement was my sanitary trowel. By the time I'd dug down deep enough – twenty or so spoonfuls – the clever worm had discovered my plan and was making its escape. I dug for the best part of half an hour. All I managed to capture was a couple of half-worms, accidentally sliced in two and slowly bleeding to death. Live bait isn't much good if it's already dead.

But there were richer pickings to be had. Beside the beach was a salt marsh, normally accessible only in wellies. Since we'd met that woman with the magic knee, the ground had dried out enough to allow easy walking and it was home to sea purslane and, even better, marsh samphire. Both are salty, succulent edible sea plants but marsh samphire is regaining its popularity and showing up on supermarket shelves. I love it. With scissors in hands, we snipped the tiny, cactus-like stalks, collecting them in bags.

Over on the cycle path, a man was walking his dog. An old woman came in the opposite direction.

"What are they doing?" she asked him, mystified.

"They're collecting samphire."

"Eh? What's that?"

"Sea asparagus," he replied, giving one of its alternative names.

"Oh," she said, none the wiser.

I walked up to them with my bag of cuttings.

"Do you want to try some?" I asked her.

She peered inside and wrinkled her nose.

"Go on. It's nice."

She took a tiny piece and inspected it closely, still not convinced. Then she put it in her pocket.

"I'll save it till I get home," she said. "And share it with my husband."

Austerity Britain seemed to be taking frugality a little too seriously.

"Take another piece for him," I said. "Have a party."

My amazement at British supermarket prices reached its zenith today with a visit to *Lidl*, although with more than a small concern for animal welfare. Y'see, one shiny pound in this budget store will buy you fifteen – count 'em, fifteen! – eggs. I can't imagine the living conditions those chickens have to suffer. What exactly is the level of life quality beneath battery chicken? They're probably removed from their cages at regular intervals and kicked around the farmyard before having electrodes attached to their little chicken scrotums. Except that chickens don't have scrotums, and neither do cocks, which is confusing if you think about it.

But this does raise an interesting moral question. How do you balance being able to feed your family on a budget with the ethical treatment of animals? I imagine the approach most people take is the one we adopted. You pretend it's not happening and try not to think too deeply while munching down your affordable omelette. For any reader who would've taken a more chicken-friendly approach, you might see what happened next as karma.

We entered the outskirts of Swansea along a flat, tarmacked cycle path. It was just after five o'clock. People on their way home from work whizzed past. The decent surface allowed me to pick up some speed. A small incline was approaching. And then, out of nowhere, everything went haywire.

I don't remember much, except the side of my helmetless head hitting the ground with the most gentle of bumps as my bike and panniers thumped into my back. All was confusion. I'd been travelling along a smooth, straight path. How could this have happened?

I jumped up quickly and checked my bones. Nothing major was broken but I felt winded and my left hand was tender. I raised it to my face and then looked at my bloodied fingers. My bottom lip felt numb.

"You just flew through the air!" Joe said, as though I wished to be judged on artistic merit.

Sabby looked at my face and winced.

"Oh my days!" he said. "Your nose doesn't look good. I'll see if I can get help."

I looked at my bike. Both my back panniers had removed themselves, shattering the strong plastic hooks that held them on to my rack. Everything else appeared to be alright until we stood the bike upright and noticed the front pannier rack was cracked and bent.

"Ah," said Joe. "That's not good."

"What isn't?"

"It's not just your rack. Your forks are bent too."

The force of the crash had twisted them a good inch.

"Can they be bent back again?" I asked.

"No, they're aluminium. They'd snap."

A fella came past on his bike and saw the wreckage.

"I've told the council about this cycle path," he said. "There have been loads of accidents here."

We tried to piece together what had happened. Where the path met the incline there was a slight dip. The bike had gone into it at speed and then immediately started to climb. There had been too much weight on the flimsy pannier rack installed on the Isle of Man – the front pannier containing my food as well as my wine experiment – and the downwards and then upwards force on the rack had cracked it, dropping it on to, and therefore locking, my front wheel. I'd then flown over the handlebars like the most useless superhero in history and, as I'd soon discover, smashed the left side of my chest into its bull bars.

"Come here," said Sabby. "This woman has some antiseptic."

He'd been busy knocking on doors to see if anyone could patch me up. Melanie, who took on the role of my nurse, came out of her house carrying a plastic washing-up bowl, some antiseptic, cotton pads and *Vaseline*. She looked at my nose.

"Ouch," she said.

"How bad is it?" I asked.

"Do you want to see it?"

"Do I?"

"Probably not."

Melanie grabbed a mirror and gave it to me. The recent sunshine had burnt my nose and over the last few days it had developed a ridge of thicker skin, which had now been completely removed and hung limply at the edges like banana peel. The exposed layer beneath was pink and wet. My lip was split and I had a large graze on my left cheek. That said, I'd been very lucky. I could easily have suffered a tour-terminating broken arm. Also, my front teeth felt a bit odd. I must've given them a knock, which was much preferable to knocking them out entirely.

"This might sting," she said with an antiseptic-soaked cotton pad in hand.

"I'll be a brave, little soldier."

She dabbed me with her cloth and then handed it to me to continue.

"You should put some of this *Vaseline* on your nose to keep it moist. And take this with you," she said, handing me the antiseptic, the tube of *Vaseline* and the remaining cotton pads. "You might need them."

I thanked Melanie. What a lovely woman!

Sabby and Joe got on their phones to find an open bike shop so we could get the damage fixed as quickly as possible. It was interesting to hear their different approaches.

"Hi, I need your help," started Sabby. "My friend has just had a terrible accident."

Joe was much more British.

"Hello there. I wonder if you could help. My friend has just had a little bump."

None of the bike shops would be open by the time we could get to them this evening. We needed to stay somewhere near the centre of Swansea or waste time cycling out and then back in again tomorrow. A bloke came out of a nearby house to see the commotion. He told us he'd broken his back while cycling, just the sort of cheery story we needed right now. More usefully, he said there were some farms on the road above the cycle track.

Sabby cable-tied my rear panniers to my rack while Joe carried my front panniers and Dave the wine. Off we went to look for a farm. When I grabbed the handlebars for the first time, a sharp, painful stab fired through my left hand. Something felt broken. I gripped as lightly as possible and cycled slowly.

After being welcomed in almost the first place we'd tried on each of our previous evenings, today it wasn't so easy, possibly because I looked like I'd just been in a fight. The first farm housed a young Chinese bloke who spoke not a single word of English and the next two were either empty or their occupants were hiding behind curtains, waiting for me to sod off.

We continued down the road. I cycled into a large chicken farm. From a hangar I could hear thousands of hens squabbling and probably waiting in fear of the farmer coming home and kicking them around the yard. No one was around. I didn't want to scrabble around sorting out this crap. I wanted to lie down and feel sorry for myself.

I saw another old house surrounded by fields. I knocked on the front door, which was also the entrance to a lovely conservatory. A woman in her sixties answered. In the background I could see a similarly aged man sitting on a wicker chair with a blanket over his legs. I explained where we were travelling and the pound-a-day budget. The woman looked at her husband.

"I don't think this is a very good time," she said.

"But," said the man, with a kind smile, "if you can't find anywhere else then please come back."

"He's just had a heart attack," she added almost like an afterthought.

Oh bloody hell. I don't know if by 'just' she meant in the last five weeks or the last five minutes but I didn't want to impose on someone in such a delicate state. I apologised and turned to leave.

"Why did you want to camp around here?" he asked.

"Well," I said, "I've just had an accident." I pointed to my face but I think they could probably see the problem without my direction. "And we need to be in Swansea tomorrow to fix up my bike."

"Ah, you should've told us before," said the man. And then he ordered his wife to show us the field in which we could camp. I still feel guilty about using this opportunity but my face and chest were aching and I didn't want to negotiate all over again with anyone else. I thanked him as warmly as I could with a lip that was growing bigger by the minute.

She led us all to a huge field with grass a metre tall that would make for the most comfortable night's sleep since the beginning of the trip.

"I wish the wine was ready," I said. "I need a drink."

Sabby made another poor man's frittata loaded with today's soft and salty samphire and the chewier sea purslane. Once again it was soy sauce that brought it alive.

Dave tried to cheer me up by telling me about a scheme he'd thought of.

"I'll go up to people and say I bet you twenty quid I've got your name tattooed on my arse. And when they say I haven't I'll show them my arse and it will say 'Your Name'."

"Genius," I said. "But it does sort of require you to get your arse out in public quite often."

We decided if he was to take this idea any further then he'd first have to sew a press-stud arse flap into his cycling shorts.

The sun sank slowly over our grassy home and turned the sky crimson. It would have been a lovely evening if it wasn't for my stiffening face and the painful breathing. It could've been worse. I could've been sitting in my tent this very minute sketching out an initial design for my brand new press-stud arse-flap shorts.

I woke up early after a painful night's sleep. The thump I'd given my chest made it difficult to find a comfortable position and it was impossible to take two complete lungfuls of air. I climbed out of my tent and saw Sabby, whose knee had given him his own sleep-free night, sitting outside his tent. He looked up at me, focussing on my nose.

"Oh my days!" he said. "That is ugly!"

"Cheers, mate."

Dave's interest was piqued.

"Crumpets! Do you want to borrow my mirror?"

The previous evening I'd heavily loaded my nose and cheek with *Vaseline*. The scabbing process had incorporated the gel, and the whole lot had gone a sulphurous yellow, lending me the air of a man with a terrible skin disease. I looked like *Blackadder*'s Ploppy the Jailer, son of Ploppy the Slopper.

Today I wore my helmet for the first time on the trip. I hate helmets. I wasn't sure why I was wearing it. It would offer no protection whatsoever if I crashed in the same gymnastic style as yesterday. The argument is always that in a bad smash a helmet could be the difference between life and death, and that's very true, but it could also be the difference between death and a lifetime with severe brain damage, and I'd rather take death. Still, I felt a little nervous today and so it stayed on my head. (In two days' time I'd be once again sick of it and take it off.) I could've imagined it but everyone set off equally tentatively. We were slower than Joey Essex.

We were on the hunt for new forks, a new front rack and replacement pannier clips. All the paths into town were flat, which was just as well because, with my painful left hand, I couldn't change gears. We tried a couple of bike shops in town without success. Finally, *Wheelies* came up with a rack and fitted it for free, but we'd have to get the remaining items elsewhere. The new rack couldn't accommodate my vat of wine and so it remained on Dave's bike. He wouldn't notice its weight, what with the seventeen medicine balls he was already carrying.

In fitting the rack, the mechanic had to remove the back panniers we'd cable-tied to my rack yesterday. We needed to re-fasten them but were now out of cable ties and the bike shop didn't have any long enough.

"Not a problem!" said Sabby.

At the nearest lamppost he used his pocket knife to remove some large, black cable ties that'd once fastened advertisements to it. He'd foraged for cable ties!

Back on the road, an old bloke on a bike passed us.

"Shame on you," he said smugly. "An 80 year-old passing you young lads."

He may have been joking but I think our 30-odd kilos of luggage and the recent accident gave us extenuating circumstances. Rather than laugh at him, with the mood I was currently in, I just wanted to tell him to piss off. But I didn't. Instead, I imagined ramming a stick into his spokes, seeing him pirouette gracefully through the air and then saying to his prostrate form, "Now, who's going faster, granddad?" I didn't do that either. I couldn't find a stick.

Swansea wasn't going to let us escape so easily. On the edge of town I was cycling beside Joe when we heard the familiar thunk of an expired spoke.

"What? No!" he whined. "This is the worst thing in the world!"

I could think of a few worse things – war and poverty and

Jeremy Kyle – but it was, so he thought, his first ever broken spoke and so maybe he was allowed this over-reaction. His annoyance was doubled when he checked his wheel and realised it was actually the second one to go.

While Joe and Sabby cycled back into Swansea to get the wheel fixed, Dave and I sunbathed on some grass at the side of the road. We were in easy reach of a large supermarket.

"I'm just going for a *Sainsbury's*," said Dave, a euphemism we'd developed.

While sitting there alone, a young bloke walked past me, saw the bikes and asked what we were up to. I told him about the tour and the accident. He looked closely at my face.

"Can't you just wipe it off?" he asked bizarrely, as though I'd stuck my nose into a bowl of custard and it hadn't occurred to me to wash my face.

It would take Joe and Sabby three bike shops before they found someone who could repair the spokes immediately, and not only did they fix it for free but they gave Joe a handful of spare spokes too. Thank you, *Schmoos*!

We finally put some miles between us and Swansea. The route was ugly, through underpasses and beside motorways for an hour.

"We'll be alright once we get past Port Talbot," said Joe.

"Where's that?" I asked

He pointed to a fortress of smoking stacks in the distance.

"That Mordor-esque place over there."

It's hard to imagine anyone wanting to live in Port Talbot. Forty thousand people do though despite all the chemical plants, heavy machinery and petrol fumes. The place stank.

We headed out of town beside the M4. A rural idyll this wasn't. But eventually we hit Pyle and a steep hill would take us to grassier lands. The bottom of the hill had its own challenges. Fish 'n' chip shops seemed to alternate with kebab joints the whole way up, their fat-filled aromas calling out to us like sirens driving us on to the rocks of budgetary collapse.

As I climbed the hill, something repeatedly clicked on my bike. I looked at it and, being rubbish like that, couldn't see the problem. Sabby whipped out his screwdriver and fixed it in seconds. Apparently, that dangly down bit of the gears at the back of the bike whose name I really should know was touching my spokes, a further, until then unnoticed, complication from yesterday's unplanned bicycle somersault.

After the waiting around in Swansea we'd only cycled 30 miles today but it was far enough. We found a friendly farmer to donate a field. He even gave us six of his chicken's eggs. As we'd also just bought another 15-pack of *Lidl*'s torture eggs we had a bit of a glut and so the logical choice of meal was yet another samphire frittata.

I suspect Sabby held personal hygiene more dearly than the rest of us. His original packing list included seven pairs of underpants, which is fine if you're going for a week in Barcelona but a bit excessive for the light packing needed on a bike tour. He'd also brought along a portable shower. He set it up on the branch of a tree at our field's edge and had a very painful-looking cold shower. Dave, Joe and I wallowed in our stench, albeit a warm stench.

Farmer Rob came out to see if we were alright. We chatted. Times are hard for farmers.

"I've 35 cows producing 1,000 litres of milk a day," he said.

"And how much do you get per litre?" I asked.

"Twelve pence."

The cheapest price for milk at *Morrisons* is 37p a litre, although you have to buy four litres to get that deal. But, depending upon the product, prices can rise as high as £1.30 a litre, and so it's clear it's not the farmers who are making the bulk of the profit.

"And how low would the price have to go before it's not really viable as a business?"

He gave a little half-smile.

"Seventeen pence," he replied.

Ah.

I had another painful night. My chest was getting worse. Maybe I'd broken something. I employed my usual everything-will-be-alright technique. If my health was still deteriorating a few days from now, I'd get myself checked.

In the morning we received a second gift from Farmer Rob, a litre and half of his own fresh, creamy milk. Well, when I say 'his own', I mean from his cows, you filthy monkey. He told us it was unpasteurised. Since all I've ever known is the pasteurised stuff I was blissfully unaware of the dangers of salmonella, E.coli, campylobacter, listeria and tuberculosis. It was gorgeously creamy, better than any milk I'd ever had. Sabby wouldn't touch it though.

"It's not safe for a city boy like me," he said.

Breakfast included the experimental use of elderflower tea to moisten the porridge oats instead of water. For future reference, and in case you were thinking of aping this recipe, don't bother.

It rained all morning. In Gavin and Stacey's Barry we stopped at *Tesco*, where a supervisor came out for a chat. She seemed a bit bored of her job and more fascinated with our injuries, my face and Dave's still badly blistered legs.

"You're doing what?" she asked.

"We're foraging."

"What's foraging?"

This was a new question for me. I described what it was, trying not to sound like I was talking to a three year-old.

"Ah right. That's what we used to do. We'd pick wild rhubarb and drink the liquid from it."

I didn't know what she was on about. Maybe she was confusing 'wild rhubarb' with 'can of *Fanta*'.

She wandered back inside the supermarket. Five minutes later, while we were enjoying our lunch of peanut butter sandwiches, she reappeared, this time carrying a plate.

"Is this foraging?"

I looked at its contents.

"Yes, I suppose it is."

She'd brought us each two chunks of juicy, succulent melon.

"They were doing a promo inside," she said. "They won't miss 'em."

It was still raining when we arrived in Cardiff. We whizzed past the castle and pushed our bikes through the pedestrianised shopping centre. I got a taste of what it must be like to suffer from a physical deformity. Walking through town I could sense people staring at my mangled fizzog. If I made eye contact they'd look away, embarrassed, like they'd been caught out. Today, in Cardiff, for one day only, ladies and gentlemen, I present to you...The Elephant Man.

Coming up was a stretch of road I'd cycled before and really not enjoyed, the link between Cardiff and Newport. The last time I'd done it, another cyclist had been killed the same day. Avoiding the deadly main road, we perused Dave's larger scale map. A quick scan had suggested plenty of farms lay closer to the coast. However, now that we cycled through the area it appeared to be one large industrial estate.

"How old is your map, Dave?" I asked.

"Dunno."

"Have a look."

He checked the sheet for a date.

"It's...ah."

"What?"

"1984."

"It's 31 years-old?"

"Yep."

He grinned.

"Well done, Dave."

We passed business unit after unit with not a farm to be seen. I saw a road turning off to the right with a leafier feel and waited for the others to catch up.

"Hey! Well done," said Sabby.

"I've not found anywhere yet."

"No, I mean these."

"These what?"

Unknown to me I'd parked directly beneath three large cherry trees, each one dripping with plump, purple-red fruit. They were sweet and delicious. We stuffed our faces and collected more for later and then cycled down the tree-lined track to discover *Seabank Farm* just as the sun came out.

Unlike our other farms, *Seabank* was a lively, happening place with kids running about. They let us use their pony jumping course. For camping, that is. I didn't saddle Dave up or anything. A young girl appeared with a donkey or some other horsey thing and jumped a few fences in a technically perfect display of utter pointlessness.

An overly friendly border collie came to visit us and insisted we play with him. He'd brought his own ball. I hoofed it a couple of times with the dog happily retrieving it.

"Your turn," I said, kicking the ball to Dave.

He recoiled his scabby leg and clumsily walloped the ball straight into Muttley's chops. We all winced. It was probably bad form to murder your host's prized sheepdog. But he quickly recovered, spat out a tooth or two and continued begging for attention.

The sun had stayed out and after a few tidal calculations we decided this would be the perfect time to fish, an hour before high tide. As we strolled down the lane towards the high sea wall our confidence was palpable.

"I'm going to catch a fish of an unknown species," I started cockily, "that when categorized is deemed to be the tastiest fish on the planet!"

Joe went one better.

"I'm going to catch a fish that brings about world peace and earns me a Nobel prize and a million pounds."

We reached the wall and Joe climbed its steps to take us to the sea. He was first to survey the state of play.

"Any good?" I asked.

"Mmm."

"How is it?"

"It could be better."

I climbed the steps and saw for myself, a huge expanse of beach with a tiny ribbon of silver far in the distance.

"Bugger."

No culinary prize-worthy fish nor peace-facilitating seafood would be captured today.

We walked back slowly to our tents. In a field we saw an improvised house, a trailer to which a wooden extension was attached. A bloke I'd seen at the farm earlier came out. He was hastily chasing his dog back inside.

"Ankle biter," he said. "Hates fishermen."

"He should have no problem with us then."

Another dog came outside, a tiny, white pup. It crawled under a fence and started to chase the guy's chickens.

"I've something for you," the bloke said.

He handed me a bag containing another twelve eggs. We already have nine uncooked ones plus four that Sabby had hard-boiled. With all this farmerly generosity, we were in danger of becoming egg-bound.

Back in our field, Sabby set up his field kitchen in preparation for the thirteen-egg omelette he'd decided to make. And then the farmer's teenage daughter appeared.

"We're going out," she said, and then followed this

statement with the best four words in the world. "You fancy some chips?"

After ten days on a restricted diet, which included absolutely nothing that could fall into the category of 'shit', and with a hollow stomach that grumbled audibly, I almost couldn't speak with excitement.

As Sabby finished the omelette, she returned to our field loaded with four bags of plump, fluffy yet crunchy chips along with four half-litre bottles of fizzy pop. I couldn't have been more thankful if she'd bought me a country estate with its own brewery and harem. The chips steamed thickly in the cooling air.

The drinks' bottles all had the same price sticker. Ironically, they cost one pound each, an entire day's budget for three or four mouthfuls of sugary water.

It'd take a better writer than I am to adequately describe how great those chips were. I really think that, once doused in vinegar and sprinkled with an unhealthy amount of salt, they were – objectively – the best chips in the history of the world. I wanted to write a sonnet to each individual cuboid of spud, but that was daft because then they would've got cold, so I just ate them instead.

Despite the warming effect of the chips and the huge omelette, the chilly evening drove us to an early night, my pains temporarily relieved by the loveliness of fried potato.

I nodded off but around ten o'clock was torn from my slumber by the roar of a quad bike. From inside my tent, there could've been more than one. It felt like that bit at the beginning of *The A-Team* when the baddies turn up. But this wasn't a machine-gun-toting ruffian soon to be defeated by an overweight, mohicanned wrestler firing cabbages from a home-made tank. I unzipped my tent.

"A present from my dad," said an unseen male, hidden by the glare of his headlights.

A loaf of bread and two cans of *Foster's* materialised through the brightness like a gift from God and plopped solidly into my tent.

The A-Team was great but *Seabank Farm* folk were better.

I don't have kids but I learnt a little last night about what it must be like to care for a baby. The elderflower wine's fermentation process seemed to have upped a gear. Within a few minutes of burping my child and squeezing its sides in, the internal pressure would cause the plastic to snap back out again. After several hours of ensuring my baby didn't explode, I took the lazy way out and unscrewed the lid enough to let the gas constantly escape. Apparently you can't do that with real infants.

It was a beautiful morning with tiny, fluffy clouds in a deep blue sky. The cycling was perfectly flat without even so much as an incline, a welcome change from the Welsh hills of late and allowed Sabby to move quickly without discomfort to his knee.

Now that I've set today's scene of bucolic beauty, let's talk about toilet time because we haven't really done that, have we? An item on every healthy person's daily tick list is, I believe it's called, big jobs. If, for some bizarre reason, you want to emulate this adventure, my top tip is that the supermarket is your friend, or at least *Morrisons*, *Sainsbury's*, *Asda* and *Tesco* are. Their toilets are always easy to find. But if it's that time of day and you feel there's one in the chamber, then avoid *Lidl*. They do have a toilet – I think by law they probably have to – but, as I discovered this morning, they don't want you to use it. Today it was located behind a security door and I had to be led there by a small, dark-haired eastern European girl who angrily punched in the code to let me through. I couldn't shake the idea that I was being escorted to the bog in some frosty Siberian Gulag. The mild terror that I felt certainly helped though.

Outside *Lidl* it became obvious Dave wasn't taking care of my baby as well as Social Services would've demanded. Lying awkwardly on its side, the bottle was leaking all over the floor. He hadn't noticed the brains spilling from my child's head. I rescrewed the lid but we'd lost a good half litre.

Not far away, and straddling the river Usk, is the Newport Transporter Bridge, a sort of car-carrying crane made out of large pieces of *Meccano*. It's a little bit special. There are only eight such structures in the world. We wanted to be on the other side – it'd save a twenty minute diversion – but the official toll was a full day's allowance. The young lad selling tickets wasn't for budging but his boss heard my plea and kindly carried us across the water for nothing.

The Usk wasn't the only river we needed to cross today. After collecting some lime blossom we approached the Old Severn Bridge. With a name like that I was expecting something Roman-looking, made of stone. It's a lot more modern than that and, like a lot of modern things in Britain, it wasn't working. Signs told us it was closed for the next two days. This would require a detour much longer than twenty minutes. It'd take a day to Gloucester and then another to Aust on the opposite shore. Fortunately, just like our Mersey crossing, we got lucky and were allowed across on the bridge's service road. With a strong side wind in the centre, we said goodbye to Wales. One country down, four to go.

Down leafy lanes, and after scoring some wild roadside horseradish, we found a farm near Easter Compton. Today was special. On my previous ride I'd met Cleo, an attractive, nineteen year-old French girl, who was backpacking around Ireland. She said she just knocked on people's doors and asked if she could sleep in their gardens. I'd been surprised that nine out of ten people said yes. I put this down, at least partly, to her physical appearance and doubted whether an older, hairier bloke would've had the same success. Today, I'd scored my tenth straight yes in a row. That is, if I ignored farms that didn't own the surrounding land or those whose tenants couldn't actually speak English, which I definitely did. I don't think it can be denied then, that this surely means I'm sexier than a young French girl. Or maybe they were just scared that if they said no, we'd burn down their barns.

To celebrate my sexiness as well as the completion of our first country, we decided to have a wine party. This decision was also made because, after this morning's unfortunate leakage, I'd become highly suspicious of what I was actually brewing. The liquid on the ground outside *Lidl* had the consistency of *Golden Syrup*.

While Sabby cooked up a rice, raisin and lentil dish, crammed full of garlic, chilli and horseradish and topped with two fried eggs each, I poured a nip of wine into my tiny plastic cup. If I were Oz Clarke I'd probably have described it as tasting like sour apples and peach blossom with a hint of battery acid that lingers on the tongue. As I'm not Oz Clarke, my analysis was less descriptive.

"I don't think we should drink this."

It was rank, a barely alcoholic, pale grey treacle on the road to vinegar. Later though I reassessed my earlier pessimism.

"Well, maybe Dave could try it first. If he isn't dead after twenty minutes then anyone else who wants it can have some."

And that's how I came to be straining the gel through an as yet unworn bandanna into Dave's cup. It was taking ages. After a while I gave up and just poured the liquid, rotting flowers and all, into his beaker. He necked it in one and smiled widely.

"It's not that bad," he said.

"Do you want some more?"

"No."

We monitored Dave's condition but there was really no need. No one else wanted to drink it. I poured the rest away in a distant corner of the field. Nothing will ever grow there.

To ease our disappointment we turned to the *Foster's* donated the night before. From plastic cups we sat there sipping half a can of warm lager apiece. We were grateful for the beer but it wasn't the party I'd been hoping for.

The next morning we woke up to torrential rain. The mood wasn't helped by Sabby's surprise announcement.

"My friend's picking me up today."

"When? Where?"

He hadn't complained much about his knee in the last few days. The route had been much flatter and I'd put to the back of my mind that he was leaving us. I was hoping he might have reconsidered.

"When we get to Bristol," he replied.

And it wasn't long before we were there. It was a sad moment saying goodbye. Sabby had fed us on a daily basis, fixed our bikes when they failed and been responsible for spotting plants unknown to us. He was gutted. He'd travelled to the UK especially for this trip and instead of lasting 100 days it was all over within a fortnight. He'd really wanted to reach Gibraltar with us.

He gave us each a hug and then cycled off to find the friend who'd drive him to London. We looked at each other sadly and felt a little lost. We were now three. But in less than an hour we would be four once again.

Days Completed: 12
Ride and Seek: **Total spend £5.84, per day £0.49**
Live below the Line: **Total spend £10.48, per day £0.87**

Chapter 6: Days of Easy Gorging

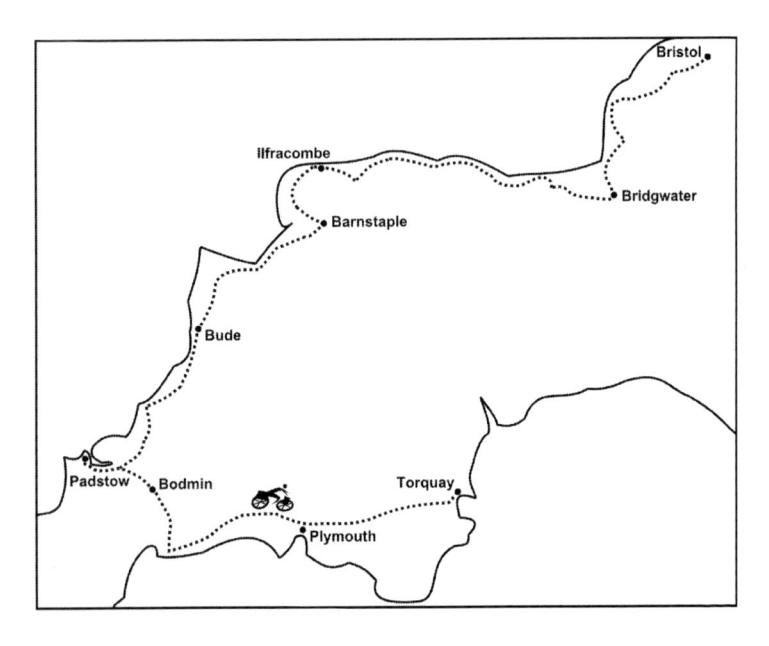

We were heading along a flat road towards Weston-super-Mare when I heard a demonic shriek and a partially Lycra-clad, middle-aged idiot threw himself out of a bush into my path.

"Surprise!"

Yes, it was a surprise and one that nearly got you run over, you numpty.

We'd arranged to meet Mark later that day but he knew we'd have to come down this road and, being as excited as a kid in a pet shop about joining us for a week around Devon and Cornwall, he wanted to get together sooner. Behind the bush was his car and his missus, Julie, the tarot card-reading fraud.

Mark set up his bike. Clearly he was taking seriously the fishing aspect of our challenge. A huge, black pole was strapped to his bike, jutting out a good two feet behind. Anyone approaching from the rear and not paying attention would likely end up skewered upon it.

"Does it work?" I asked.

"Yes, I caught some mackerel a few days ago."

Wow, mackerel, that'd be nice.

"Ask him about his shorts," said Julie.

"What about your shorts?"

"They're hers," he replied.

"Nice."

When we finally restarted, Mark set off at a sprint. Maybe he wanted to demonstrate that, despite being older than the rest of us, he wasn't going to hold up our progress. He disappeared into the distance, which meant none of us would be impaled for a while.

We hit the coast at Weston-super-Mare but even with Mark's long pole the sea was too far out. At low tide, dangerous mudflats are exposed that suck in hapless tourists like quicksand. It was better to steer clear.

My face had healed remarkably quickly. Maybe because the nose scabs had been loaded with *Vaseline*, they'd reduced in size over the last couple of days. Today, in a *Sainsbury's* bathroom, I peeled off the final one. My nose was back to normal. I was no longer a monster. Dave's legs were still a mess though.

We carried on to Burnham-on-Sea, once the home of the longest married couple in Britain. Walter and Beatrice Postings were hitched for over 80 years. If 50 years is your golden anniversary and 60 diamond, you'd expect something pretty bloody special for your 80th but you'd be disappointed. Officially, your anniversary gifts should be made of oak. Perhaps the thinking was that, unlike expensive precious stones, at least from hardwood you could manufacture your own false teeth. Or a penile splint.

We found a house next to a huge, under-utilized field. I knocked on the door, hoping my streak of sexiness would continue.

"It's not our field," the old bloke said.

"Ah, right. Sorry to have..."

"But we've got a paddock you can use."

While we set up amid large apples trees, John, our host, came out and kindly gave us a packet of digestives and some *Mr Kipling Almond Slices*.

It was a lovely spot but it raised a question. Why did John keep a single magpie in a cage at the bottom of his garden? Perhaps he was very superstitious and always wanted the option of seeing 'two for joy'.

I used my portable washing machine for the first time on the trip. The rubble sack I'd brought with me, along with a few cupfuls of water and a squirt of shower gel, didn't achieve that 'bluey whiteness' required of detergent commercials but then again most of my clothes were black, as was the water by the time I'd finished.

With no Sabby to orchestrate our dinner we had to make other arrangements. He'd also taken the only big pan we had. As a result, Joe cooked pasta on his stove while, on mine, I made a satay sauce with peanut butter, garlic, chilli and horseradish. It went down alright. We weren't going to starve. Not yet, anyway.

In his rush to pack and the excitement about wearing his wife's pants, Mark had forgotten to bring any warm clothes. As the evening chilled, he had to huddle in his tent for warmth. But, according to John, his chills would soon be alleviated as another heatwave – hopefully one that lasted longer than a day – would start tomorrow. I didn't bother checking *Accuweather*. It would probably have predicted a blizzard.

Mark had a terrible night's sleep and he didn't mind telling us.

"I was freezing," he said. "And what was with those bloody owls?"

In the early hours, two of them had moved into the trees above our heads and held some sort of horrible screeching competition. They sounded like they were being electrocuted.

Despite being unable to locate front forks and pannier hooks in Swansea, our route fortunately took us through Bridgwater, home to the UK's largest supplier of touring bike spares. Once repaired my bike was better than new, with much stronger, steel forks. I could now crash into solid objects at will.

Despite being the only A-road through the Quantock Hills, the A39 isn't really up to the job. There's too much traffic. We cycled slowly over its pretty undulations. Mark cycled like a man possessed but unlike yesterday now he seemed possessed by the spirit of a giant sloth. He'd perhaps worn himself out after yesterday's blazing start. He wasn't enjoying himself very much. He didn't mind telling us that either.

After yesterday's lack of fishing possibilities we headed for Watchet at high tide. The water was churned up and muddy. A local fisherman pointed out the obvious to us, that fishing with spinners in such dirty water was pointless; the fish wouldn't see them. At least it would've been obvious if we weren't such rubbish fishermen.

Instead we headed to Blue Anchor and had an hour lying in the sun. A bloke cycling the coast of Britain saw our tents and asked which campsite we were going to. It made me realise how incredibly convenient our arrangements were. We didn't have to hunt out a distant campsite. We could stop wherever there was a kindly farmer, which, in our experience, was just about everywhere. And not far away, in Carhampton, we found the kindliest of all.

Eric pointed out a comfortable field and told us where we could find the farm workers' toilet. We would've been well satisfied with that, but then he uttered a glorious statement.

"When you've finished setting up, go to the pub and tell them Eric sent you."

We got excited. Supermarkets aside, we hadn't done much mingling with the public and felt tonight we should make an effort. For the first time on the journey, Dave put on the jeans he'd brought with him. Quite why anyone would carry a heavy, bulky pair of jeans on a foraging bike ride I've no idea but that's Dave for you. It was either the jeans or one of the 73 pairs of tweed trousers he'd brought along. I put on my tuxedo, by which I mean my second t-shirt, the cleaner one.

Once inside *The Butcher's Arms* we presented ourselves at the bar. I felt a bit like a spy.

"Eric sent us," I said.

Sandra, barmaid and owner, looked blankly at me. Maybe it'd all been a trick. Perhaps right this very moment Eric was cackling maniacally and rubbing his hands together while loading our bikes into his van. Damn you, Eric!

But it wasn't a trick and the confusion was quickly sorted out. We had a choice of barbecue ribs or a hamburger, and a pint. This being Somerset I opted for an ice-cold cloudy cider that was so fantastic it should have been illegal. In a world where something tasted this good, who would ever get any work done?

We sat at a picnic bench in the sunny beer garden waiting for our food.

"I think these hills are too much for me," said Mark.

"Do you want to complain some more?" I asked.

He pulled a face.

"Besides," I added. "you can't give up so early. You've only been cycling for a day. And you're a lucky charm if Eric's anything to go by."

The food arrived. My ribs were mighty tasty. Our plates were clean within seconds.

"I wish I'd had the burger," said Mark.

"Shut up, girl pants."

Eric came to the pub and sat with us. Apparently, his farm was rented from the Crown and so it was the Queen who was really our host for the evening, which was nice of her. Eric wasn't sure what would happen to his farm when he retired. His son was studying engineering at Cambridge and had no interest in taking it over. Having seen loads of farms and farmers over the course of the last few weeks it seemed like a lot of hard work. Eric went inside and Sandra appeared carrying four halves.

"They're from me," she said.

We left the pub shortly afterwards with another gift from Sandra – for a reason I can't recall, several packs of *Haribo* – and returned to our field. I climbed into my tent and slept a happy, cider-fuelled sleep.

The promised heatwave was here. By seven o'clock in the morning, the tent was already roasting and I crawled out into the cool morning air.

Eric wasn't finished with his generosity yet. The previous evening he'd also invited us to breakfast. We sat on his patio in the sun while he emerged from the kitchen carrying a large pile of bacon, beans and scrambled eggs. Lubrication was provided by a jug of yet more deliciously creamy, tuberculosis-filled unpasteurized milk. The calories were particularly welcome, for today we would climb one of Britain's most stupid hills.

What is it that the French, Italians and Spanish, in fact the entire planet, knew about building roads that never made it as far as Britain? Our European neighbours have proper mountains soaring two, three, four thousand metres into the sky, and yet their roads rarely exceed a gradient of 10%. Compared to these rocky monsters, England's hills are pimples and yet the gradients are crazy. Today's Porlock Hill, Britain's steepest A-road, is a whopping 25%. If the Brits had been responsible for the roads through the Alps, there would've been no switchbacks, just 75% slopes from the bottom straight to the top. I could hear the voice of the eighteenth century British foreman while some hapless sod stood forlornly at the bottom amid shattered carts and a pile of dead horses.

"Don't be soft, man! It's only a little hill."

From experience I was aware that, fully loaded, I can only manage a gradient of 15% before I have to push. I knew ahead of time that Porlock would defeat me, but Joe and his super-gears wanted to reach the top without dismounting. There was an easier option. Mark wanted to take the less steep toll road, but that would've cost money we preferred to spend on food.

I was about three metres into the hill when I climbed off my saddle.

"Bollocks to this!"

Dave and Mark, just behind me, did the same.

While I knew some hills were beyond my capacity to pedal up them, it never occurred to me there could be a slope I'd be unable to push my bike over. I mean, I could shove it along a flat track but I couldn't push it up a wall, so there was obviously a tipping point, some gradient in-between where I'd have to give up. It felt like 25% was damn close. The technique was basic. I'd push using all the strength in my arms, which was very little, and with all my body weight, which was considerable. I'd then take three or four steps before swearing and then squeezing the brakes to prevent my bike from rolling back down to the bottom. Stop and repeat. For two long, long miles. By the time I reached the top, five days later, I'd climbed 400 metres.

Joe was already at the top. The combination of young legs, quality gearing and a style that involved weaving from side to side like Gazza on his way home from the pub had made his no-push attempt successful.

Mark's was less so. He was still a long way behind, employing his own pushing-cursing-stopping technique. His reaction at the summit was little surprise.

"I'm going to hire a van and go home."

The exertion was worth it though. Once on top, the road floated high over Exmoor for twelve miles with stunning views down to the coast illuminated by a dazzling sun. We crossed into Devon before tumbling down to Lynmouth and facing an even dafter slope. Lynmouth Hill, the road from Lymouth to Lynton, has stretches with gradients of 33%. Fortunately, it's a lot shorter than Porlock Hill.

Mark decided on a different approach this time. Rather than grumbling, he got playful. As we neared the top my bike seemed harder to push than before. I looked behind and saw Mark very close. I faced forward and pushed again. After a second or two the ascent again got harder. He was right behind me again. I knew what he was doing. He was rubbing my back tyre with his front one.

"What are you doing?" I said.

"Nothing!" he said with mock innocence.

I pushed my bike up on to the pavement at the side of the road. Pushing was easier now and then suddenly it wasn't. Mark had climbed the kerb too.

"Knob."

I bumped my bike down on to the road and legged it as

fast as I could, which wasn't very fast at all. He tried to keep up but couldn't.

"You crazy fool!" he said, laughing.

But his mood changed once he got to the top.

"I'm not doing this any more," he said.

We ignored him. He'd already said it about 30 times in the last two days.

"I've got a dodgy hip, y'know?"

He hadn't. He was merely planting a seed of failure in case he needed to nurture it to a fully grown Tree of Surrender later on.

We had inspiration to get us up this hill. We'd been told how, at the turn of the twentieth century, a massive storm had stranded a nearby ship in tempestuous waters. Because the weather was too awful to launch a lifeboat in Lynmouth, a group of women had carried it over this hill to a safer harbour. Imagine that – malnourished Victorian girlies in gowns, petticoats and clogs carrying a heavy, wooden boat up a long, 33% slope and we could barely push a bike. Anyway, having now checked, this story isn't even true. The women carried the boat up the *other* hill out of Lynmouth, Countisbury Hill, and that's only 25%, the pussies.

Soon afterwards, Dave was nearly hit by a car that came careening around a tight corner. It spotted him at the last minute and slammed on. Despite the acrid smell of burning rubber, Dave was completely unaware of what had just happened. He cycles in a dream world. The bloke in the car had a lucky escape. Dave's concrete tank would've left a bicycle-shaped hole in his bonnet as the driver was catapulted through the windscreen and over Dave's head.

Undamaged, we cycled on a flat straight near Combe Martin. A little kid stood by the side of the road with his mum.

"Look," he said, spying us. "It's like the *Tour de France*."

He wouldn't have said that if he'd seen us on the hill stages.

Tonight we had an appointment. Via one of the cycling forums, a very kind lady called Maureen had written to say she wanted to help. One way she did this was to arrange a garden camping spot for us in Ilfracombe at the house of Campbell, a friend of hers. Campbell's wife, Catherine, answered the door and showed us to the garden. We set up our tents and then had our first shower in nine days. Separately, that is. We weren't all in there together, soaping each other's pasty white bodies.

Campbell was working late but we all sat around the dining table, along with Catherine, her children and a couple of exchange students, and ate a massive chilli con carne. It felt weird being inside again.

"So how do you know Maureen?" Catherine asked.

"I don't," I said.

"Ah. I thought you must be good friends."

"No, I've never met her. So, are you and Campbell into touring too?"

"Us? No. We don't even have a bike."

"Then why did Maureen suggest we stay here?"

"I don't know."

When Campbell came home later it was clear Maureen had fixed us up because they were such a friendly, accommodating couple used to a houseful of guests. But Campbell wasn't home just yet and I was sitting in the garden next to Mark. He was pulling his face.

"When Campbell comes home, tell him I'm not feeling so good," he said, climbing into his tent.

"What's wrong with you?"

"Nothing."

"Don't go to bed. Just think how kind they've been."

"I can't be arsed with it."

Go on, wind him up.

"Your loss then," I said.

"Why's that?"

"Well, Catherine said, with a name like Campbell, it's no surprise he's very, very Scottish."

"So?"

"Maybe he has a large collection of whiskies. Perhaps once we get chatting, he'll crack open his giant chest of single malts."

He thought for a minute.

"Yeah. Alright then. I'll stay up."

"Mercenary git."

Campbell came home shortly afterwards and was possibly the most enthusiastic person I've ever met. He'd recently been promoted to Vice Headmaster at his school and I can't imagine anyone better to inspire the kids. We never found out whether he collected whiskies and so Mark's greed wasn't rewarded in that way, although he did get a beer out of it, the cheeky sod.

The next morning Mark was perusing the map. He was looking for ways to reduce his workload.

"You could cut a big section out today if we got a ferry across the river Taw."

"No can do. They cost money."

"I thought you said you were under budget."

"We are."

"Well, spend it then."

"No. We're saving it for a party on the last night."

"Is a party allowed in your stupid rules?"

He didn't like the *Ride and Seek* regulations. He didn't like how the budget limited our access to alcohol, although we weren't doing too badly this week.

"If we're still on budget at the end we can do what we

want. We could hire a cannon and fire a donkey out of it."

After a breakfast of cereal, and each armed with a pack of sandwiches made by Campbell, we were back on the road, or rather a track. The Tarka Trail uses the old railway network – with the tracks removed, obviously – and so the gradients are shallow and manageable. Mark was unusually quiet.

We cycled along the river and through Barnstaple, heading towards Bideford. The heatwave had once again been oversold and had lasted for a single day. The skies filled with black clouds and grumbled more loudly than Mark. Then the rain came down. We hid in a bus shelter near Fairy Cross and ate our gifted lunch.

"These sandwiches are a bit dry."

I bet you can't guess who said that, but he was also smirking. His complaints had become a wind-up.

"Don't be so ungrateful," I said.

"They are though," he said peevishly. "They need more butter."

We continued through Bideford and on to the coast at Bude, now in Cornwall, collecting more samphire along the way. Today we had another appointment, this time with Maureen herself. Ever since getting in touch she'd said she wanted to give us a goody bag. Its contents had never been specified and so we each speculated over what would be inside our fantasy bag. Dave would surely be disappointed. It was unlikely there'd be any *Sherbet Dib Dabs*.

Our meeting spot was an isolated cricket ground in Bude. There was no one else about. It seemed an unlikely place to meet. Suddenly, a dark car appeared and rolled slowly along the edge of the pitch towards us. It felt a little like a hostage handover. Dave was their kidnapped son. We were going to trade him for the money we'd demanded. That tenner would be useful.

Maureen and her husband, also called Dave, climbed out of the car. They were older than us but more athletic-looking. Maureen wore a huge smile. Dave opened his boot while she extracted a couple of carrier bags. Their contents were amazing. There was a roast chicken, a home-made sour dough loaf and a salad with what turned out to be an amazing, herb-loaded balsamic dressing, carrots, beetroots and peas from their garden, biscuits, flapjacks, a packet of custard powder and a rhubarb nut mix that'd improve our porridge no end. There were also sachets of energy drinks donated by the kind but, given their name, seemingly unimaginative owners of *The Bike Shop* in Tiverton.

"And there's this," said Maureen, reaching for a plastic bottle. She'd seen a photo of some blistered body parts on *Facebook*. "Which one of you is Dave?"

He raised his hand a little.

"Come here, you. Put this on your legs."

Dave's pins had never really improved from the initial assault of sunshine and pedal-battering and still looked like they were heading dangerously towards infection. Maureen had the solution.

"Where are you staying tonight?" asked Dave Two.

"No idea."

"We should ask at the cricket club. I used to be a member."

I thought perhaps he was going to see if we could camp in the middle of their pitch but he wasn't. They suggested asking the local campsite for a freebie, a prospect I thought was pushing it a bit.

"The campsite people, they're very kind," said an old guy who seemed to be in charge.

Maureen and Dave Two took us to a bar for a chat and bought us a round. I opted for cider again, this time a gorgeous 6% *Rattler*. Then Dave Two and I jumped in his car and headed, a little reluctantly on my part, to the campsite. Fortunately, that pint of powerful cider have given me a little extra bravado as I walked into reception.

"I know this sounds cheeky but I've been told you're very nice people..." I started and two minutes later we'd been given a free pitch for our four tents. Wonderful.

We returned to the pub where they bought us another round. Kinder, lovelier people you couldn't hope to meet. We christened Maureen as *Ride and Seek's Official Mum*.

"I wish you wouldn't do that," said Mark once we'd all said goodbye.

"Do what?"

"Tell them I'm only here for a week."

"But you are."

"Yeah, but it makes me feel like a fake."

"I thought you'd be used to that by now."

"You told Catherine yesterday, and Maureen today."

"Shut up, girl pants."

We cycled up the hill to Lynstone campsite, our donated home for the evening. Not all of us would be staying the night. Joe's girlfriend was on a nearby surfing trip and he'd be foolishly walking away from a giant bagful of free food and leaving Dave, Mark and me behind.

"Have you got a girlfriend?" I asked Dave.

"Nah," he said, "I'd be lucky to get a dead goat."

"A *dead* goat?" said Joe.

"C'mon, Dave, set your standards a little higher. At least go for one that's alive."

Joe disappeared and the rest of us had a feast, polishing off nearly Maureen's entire bag. We laid around under the now pleasant evening sun and wallowed in our excess. Having a stomach close to bursting clearly pleased Dave. He walked up to me with a giant grin on his face.

"This is the best holiday I've ever had," he said.

"Just wait till I find you a goat."

In the morning Mark had something new to complain about. During the night, the single pole forming the backbone of his tent had snapped. He looked like a man trapped in a bin bag.

"How much was your tent?" I asked.

"Twenty-five pounds."

"Mmm, maybe you get what you pay for."

"It was reduced from thirty-five."

"Bargain."

We quickly threw down some breakfast and went to find Joe. It was raining again. This was the worst heatwave ever. We took the coast road to Tintagel to see King Arthur's gaff and then headed towards Wadebridge. It was an uneventful ride except that a shortcut up a narrow, very steep hill became the first to defeat Joe and force him to push. Oh, and we saw a burger van in a lay-by called *Nice Baps*. Classy.

Our mission today was to go fishing in Steintown, or Padstow as it's more commonly known. We wanted to nick some of Rick's fish. Padstow was full of tourists looking for the man himself or sampling the seafood in his restaurant, or his chippy, or his café, or his fish market, or his pub, or his hotel, or his culinary school. This is Rick's empire. If he were only a little bit more Heston Blumenthal he'd probably have a fish-based ice-cream parlour too.

"Yes, sir?"

"One scoop of mint 'n' herring and one of cod 'n' chocolate, please. And some starfish sprinkles."

Today I discovered just how hideously heavy Dave's bike really was. While he popped to the loo, Mark decided to give Dave's bike a test run. He started to laugh.

"This is just ridiculous," he said.

I gave it a go. I reckon he had more weight on his front

wheel than the rest of us had on our bikes in total. I couldn't even turn the handlebars. I had to stop before I crashed into a wall.

The plan was to find somewhere to stay and then hit the water and extract our dinner. Hunting for a farm took us up on high. Before we knew it we were overlooking the next seaside village of Trevone.

The farm's front door was answered by Neil, a softly spoken bloke in his 30s who allowed us to camp in his front garden. It wasn't huge but, carefully arranged, there was enough room for four tents, although my tent's guy ropes proved too much of a challenge for Mark.

"Oouf!" he went as he tripped over them for the eighteenth time.

Neil came out for a chat.

"I've just been looking at your web site," he said. "And I saw your rules. So it's allowed for me to give you something."

"It is," I replied, "and it's very kind, but please don't. These last few days have felt more like a freeloading trip than a foraging trip."

And they had. All the free food would get factored into our final reckoning but having confidently told my mum we'd be given nothing in western Europe, England had proved me even more wrong than Wales.

"Alright," he said. "But surely you'll accept a beer."

Some things would never be refused.

The tide was in and there were rocks nearby from which to fish. Neil told us his favourite spot. We strolled across a cliff-top field jammed with wild carrot and clambered down to the rocks below.

Mark took out his rod for the first time since joining us and employed his mackerel feathers. There was an air of quiet confidence about him, which made a welcome change from the usual air of noisy whinging.

Others were confident too. Joe had got his parents to post his spare, better-but-heavier reel to Mark's before we met up and he was using that. This freed up the handle from his crap reel to replace my missing one. My full-size rod was back in business.

We were four men with four rods and four reels. And, as it turned out, no fish. No one had so much as a bite and Joe managed to fling yet more equipment into the sea. It was a good job we weren't depending on our fishing skills for survival. With everything we'd donated, Neptune could have opened a fishing tackle shop.

We traipsed back to the garden and cooked up some spaghetti mixed with the final vegetables from Maureen's goody bag and the samphire we'd collected the day before. Mark got up to collect ingredients for a cup of tea and tripped over my guy lines again.

"Right, I'm gonna charge you five pounds each time you do that," I said.

It was morning and I was awake in my tent. Someone was moving around outside. Then I heard a squeal and the tent shook as someone tripped over a guy line.

"Five pounds!" I yelled.

Two minutes later it shuddered again.

"Ten pounds!"

He was doing it on purpose, the pillock.

We trundled back down the hill into Padstow and back along the cycle path to Wadebridge. I cycled beside Mark. Something had happened to him. Oddly, he was in a positive mood. Possibly because he was nearing the end of his ordeal.

"There's a small part of me that's enjoying this," he said. "But I can't locate it to let it out."

We now changed direction. Instead of crawling all the way

to Land's End, we were going to leap across Cornwall and head for the south coast. We continued on the cycle track to Bodmin, at the end of which was a *Sainsbury's*. I'd never lived anywhere where supermarkets had self-service checkouts.

"I'm not sure I like 'em," I said as we waited in line to be served. "I'd rather have a checkout person to talk to."

"Not me," said Joe. "I'd rather not talk to anyone I don't know unless I have to."

"But you might see a girl on the checkout and fall madly in love with each other."

He shook his head.

"I won't. I've seen her."

I looked at her.

"Maybe she has hidden beauty."

"If she has, it's very well hidden."

It wasn't far to the south coast but the route was full of tiring lumps to climb and quick descents giving us no time to get back our breath. As usual, Mark was trailing behind. Near Trebyan we stopped and waited for him but he didn't appear. Maybe he'd given up and caught the bus home. Ten minutes later he still wasn't there. We gave him a call. He'd missed a turning and was now three miles away in the wrong direction. Eventually he arrived, red-faced and out of breath.

"I thought even though this is my last full day," he said, "they're trying to ditch me."

"C'mon. As if we could survive without your uplifting positivity!"

We stopped for water at a public toilet in Lerryn. Outside was a community notice board whose summer fête included an activity called *Splat the Rat*. Is that a version of *Whac-a-Mole* or an opportunity for the village to beat to death its local adulterers?

A huge storm had been predicted for the evening and so

we wanted to set up camp early to give us time to fish. On the advice of the owner of a field-less farmhouse, I tried another campsite, this time without the cider to spur me on. Two minutes later we were setting up our tents on a lovely, well-maintained lawn. We seemed to get better treatment than the paying guests.

"There's a picnic bench over there," said Chris, the site owner. "Bring it over to your pitch if you like."

Wow, a dining table! We weren't used to such comfort.

"What time are you off tomorrow?" asked Chris.

"About ten," I replied.

Mark leaned in and whispered.

"You should've said, 'Tomorrow? What are you on about? We're here for a week, mate!'"

Chris told us of a great place by the nearby harbour where, apparently, we couldn't fail to catch fish. But he didn't know us, did he? Off we trotted. Surely this time we'd catch something. And we did. With a particularly clumsy cast, Dave caught a small boat. He wrestled with it like he'd snared a marlin until his line snapped.

The rest of us weren't as lucky. At least the other two people fishing at the same spot didn't catch anything so we couldn't put our lack of fish down entirely to our rubbishness. I was, by now, utterly sick of fishing.

The predicted storm was warming up and so we returned to the campsite and started to make some food. Joe got the rice started but Mark was up to something.

"What's the matter with you?" I asked.

"Nothing," he grinned.

Joe continued with the rice for a couple of minutes.

"It's here!" said Mark.

"What's here?"

Suddenly, from nowhere, our picnic table contained a pot of sweet and sour chicken, rice and eight flour tortillas.

"Where've they come from?"

"Plot 34," he said.

"Who?"

"I was speaking to them earlier. It's their leftovers. They said we could have it."

I'm not sure how that conversation started and I didn't want to know. We wolfed down the lot and took the pots back to Plot 34.

"We're off in the morning," said our caterers, "and we've got loads of cold cuts left over. Come over in the morning and you can have them."

There was something about Mark's presence that had turned this week into one giant charity gorgefest. There hadn't been a single day when someone hadn't given us something and now it looked like it'd continue into his final day tomorrow. Just imagine how much whining there would've been without all the free food and alcohol.

The next day we found the A38 and pointed the bikes towards Plymouth. This must be one of the most tedious rides in the world. Each long, steep, tree-lined uphill, of which there were thousands, was followed by a quick plummet to sea level. Despite all the climbing we never got high enough to see anything worth looking at. I wasn't expecting the ice shelves of Antarctica or Machu Picchu, but still.

In Saltash we met up with Mark's son, who was going to whisk him away to a land of warm baths and comfy beds.

"I've enjoyed myself," he said as he was about to leave.

That was hard to believe.

"Really?"

"Except the camping. I hated the camping."

"Ah."

"And the hills. The hills were terrible."

"So you enjoyed the flat bits?"
"Yes. But there weren't really any flat bits, were there?"
"Did you enjoy the fishing?"
"Let's forget about the fishing."

A sizeable body of water separates Saltash and Plymouth. Dave, Joe and I made our way to the Tamar Bridge, once the UK's longest suspension bridge at nearly 600 metres, connecting Cornwall to Devon. We'd been lucky on our previous river crossings, getting over the water despite roadworks and closures. Surely the Tamar bridge would be fully functioning. And, yes, the road bridge was open. Unfortunately for us, bikes weren't allowed on the road bridge and the cycleway was closed, and for a full three days. We stood there, gawping at the sign, frozen by indecision. This detour was going to be massive. It would be quicker to wait for it to reopen.

"It's a good job Mark's not here," I said.

"Do you want a lift?" came a voice from behind.

We spun around to see a young bloke sitting in a minibus. A shuttle service had been set up to get cyclists and pedestrians to the other side. Our luck continued. Once in Devon, the view down to the river beneath was spectacular, with the water turned golden by the summer sun. It looked like a Norwegian fjord.

We started to look for a farm. I spotted one crumbling mess and asked the 200 year-old fella inside but he just said no and closed the door in my face. Clearly I was no longer as sexy as a French girl.

A young lad was looking after the next farm on behalf of his parents and said they wouldn't be happy with campers. He suggested we wild-camp on Dartmoor whose dark hills we could see in the distance. We'd already suffered a day of slopes and no one felt much like cycling uphill any more. We tried at a third farm but they didn't own the surrounding land. A night on the moors was our only hope.

We started up another stupidly steep hill, Dave and I pushing from the off. Looking up, the hill seemed endless but it passed the entrance to another farm and, not wanting to be beaten, I figured I'd give it a go.

"Aye, of course. Follow me!" said Phil the farmer.

He led us farther up the hill into a rocky field that maintained the slopey theme. We set up our tents as best we could. The angle of the ground would make it an awkward night's sleep. With our tents on such a slope, especially with its packed mud surface, we definitely didn't want rain tonight.

The camp was quiet. It was the first time it'd just been the three of us. Dave and Joe didn't talk much at the best of times. Mark had limited his negativity to the hours spent cycling. He'd been entertaining company in the evenings and now he'd left a hole. And after a week of varied meals lovingly prepared by someone else and sometimes accompanied by beer or cider, we were now back on stove food and water. But at least there was delicious elderflower tea to cheer us up. Well, for me and Dave. Joe didn't like hot drinks.

"It's not really fair to use our communal fuel to make tea when only two of us drink it," said Joe.

He had a point, damn it. So now there was no elderflower tea either.

To rub chilli powder into the wound, we could hear live music from a distant beer festival we'd passed earlier. The band was murdering a range of eighties rock anthems but it sounded like they were having more fun than we were.

Joe cooked up spaghetti while I made a sauce using tomato purée and this morning's donated meat. The slope made food preparation difficult. Joe was struggling. The pan of boiling pasta started to slide off his stove. He grabbed its handle.

"Owww!" he yelped. "Who makes a pan handle out of metal?"

With singed fingers he quickly let go of the heated handle and tried to use his fleece as an oven glove. The pan was still sliding.

"This is the worst thing in the world!" he wailed.

He finally managed to manufacture a heatproof glove and stabilise the stove but not before burning a hole through his fleece.

The mood was eventually raised when we had our first home-made dessert of the trip. We'd collected cherries earlier today as well as a few handfuls of wild plums. Although the plums were green and under-ripe, when cooked with the cherries and plenty of sugar and then topped with broken biscuits and Maureen's custard, we had ourselves a bowl of warm happiness on an otherwise chilly evening.

We ate our fruit while watching a bank of cloud move across the fields beneath us. In the distance we could see rain and it was coming our way. We climbed into our tents and prepared for the worst. I expected to wake up at the bottom of the field wearing a sleeping bag made of mud.

Unusually for this trip, the rain never arrived. Despite this, I'd still slipped down the hill and ended up crushed into the bottom half of my tent by the time I woke up.

We pootled onward and hit the coast at Paignton, not so much a town as a real-life saucy seaside postcard. Everyone looked unhealthily English. It wasn't a place troubled with beautiful architecture either. It felt like someone had given a fiver to the town planners in the 1960s and asked them to do their best.

We got a phone call from Mark. He sounded much happier now he wasn't cycling and had a surprise for us in

Torquay, twenty minutes away. We raced along the coastal cycle path under a sunny sky. Compared to Paignton, Torquay looked like the south of France, although possibly only because it had a palm tree.

We found Mark and Julie sitting outside *The London Inn*.

"Now that I'm not part of the team, I'm allowed to give you something, aren't I?" Mark said.

"I suppose so."

"In that case I want to buy you lunch."

"That's very kind. Thank you."

"And to give you this."

He reached under the table and struggled to lift a two-litre glass flagon of 7.5% cider.

"Is that as heavy as it looks?" I asked.

"Yes," he smirked.

It weighed approximately the same as a medium-sized cannonball. That was going to be a joy to lug around.

We went into the pub and had a lovely roast dinner and another *Wetherspoon's* pint.

"I told Julie I'd lose weight on this trip," said Mark.

"Did you?"

"Not an ounce."

Despite all the hills, it was hardly surprising. I'd already lost about a stone (7 kg) in the two weeks before Mark arrived but the weight loss had come to an abrupt stop since then. But our days of easy gorging would soon be coming to an end.

Days Completed: 20
Ride and Seek: **Total spend £8.84, per day £0.44**
Live below the Line: **Total spend £15.64, per day £0.78**

Chapter 7: Coasting to France

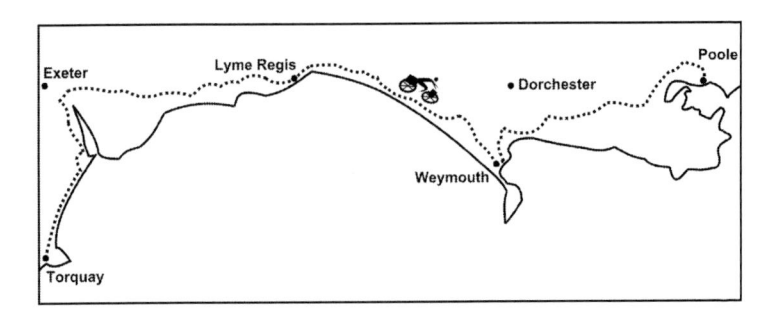

We climbed the large hill out of Torquay and made our way to Dawlish. A few cars were parked in the lane outside a farm. Hearing chatter coming from the back of the farmhouse I walked around to be confronted by twenty people sitting at a table. In what felt like a presentation for *The Apprentice* I explained what we were doing as forty eyes watched on. Luckily, I wasn't fired. Steve the farmer was in a good mood. It was his daughter's birthday barbecue.

Our tents had only been up for a minute when Steve came to our camp carrying a party pack.

"I thought you might like these," he said, as he handed us each a hot dog, a cupcake and a can of *Carling*.

This set the tone of the evening. With Mark's cider to drink, we were having a party of our own.

A farmer in the next field put on a show while we prepared to sup. He'd piled high the bundles of hay on his trailer and was using his tractor to pull it up a sloping field. But he hadn't secured the grass and a couple of dozen bales tumbled off the back, one or two splitting as they hit the ground. He got out of the tractor and stood over the mess, scratching his head.

We poured out a first glass of cider. Dave necked his immediately.

The farmer disappeared for a while and came back with a forklift truck.

We poured another glass and Dave downed it in one again. He was obviously missing the alcoholic pop. It had, after all, been a full six hours since his last drink.

The farmer didn't look like he'd used a forklift before. Each time he lifted a bale and attempted to reposition it on his trailer, it'd fall off again and split on the ground. His carefully packaged bundles of hay were slowly turning into a giant haystack.

The cider was eventually finished, its ethanol lubricating the conversation. Dave told us about a series of stories he'd once written about a delinquent, alcoholic teddy bear. This sparked Joe to divulge the wonders of vodka-soaked *Gummi Bears*. The cider, as is often the case, had us talking shite.

Three hours after he'd first tried to leave the field, the farmer had finally reloaded his trailer and managed to carry his hay away. After the evening he'd suffered, I bet he'd also be downing a pint or two.

Steve's farm was called *Highwinds* and its name was well-deserved. With a hard-packed ground that made it difficult to secure the pegs and a strong breeze in the night, I woke up to a collapsed tent. Tonight though I'd have no such problems because we'd be sleeping in a church, Dave's church in Lyme Regis to be precise.

But we had to get there first. Eight perfectly flat miles on a cycle lane beside the river Exe's estuary were a nice start. But the temperatures felt more like February than July and were followed by light drizzle as we reached the angrier, traffic-stuffed roads near Exeter. Ah, the joys of the English summer!

"Don't worry, Dave. There'll be no rain once we get to

France," I said.

The route to Lyme Regis passed through the cutesiest monikered village of the trip so far. That wasn't its only accolade. Newton Poppleford was recently christened the kindest place on Earth by Jeremy Vine. Because of its inhabitants' huge charitable donations? Because of the shelter they provide to hundreds of terrified refugees? No, because someone put a plastic chair at the end of a garden path displaying the stencilled words: "OAPs, please take a seat". A nice gesture definitely but not really worthy of Jeremy Vine's Nobel Peace Prize.

We finally reached Lyme Regis and headed to the Bethany Chapel, the small church Dave has attended with his parents for a number of years. They only have a tiny congregation. I picked up a leaflet about the place as we pushed our bikes inside.

"Two doors up from Lyme's *Fish Bar*, opposite *The Ship Inn*," it said on the front cover, squarely taking their aim at those guilty of gluttony and over-indulgence.

The chapel's main room was fairly ordinary with chairs rather than pews and a small, wooden stage, but the building contained everything we needed, including a shower and a fully-featured kitchen. On the kitchen table was a copy of the local paper. I love local papers. You can sense the desperation the poor reporters have felt trying to wrestle a story from the week's non-events.

One of the main stories didn't show Lyme in a particularly good light. A woman in a local care home was celebrating her 107th birthday. She hadn't always lived in this area but had moved here when she got married aged 30. She was asked whether she liked living in Lyme.

"I'm only just getting used to it," she replied.

Seventy-seven years seems like a long time to settle in. But it got worse. When asked to explain her longevity, she put it down to not having any excitement in her life, the poor sod. Come to Lyme Regis and live forever, bored out of your skull!

Also on the kitchen table was a present from Dave's dad. He'd left some money with instructions to buy a fish 'n' chip dinner. I'd never met Dave's dad but I liked him already.

Dave planned to give us a tour of Lyme but before he did, Joe wanted to do Dave a favour. Now that Dave was on home territory, Joe was convinced, justifiably as it turned out, that he could prune Dave's gear and leave some of it behind. When Joe had finished, the table was straining under the weight of the redundant equipment. It included six incorrectly-sized inner tubes, a garden fork, a useless solid-fuel stove and eight heavy packs of fuel blocks, two bottles of lubricant, four pairs of socks, wire clippers, a set of spanners that didn't seem to fit any of the nuts on his bike, pliers, a spare set of lights and a giant pile of maps. When repacked, Dave's bike was much lighter, but still weighed approximately the same as a bison.

We left the bikes in the church and went for a wander. Past the pastel-painted doors of the beach huts and down at the sea wall, we looked farther east, towards the cliffs and the surrounding collapsed hillside. On to the pretty harbour, a port pub had its blackboard outside displaying its specials. You could buy half a lobster – about three mouthfuls of food at best – for £24.50. I hadn't spent that much since I'd set off three weeks ago.

While giving us a tour, Dave told us a local story. Following the Duke of Monmouth's attempted coup, the Hanging Judge, Judge Jeffreys, was sent to Lyme to deal with all who'd assisted the traitor. Jeffreys stayed in what is now *Boots the Chemist*. One evening, the Devil himself turned up on a ship and, when asked by a harbour worker why he was there, said he'd come for what belonged to him. Old Satan hotfooted it 'round to *Boots* and kicked down the front of the building. Seeing his assailant, Jeffreys immediately died of fright. The Devil grabbed his soul, returned to his vessel and disappeared forever. It's a great story, except that, more prosaically, in real life Judge Jeffreys died of liver disease while serving time in the Tower of London. The stories *Boots* will tell to sell more cosmetics!

Along with the old lass who hadn't had much fun in Lyme Regis, the local paper had also told about gangs of gulls terrorising holidaymakers. One woman had written in to say she wouldn't be back unless a 'solution' was found. Given that it's unlikely anyone is going to train the gulls to change their behaviour, her request does sound a bit holocausty. We passed a beach. It was divided into sandy quadrants, each with its own terrifying bird standing in the centre and ready to steal the chips or rip out the throat of anyone who dared to enter. Say what you will about Lyme's bird life, they were very well organised.

Speaking of chips, we wanted ours and along with a crisply battered fish they were heavenly. We were allowed to spend the change and, unsurprisingly, it went on more cider. For the second night in a row we got a tiny bit drunk. Was that wrong in a church? I don't know. I seem to remember the vicar at my school church taking more than his fair share of communion wine. Don't get me wrong. He didn't stumble down the aisle putting people into headlocks and slurring "I fuckin' love you" but he must have got a bit tiddly.

And then, all too quickly, it was bedtime. I slept on the floor of the main room. Robbed of a soft field to cushion my back I had the most uncomfortable night's sleep of the journey. With three weeks in the open air I now belonged outdoors, like an adventurer. Or, perhaps more accurately, like dog poo.

The next morning we ascended the big hill out of Lyme

Regis and continued east, bus-sheltering from more rain along the way. We left the busy main road and headed to the beach at West Bexington. Our rods were too short for beach fishing and so we searched for seaside plants instead. We managed to find some gnarly-looking sea kale and what might have been alexanders. You don't mess with alexanders or any of the Umbelliferae family unless you know what you're doing. It contains fool's parsley and hemlock, both of which can seriously ruin your day. In the end we came away empty-handed but alive.

Down the road we cycled through the stunning village of Abbotsbury, crammed with sixteenth and seventeenth century houses. In order to maintain its traditional charm there isn't a single street light in the village. I imagine for those walking home at midnight, the inky blackness is a little less charming. So pretty is Abbotsbury that it feels more like a museum than a real-life village. The entire place is owned by the Ilchester estate, who presumably encourage its toy town atmosphere. All it's missing is a bunch of actors in period costume, meandering up and down the main street, painted with boils and buboes. But maybe it was their day off.

Beyond Abbotsbury is a small town called Chickerell. It's quite a modern town and, as such, a quick google gives the impression not much of interest lies within. This is strange because it contains something genuinely unique. In a garden next to the town's main road, there's an evil-looking, ten foot tall, steel bear – a Cyberbear – standing erect with its killer claws out. This *Doctor Who* prop seemed appropriate down here. After all, the coastal resorts we'd seen so far felt like we'd gone back in time.

We added another English seaside resort to our collection at Weymouth, which seemed a lot classier than Paignton. Its wide coast road was lined with tall Victorian houses and felt like the Isle of Man's Douglas but with a lot more going on (i.e., something going on). It had finally turned into a nice afternoon. Dave even went for a little paddle.

Not far from Weymouth is Preston and it was near here that we found a field close to the Osmington White Horse, the huge, chalky equine cut into the hill. This farm had a much more professional air than the previous ones we'd visited. They even had an office. We were told they didn't have a licence to accept campers but if we set up in a distant field all would be fine. Obviously if we were eaten by wolves or murdered by bandits they'd deny all knowledge of our stay.

They gave us directions to the distant field in which we hadn't really been given permission to stay. This was my favourite camping spot so far. The wind was increasing to the speed that knocks over large trees but we had a tall wall to shelter from it. But the best feature was three foot tall, duvet soft grass. It was awkward to pitch the tent but once inside it was more comfortable than Brangelina's mattress.

Dinner was also a challenge. We had to cut a hole in the grass to make room for the stove. Joe made pasta while I made a pan of lentil curry sauce and a dish of scrambled eggs. Drowned in soy sauce the ensemble was much better than you're imagining. No, honestly.

Once again we had dessert. A huge bag of cherries we'd collected the day before was cooked with sugar and topped with broken digestives and a cheap tin of custard. We worked out that a portion only cost 12p although, according to *Aldi*'s prices today, we'd foraged around a tenner's worth of cherries. However, I suspect if we'd bought *Aldi*'s fruit it wouldn't have suffered from the problem that ours did. We noticed tiny maggots in the cherry-stoning bowl. We'd eaten some of the cherries yesterday without any ill-effects and so we put the bugs to the back of our minds and scoffed the lot regardless.

This evening we noticed a flaw in Dave's crockery hygiene

technique. He was still eating from his yellow Tigger bowl. Rather than wash it up he simply licked it cleaned, much like a dog would do. Unfortunately, his tongue wasn't long enough to reach the centre of his bowl and so that part always went unlicked. Each subsequent meal added another layer of flavour to the central square inch of his dish, and they weren't always complementary flavours. Tonight alone, cherries and custard had been added on top of curried lentils. We could've taken a cross-section from the gunk in the middle, analysed it and had scientific proof of each breakfast and dinner we'd eaten on the trip so far.

"Do you reckon your bowl-washing technique explains the quantity of food living in your beard?" I asked Dave.

He smiled broadly with cherries all over his stupid face.

Our original plan was to get the ferry from Portsmouth. However, all the ferries leave there in the afternoon, dumping their passengers in Cherbourg mid-evening, which would've given us precious little time to find somewhere to sleep before it got dark. Instead we would head to Poole, knocking two days off our journey, and take the early morning ferry. Today we'd cycle there and buy a ticket for tomorrow.

Yes, buy a ticket, I said. I'd hoped we could cross the Channel within our pound-a-day budget but with only two ferry operators, Brittany and Condor, at this end of the coast and both of them refusing to help us – actually Condor didn't even bother to answer the enquiry – we didn't have much choice. This didn't matter much. Scoring free tickets would've fallen into the blagging category of cheap travel and this trip wasn't about that. This trip was about something more noble. Like being so hungry that we'd gladly eat cherries crawling with maggots.

The ride to the ferry port and our exit from England was pretty near perfect with little traffic, gently rolling hills and even a strong tailwind. If Newton Poppleford had provided a pretty village name, we passed its opposite today in Poxwell, although its inhabitants pronounce it Pokeswell so as not to feel constantly itchy and plague-ridden.

We reached the edge of Poole and the road forked, taking traffic to different sides of the harbour. I stopped and asked a local which was the better one to take. He went off on one.

"You want this one but the cycle path is a farce. It stops and starts at will. And you can't buy tickets from the ferry terminal any more. You have to go to the tourist office."

We thanked him for the information.

"But, mind," he continued like The Riddler, "everything I've told you might be wrong."

Which sort of undermined what he'd said.

"And watch the ferry company. They have a tendency to crash the boat into the quayside."

"Have you ever thought of working for the tourist office?" I asked.

He told us to take a shortcut through Upton Park, which took us beside a well-kept lawn and along a wooded cycle path beside the sea. We stopped to gather more samphire, which was becoming one of our favourite forageables. Near the centre of Poole, we found a 24-hour *Tesco* and bought a few things we doubted we'd find in France at prices we could afford, including plenty of porridge oats, a couple of jars of cheap peanut butter and some 22p, almost lemon-free lemon curd.

We found out which facts our earlier assistant had been wrong about. Despite what he'd said, tickets *were* available from the ferry terminal. Unfortunately, the happy bloke on the desk had bad news for us.

"Tomorrow's ferry is full," he said.

"You can't squeeze on three foot passengers and their bicycles?"

"No, it's already over-booked by eleven people."

"Ah."

"But if you buy a ticket for Friday instead and come down here tomorrow morning we can get you on if there are enough no-shows. It's first-come, first-served. Your best chance is to get here at six-thirty."

That was three hours before the ferry left.

"But," he continued, "there'd need to be fourteen no-shows to get all three of you on."

Bollocks.

We sat outside the terminal deciding where we could spend the night and, in all likelihood, the next one too. If our chances of getting on the boat tomorrow were so slim as to be not worth attempting, we could cycle out of town and find a farm. But if we were going to take our chances in the morning we'd need to stay in town, something we hadn't tried yet. I had an idea based around the 24-hour supermarket.

"Maybe we could go to *Tesco* and take turns pushing each other around while they sleep in a trolley."

But Joe had a better idea. We cycled back to the woods we'd been through earlier and he found a clearing deep within the trees invisible from the path but large enough to accommodate three tents. For now though, and until it got dark, we'd have to amuse ourselves. With an entertainment budget of zero pence, it involved a lot of lounging about.

We explored Upton Park's lovely walled garden and even managed to forage a few apples from the bushes inside. The sun was out and so we took the opportunity to charge our electronics and take a snooze while, as we later learned, the local squirrels ate most of our loaf that was strapped to the front of Dave's bike.

In the evening, we returned to the clearing and cooked dinner. Yesterday's lentil dish had been such a hit we repeated the meal, this time adding flour to the eggs to make them more substantial and calorific. After dinner, we ate some left-over digestives, but they wouldn't share out evenly and so Joe took his knife and, with mathematical precision, sliced two digestives each into three identical pieces. With hungry bellies, no one wanted to be cheated out of a crumb. It was only two days since we'd stuffed ourselves at someone else's expense on fish 'n' chips but we were already obsessing over food again.

The sun set and the night started to descend. I packed away the cooking gear and, by the time I was finished, someone was missing.

"Where's Joe?" I asked.

"I don't know. I'll have a look."

So then Dave disappeared too. The woods continued to darken. Maybe this was a cheap horror film with one hapless dolt being picked off after another. Never having camped in the woods at night before, these were the stupid thoughts that crept through my brain.

In the twilight I set up my tent. It was too cold for a July evening. I crawled inside awaiting their return or the sudden appearance of the local axe murderer. I wasn't sure I was going to enjoy wild camping.

My phone's alarm clock screamed me awake at a quarter to six. We had an early start if we wanted to try to sneak on to today's ferry, and we wanted that a lot more than kicking around Upton Park for another 24 hours and having the squirrels eat the rest of our dinner. Fortunately, Joe and Dave had wandered back to camp later last night alive or at least reanimated.

We arrived at the ferry terminal at half past six and went to the vehicle check-in expecting a long wait. The smiley bloke who had served us yesterday was there.

"Good news!" he said immediately. "You're on."

"Eh?"

It was too early for him to have known about any potential no-shows.

"We, er, modified the ferry's upper limit," he said.

Modified was a strange word to use. What did they do? Add any extra three metres to the length of the boat?

"Does that mean there's no place for us on the lifeboat?" I asked.

He laughed, but didn't confirm or deny that. Let's hope it wasn't going to crash into the quayside again.

It didn't matter. We were finally on our way to France, with better weather and different plants as well as a language that I hadn't studied for 30 years, that Joe was reluctant to speak and of which Dave knew not a single word. We had a lot to learn. For example, would French supermarkets turn out to be as cheap as their English counterparts? No, they bloody wouldn't.

Days Completed: 23
Ride and Seek: **Total spend £11.73, per day £0.51**
Live below the Line: **Total spend £19.85, per day £0.86**

Chapter 8: Lost in the Ker-Zone

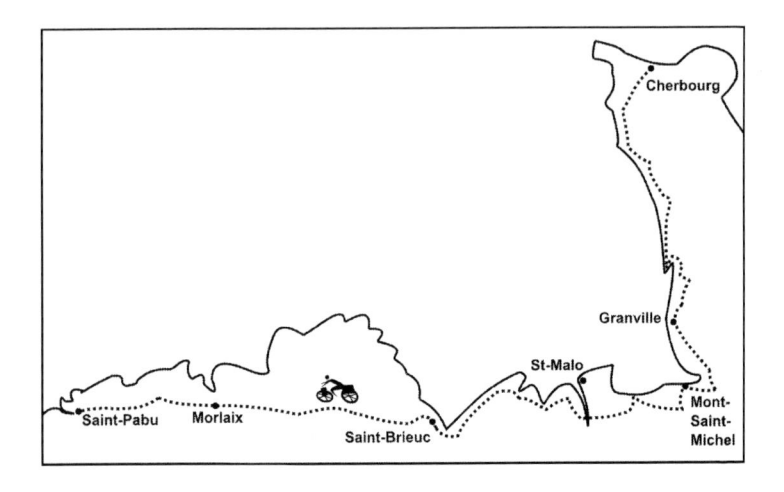

While waiting to board the ferry, we'd chatted to a couple of cyclists who were travelling to watch the *Tour de France*. On the boat, one of them found us again.

"Is this any good to you?" he asked. "It's what's left of my full English breakfast."

Full English? Bacon and sausage and black pudding and beans and mushrooms? My mind fizzed with greasy possibilities. Never mind that this was someone else's leftovers, that we were now a source of pity. It was our choice to live like tramps. If someone was generous enough to donate a full English then we'd accept it and enjoy it. I looked for the first time at the plate in his outstretched hand. Actually, it was more like a small saucer. On the little dish was a tiny triangle of toast covered with a similar-shaped piece of thin hash brown topped with a sliver of tomato. It would've been a snackette for one of us, let alone three, but it's the thought that counts. Joe once again took out his knife and carefully dissected the morsel equally. Dave watched him carefully.

"Joe should've been a brain surgeon," he said.

"Yes, because brain surgeons spend all day slicing brains into three exactly equal pieces."

We were lucky to have our knives at all. Passing through customs, some of our bags had been searched. My silly, little penknife was acceptable but both Dave and Joe had more substantial weapons with blades that could be fastened in place. For some reason, the amiable customs officer demonstrated how to lock Dave's knife – Dave already knew how, obviously – and broke the mechanism, the clumsy git.

"You know, I should confiscate these knives," he said. "They're illegal." We waited for him to pocket them. "But you could just buy some more in France."

Is that normal border guard behaviour?

"Yeah, I know you're carrying a kilo of heroin, but if I take it off you, you'd just go and score some more, wouldn't you, you little scamp?"

"What? You've got an Uzi? No problem. Every bugger's got an Uzi in Cherbourg. Welcome aboard!"

So the knives were returned and Joe's career as a breakfast brain surgeon was still intact. We each ate our allotted share. I got mine stuck in a tooth.

After the strong winds of the past two days, the luck we'd experienced during all our previous water crossings continued. We arrived in Cherbourg through a glassy sea on a breathless, sunny morning.

In the past I've noticed a strange gravity surrounding French port cities that spins you around and around and prevents you from leaving town until you've done three or four circuits. Today was no different. Eventually though, we found the road to Les Pieux and the French leg of our hunger games could properly begin.

"This is the weather I told you about Dave," I said with ill-deserved confidence. "You've used your raincoat for the last time on this trip."

Dave smiled. He hadn't travelled abroad very often and you could see on his face that France felt exotic. The sexy part of the journey had arrived.

The roads south down the Cotentin Peninsula were gently undulating. There was none of your 25% gradient nonsense here. And the traffic was behaving very French, keeping their distance when overtaking. As cyclists we felt loved, unlike in the UK. As a cyclist in Britain you often feel about as popular as Ebola.

We had no plan for the evening and no idea how we'd arrange a camping spot. We monitored the scenery. A lot of France's fields seemed to be lying idle, which was a positive for us. On the other hand, the farms we saw invariably had huge, seemingly impenetrable gates, often with Keep Out signs. They looked more like concentration camps.

We cycled 25 miles and, around sixish, stopped at a large picnic site in Saint-Jean-de-la-Riviere with views down to the coastal plain and the rocky lump of Jersey nestling in the sea beyond.

No one else was around. As we hadn't found an approachable-looking farm, we figured we could cook up some food while sitting on the picnic benches and, as the light failed, pitch our tents in the neighbouring field. Like many we'd seen today, the field was surrounded by hedges and was lacking a gate.

This would be our first foray into trespassing. Our two previous wild camps had been on that public beach near Tywyn in Wales on Day Four and last night's stay in the woods beside a public footpath. On every other occasion we'd sought and received permission. Tonight would be different. There was no obvious farmhouse attached to the field but, like land everywhere, it belonged to someone.

My parents had long since instilled a respect for the law in me, which had morphed into a fear of authority at age nine when a policewoman knocked on our front door and asked for me by name. I'd been playing out on the field at the back of our house with Neil Duxbury, the local ne'er-do-well who lived across the street. We'd lit a small fire and, for reasons that escape me now, were poking it with sticks. An old Polish woman, locally famous for moaning at kids and whose land abutted the field, came out of her house. She said the fire was too close to her fence and threatened to call the fuzz. She asked for our names and addresses. Neil wisely legged it but I, like a lemon, stood there and told her. Now, you might think this means Neil was a smart cookie but a few days later, in a moment of anger, he would pick up a fresh and none too solid dog shit with his bare hands and lob it in my direction, missing comfortably and leaving himself with a very stinky paw. Not so clever now, eh?

All this is longhand for saying I wasn't entirely comfortable with this sort of wild camping and so I had to find some moral justification for it. Forgive me if this all sounds a bit like an idealistic sixth-former, but it worked for me.

Despite my childhood brainwashing, as I've aged, my politics have become increasingly anarchistic. I don't mean that angry teenage, let's-smash-everything-up sort of anarchism. No, it's the hope the government should be reduced to a minimum until it melts away completely, and where there's no social welfare except that provided by a well-functioning community of kind, honest individuals. Yes, I know it can't work. It goes against selfish human nature. But that doesn't mean I can't still want it. Told you it was idealistic.

Another anarchist was Pierre-Joseph Proudhon, a man

from this very nation, famous for his maxim: Property is theft. Some people argue the land in question would have originally had to belong to someone for it to be stolen in the first place, and back then it clearly didn't. But that's the point. It was taken from the communal stock of land once available to everyone, stolen from my ancestors and yours. In centuries gone by, I could've visited tonight's field and slept without worrying about disembowelment by a farmer. I'd still, however, have had to worry about disembowelment by a sabre-toothed tiger.

A related idea is that of usufruct, the use of someone else's property as long as you don't damage it or wear it out. It's an awkward concept for us selfish individualists to grapple with. For example, imagine you discovered that, while you were away, one of your neighbours – one you didn't know – had used the plastic bucket you keep at the back of your house without your consent. Later, he'd replaced it in exactly the same spot and left it as clean as he'd found it. Would that make you mad or not? I mean, you can't really wear out a plastic bucket and his actions have cost you nothing. Perhaps you think good luck to him. Alternatively, you might simply recoil in horror at someone touching your stuff and say, "It's mine. Go and buy your own!" Your answer here will probably determine whether or not you buy my usufruct argument for sneaking into fields. We'd sleep there, cause no damage and leave no trace behind. If a field had a gate or Keep Out sign, we'd camp elsewhere, assuming the landowner fell into the "Get yer filthy hands off my stuff!" category of human. Otherwise, it was fair game. If that makes us monsters and you can't accept this sort of behaviour then you'll probably want to stop reading now because we're going to be doing a lot of it over the next few weeks.

Back to the picnic area. We had an hour of tranquillity during which I discovered I'd passed the exams I'd taken in

June and was now the owner of a maths degree, most of which I'd studied for while cycling around Europe. I was in a mood to celebrate but without the tools to do so.

My individual joy and our collective peace were suddenly shattered by the arrival of what were possibly the local bad boys, three knobheads aged around twenty, in two battered cars that proceeded to tear up the well-maintained lawn of the picnic area by skidding around it with over-revved engines like they were auditioning for *Fast & Furious*. We hoped this would only be a five-minute show but then they parked up, unloaded a crate of beer, ripped down part of a tree for some reason and set up a barbecue. They cooked meat to the rhythm of loud, distorted techno.

Oh well, we thought, we may as well eat too. Today we'd discovered three affordable supermarket items that could, tastily if boringly, form a dinner anywhere in France. Everything else on their shelves was too expensive to make a meal with enough calories, protein, fat and carbs. First of all, every supermarket sold two large tins of budget ready-meals – one, lentils with sausage, and two, cassoulet, which is white beans and surprise meat – and these could be had for approximately €1 each, or 71p at the exchange rate we'd managed to get. We'd also discovered French *Lidl*'s special offer on a wannabe soy sauce, sweeter than normal, for 25 cents (18p) for a large bottle. Soy sauce had already saved many a meal on this trip and it wasn't going to stop now.

Add pasta to these ingredients, which wasn't too expensive, as well as eggs and we had pretty much the meal we'd had for the last two nights but with a French twist. We could alternate for variation if required, with lentils on one night and beans on the other, although, to be honest, it wasn't much variation.

Tonight was the turn of cassoulet. Proper cassoulet, the more expensive stuff, is a sumptuous bean and vegetable stew containing pork sausages, goose and duck. Our cut-price tin had various unidentifiable blobs of processed animal death, but it tasted alright.

We finished our dinner and hoped the three French yoofs would be done soon but they'd taken to playing football with a three-litre bottle full of water and screaming loudly.

I decided to go for a wander. A car passed me, belching thick smoke. For a moment I thought it was on fire. The young driver gurned gormlessly at me through the window like he'd just won a competition to drive a steam engine. What was wrong with this town?

I returned to the picnic area and, after an hour of water bottle football, the lads suddenly remembered they'd brought an actual football and so switched to that, repeatedly hoofing the ball as hard as they could against their own, already badly battered cars. Perhaps we'd found three French Neil Duxburys. It's a good job there was no dog poo about.

It started to get dark. We didn't want to set up our tents while they were still hanging around. After all, maybe one of them was the Chief of Police. But we were getting cold and so we sneaked next door and built our homes. After ten more minutes of yelping, they packed up and drove away, pissed up and blaring their horns.

Welcome to France!

There's a piece of wild camping advice often disseminated on cycling forums: Set up late; pack up early. If your tent only occupies its space during the hours of darkness, you're unlikely to get rumbled. I woke up just after seven, dismantled my dew-sodden house and returned to the picnic site next door, now with tyre marks gouged out of the grass. It was a lovely morning. The clear air made it look as though I could've swum to Jersey. I waited for Dave and Joe instead.

An hour and a half later I was still waiting. Perhaps they

hadn't read the same advice I had. I could hear the hum of industrial equipment. In a field above last night's camping spot, a fella with a chainsaw was trimming his hedges. He must've been able to see Dave and Joe's tents. He disappeared from view. Maybe he'd gone to saw them in two.

Fifteen minutes later, Dave and Joe emerged, unchainsawed. We had our first French breakfast – more British porridge – and continued on our way. Since landing in France, a switch had clicked in my head. I'd suddenly felt energised. The West Country's lumps and drizzle had been replaced by flatness and sunshine and I wanted to fly.

We passed fields containing thousands of perfectly aligned spring onions, first in soil and then, as the ground dried out, in sand. Later, these were replaced by wheat, sweetcorn and purple lavender.

We stopped at a supermarket to buy some cheap methylated spirit for our stoves. Standing outside the shop, Dave inadvertently blocked access to a French bloke's bicycle leaning against the wall. The man, politely and in French, asked Dave to move. Dave reacted as though he'd been confronted with a rabid Doberman chewing a baby's severed arm. He jumped out of the way with a terrified look on his face. What was this strange breed of creature that spoke no English?

Untravelled as he was, Dave was suffering a steep learning curve. A lot of what he thought he knew about the locals seemed to have come directly from Al Murray's Pub Landlord.

"Is it true that Frenchmen just piss wherever they want to?" he asked.

"Well," I attempted to answer, "given that most Frenchmen probably want to piss in a toilet rather than, say, all over their dinner table or their children's faces, then, yes, I suppose they do."

In my newly energised state, we seemed to be travelling very slowly. So far on the trip, we'd cycled closely together, almost always within sight of each other. But here, with Joe in front, I found it difficult not to hover constantly on his back wheel. I would stop pedalling for a minute and let him get a hundred metres ahead but as soon as I restarted I was instantly shadowing him again. I think my proximity was annoying him, although he said nothing. It was beginning to annoy me. I wanted to go a lot faster.

Now that I'd been alone with Dave and Joe for a few days, other personality traits became noticeable. For one, Dave would agree with absolutely everything that either Joe or I proposed.

"Shall we stop for lunch?" I might suggest.

"Yes, I'm happy to stop for lunch," Dave would reply.

"Do you want to cycle for another hour?"

"Yes, I'm happy to cycle for another hour."

"How about we all go and stick a spear in our heads?"

"Yes, I'm happy to stick a spear in my head."

We decided to have a first attempt at French fishing. Looking at the map, we saw a lighthouse in Agon-Coutainville. We assumed it would be located on a jetty or something. We cycled miles out of our way to get there only to find it was about 200 metres inland from a shallow bay and, despite our calculations, the tide was out once again. Still, it was a sunny day and this was a great spot for a snooze and to dry out our tents. Dave rested his bike against a tree. It toppled over with a crash.

We cycled on to the port town of Granville. It appeared to be the accident capital of France. Within a minute of arriving I'd spotted three people with broken arms and one with a broken leg. What could be the reason for this?

I'd been in France for over 24 hours and not yet had a

proper chance to use my rubbish French. In Granville, a young fella came up to us and we had a conversation of sorts.

"Chelsea!" he began.

"Yes," I replied in French.

I think it's fair to say he hadn't given me a lot to work with.

"Arsenal!" he continued.

"Mmm."

"Liverpool!"

"Yes, Liverpool!"

Finally, I thought, a rope to grasp hold of. I tried to explain we'd left that very city 25 days earlier and we were cycling to Gibraltar. He simply nodded and walked away. Maybe it'd been a game and I was supposed to reply with "Paris Saint-Germain!" or "AS Saint-Etienne!", each of us trading a football team from the other's national league until one of us could go no further. Or maybe he was just supposed to keep naming teams until he mentioned one I didn't like, at which point I was meant to break his arm or leg.

For such a rainy country it hadn't always been easy to find water in Britain. Public toilets weren't very common and miserly petrol stations usually charged for the water normally destined for cars. In France it was much easier. As well as more numerous public conveniences, nearly every village had a cemetery, and cemeteries always had taps. We filled our water bottles in the dead centre of coastal town Jullouville and hunted for a place to sleep.

After a long hour of searching, we found some bins standing in a little field. No, we weren't going to sleep in them. I'm not *Top Cat*. But the hedge separating this field from the neighbouring one had a small opening that provided access to a perfectly concealed space. Even better, the site looked out across the bay and the beautiful, abbey-dominated island of Mont-Saint-Michel was clearly visible, wallowing in a shallow sea. Had this been the view from a hotel window you'd have paid a fortune. Since it was a field near some bins, we didn't.

Despite our good luck, finding somewhere to stay was a huge hassle, an obvious consequence of having no money to spend on accommodation. I lay outside my tent watching a gull fly overhead, envying its freedom to land wherever it wanted without fear of being arrested or moved on by the Pigeon Police. Civilisation comes at a price, and it was a bigger one than our current budget could afford.

The next morning we woke up to grey skies. This wasn't supposed to happen. It was meant to be sunny from now on. We had breakfast. Our porridge lacked its usual raisins. Dried fruit is stupidly expensive in France. Most families here have to choose between owning a car or buying a small bag of sultanas.

Today we were heading to Mont-Saint-Michel, the island we'd looked down upon last night. First, though, we had to complete the Cotentin Peninsula. I'd had enough of slowly tailgating Joe all day and so I decided to go at my own speed and then wait for them later.

At Pontaubault, where the peninsula meets the rest of France, I changed direction, turning from south to west. Some old women were playing *boules* on the cinder cycle path. They stepped aside as I approached and I weaved between their metal globes. As I passed, I stuck out a foot and pretended to kick a ball to bugger up their game. I received a lovely whoop of joy. Around the next corner I was confronted with a squadron of 30 young blokes on 50cc mopeds, dressed in costumes, wigs and comedy glasses, thrashing their legs about and screaming. Their little bikes farted rather than roared. The Pontaubault branch of *The Hell's Angels* had a lot to learn about intimidation.

We regrouped before making our assault on Mont-Saint-Michel. In the time we'd spent apart, and clearly more observant than I was, Dave and Joe had stumbled upon cherries and plums. We cycled together. The bike path to the island was sporadic at best and appeared to have been designed by Mr Magoo.

It was mid-morning when we found the track to the island. Beside the path were low bushes of wild raspberries, heavily loaded with fruit. And they were sweet. We'd already scoffed a few handfuls when an elderly French couple approached and, after a misunderstood attempt at a verbal admonishment, took the more practical approach of miming a dog having a piss. The penny dropped. We gathered a few bagfuls of fruit and promised to wash them later before eating the rest.

Once free of the urine-soaked raspberries, we hit the new, half mile-long road bridge to the island. According to legend, it was Archangel Michel who commanded St Aubert to build the church at Mont-Saint-Michel. Because St Aubert was the patron saint of bakers, and presumably like loafing about, he refused. Archangel Michel kept on at him and only eventually managed to motivate him by burning a hole in the saint's skull with his finger, which all sounds a bit unchristian to me.

It's fitting that St Aubert is the patron saint of bakers because Mont-Saint-Michel is like a *Great British Bake Off* showstopper built out of granite. There's building piled on building and the abbey balanced on top. It's really quite impressive. We weren't the only ones who thought so. It receives three million visitors a year and most of them were here today. This must be somewhat overwhelming for the locals. There are only 44 of them.

We pushed our bikes through the small archway into the citadel and quickly realised we weren't going anywhere, blocked by the heaving masses. Even without the hoards, the place was full of steps and staircases. Visiting a historic site with a bike poses the same problems it would if you were a Dalek. We turned around with difficulty and pushed the bikes back outside.

We left Mont-Saint-Michel behind and passed through flatlands loaded with sweetcorn, lettuce, onions and carrots. When the sun came out, the green fields shone, but without hedges to separate them we were at the mercy of the wind.

We'd originally planned to stop at Cherrueix but it was still early afternoon. We pedalled to the beach and watched an impressive display of dozens of multi-coloured kites dancing in the strong breeze. These weren't your run-of-the-mill, hand-held ones. They were fastened to the ground, some spinning like windmills, other soaring high. There was even one giant, tubular alien-worm flying over the car park that flapped wildly and occasionally smacked a passer-by in the face.

On the wide beach in the distance, kids were trying out their land-sailing skills. They each sat in a little go-kart with a sail attached and raced merrily around a circuit. A little later, a bloke turned up in a much more impressive model. Its car was larger and fitted with a huge sail. He screamed across the sand and looked about to plough into a crowd of onlookers, but at the last minute he performed an impressive skid, missing them by inches and then undid his coolness by turning his car over.

We'd noted the tide time posted near the entrance to Mont-Saint-Michel and calculated we'd now have a few days when the optimal tide for fishing would be early in the morning or late at night. Since finding a camp spot directly on the coast was posing a problem we decided to abandon fishing for a few days and cycle further inland. It wasn't as though we'd miss the huge quantity of fish in our diet.

Before we could stop for the day we needed to cross the estuary of the Rance, the wide river that eventually empties into the sea near St Malo. On the busy main road approaching the bridge, an arse in the passenger seat of a passing car decided it'd be funny to shake up a can of beer and spray it at me. And he was right. It was hilarious when he covered the back end of the car and his own face in frothy hops, the gobshite.

Close to the bridge wall, we found several trees loaded with small, ripe, sweet plums. Dave leant his bike against the bridge. It instantly crashed to the ground. Dave and Joe went into Spiderman mode and scaled the wall in an attempt to collect more fruit. I loaded up the pocket on the back of my cycling shirt with fruit and ate them like sweets while cycling along until my guts started to gurgle in a distressing way.

It was close to eight in the evening. We'd been cycling since early morning and even with our break for Mont-Saint-Michel and various forays into fruit foraging we'd cycled well over 60 miles. We were slowly getting ahead of schedule.

In Pleslin-Trigavou there's a stone circle signposted with the enticing label *Megaliths*. Sounds impressive, doesn't it? And it *is* impressive because this site, properly called *Champ de Roches*, is apparently – get this! – the *third* most important stone circle in Brittany. Champ de Roches translates as 'field of rocks', which sounds less impressive but is, sadly, more accurate. The tourist website states these rocks were "erected between 6000 and 2000 BC", although a more appropriate verb would've been 'dumped'.

It was the next day and we were reading the on-site information sign. It stated the purpose of the stone circle was an enigma. We had our own attempts at interpretation. Dave suggested it was a primitive adventure playground. Joe clambered on to one of the larger rocks to demonstrate the fun that could've been had by a cave toddler. It looked to me like a religious site. I could imagine the head druid beside the largest rock conducting a ceremony to a congregation of men, women and lesser priests and, in the far corner, an ancient version of Dave molesting a recently sacrificed goat.

Today was Sunday. When cycling through Britain, the day of the week doesn't make much difference to your experience. Not so in France. Supermarkets don't generally open on Sundays here. Imagine that! A day when you have to do something other than shopping. Sadly for the French worker, this is changing, with larger supermarkets beginning to open on Sunday mornings. That's not all. With only a few exceptions, trucks are banned from the road network on the Sabbath. Sunday is the perfect day to hit the roads in France, as long as you remember to bring a sandwich.

The initial sunshine that France had provided had been replaced by a solid grey sky. Approaching Saint-Brieuc, it started to rain.

"Don't worry, Dave. Once we get to the south of France, the weather will be glorious," I said confidently.

How *couldn't* the south of France be sunny in July?

I'd collected a load more plums, sweet yellow ones and tarter purples. They filled the pockets in the back of my cycling shirt, making it hang low, giving me the appearance of a man with the world's worst haemorrhoids.

The fruit may have been lovely but you needed to be careful foraging around here, especially on the beach. In 2011, over 30 wild boar were found dead, suspected of ingesting poisonous algae. The algae's over-production was blamed on the fertilizers found in agricultural run-off. And it wasn't only pigs that suffered. In 2009, after the death of a horse and some dogs, a council worker was sent in a truck to clear the huge amount of rotting sea lettuce from the beach. The council had underestimated the quantities of hydrogen sulphide gas –

that farty smell at the seaside – that can be produced by such quantities of weed. The driver was found dead in his truck.

On the other side of Saint-Brieuc, the roads got lumpier. We'd been warned that, geographically speaking, Brittany was the Cornwall of France. So far, the French road builders had coped better with the gradients that their English counterparts. Moving westwards, Dave started to titter.

"What's the matter?" I asked.

"Whenever I see a signpost for Brest it makes me giggle like a schoolboy."

I should take him cycling near Cockermouth.

By early evening, we'd had enough and found an empty field in the village of Plouvara. A hedge hid us from the road that ran through the centre of the village. We wondered if drivers could still see us somehow. They always slowed down as they passed. It turned out there was a speed bump on the road. I didn't like to be constantly on my guard like this.

I don't need to tell you what we had for dinner. We'd eaten the same main course, or a variation of it, every day for nearly a week and, as good as it was, I was getting tired of it. Hopefully soon, high tides would align with when we'd be near a fishable bit of coast. All the edible leaves we could identify – like dandelions and nettles – were already past their best and wouldn't have provided many calories in any case. We were dependent on the few bargains we could find in expensive supermarkets. It was certainly harder to survive here than in the UK.

Fortunately, foraging was doing us well when it came to desserts. We made a delicious biscuit-topped plum stew. Joe's approach of precisely slicing each plum with his knife, surgeon-like, and then carefully removing its stone would have taken ages for the amount we needed. I just squashed the soft fruit, ripped out its heart and threw the flesh in the pan. After all, we were sitting in a field, caked in crap. We didn't need to be quite so prissy when it came to kitchen technique. This wasn't *The Ivy*.

Despite this lack of showering, I don't think we were particularly smelly. The previous day I'd walked past a woman who stank. I took this to be a good sign. If she could out-stink us then we probably weren't doing too badly. Either that or we'd become so used to our own stench we could no longer recognise it.

But it wasn't all good news. I'd come to realise that using a smart phone in rural France is a bit like using the internet in 1995, lots of waiting around followed by a slew of error message. The signal was sporadic unless we were close to a large town. I assumed Dave had a smart phone given how many hours he spent on it, but why, I wondered, did his appear to perform a lot better than mine?

"Are you online, Dave?"

"Eh?"

"Are you online?"

He looked at me.

"It's not a smart phone," he said.

"What are you doing then?"

"I'm playing *Snake*."

For hours, and hours, and hours.

Dave was up first. I wasn't sure why he'd packed everything away so quickly, especially given that he knew we used his larger pan to boil the water for our morning porridge. I set up my stove.

"Dave, I need your pan."

He looked pensive for a moment.

"Yeah, I thought so," he said.

He then had to remove almost everything from his panniers to extract the saucepan.

Not long out of Plouvara we fell foul of one of Brittany's dreaded 'squiggle maps'. This *départment* has a curious approach to road signage. Wherever there's a snake pit of minor roads in a rural area, then at its entrance they play a game with you. They place a huge sign of such complexity that should you find you way through it, you'd expect the minimum reward of a chest of treasure.

The map contains dozens and dozens of labelled places joined by a mess of squiggly lines. I've no idea who the sign is aimed at because the typeface is too small for drivers to see and, besides, they'd have to block the road for several minutes while they work out the complicated series of lefts, rights and straight-ons that'd take them to their destination.

Our route however seemed relatively simple. A right turn and then a left and we'd be through to the other side. It didn't work out like that. The turnings on the map were a stylised depiction of their real-life versions. What was portrayed as a right-angled, ninety degree turn on the sign could in reality be a turn of any angle at all. Counting turns didn't help either, since what appeared to be a lane might actually be the long entrance to a farm. We got very lost.

Occasionally, while within the bounds of the original sign, you get an additional squiggle map that serves only to baffle you further. We tried to relate the supplementary information to our not undetailed road map. Nothing seemed to match. First of all, all the villages mentioned on the sign began with the prefix "Ker", whereas only the odd one did on the map.

When the map failed to help, we tried other approaches. I always carry a compass. Needing to go westwards, we aimed in that general direction but we would follow a road that started going west only for it to bend right around and head off in an easterly direction. Roads went around in circles, doubled back on themselves and disappeared off into the sky.

Our next approach was to realise we were quite high and,

knowing our destination was lower, if we headed downhill then it had to be correct, except it wasn't because we'd go down only to climb again a minute later.

We cycled around and around and started to despair. We had slipped into the Ker-Zone, where time appeared no longer to function properly. Turning a corner, we came across three ancient cyclists dressed in clothes like ours yet tattered and torn.

The oldest with a long grey beard, speaking in a Blackburn accent, gave us a warning.

"Do not take the next left," he said.

We thanked them for their help and set off again, but the next left turning felt so damn right and, not heeding his advice, we went down it. We became even more lost. We cycled around those lanes for 50 long, hard years, until our beards reached our crossbars and our clothes were ragged. We eventually stumbled across a younger version of ourselves. I offered them some advice.

"Do not take the next left."

The silly sods cycled off in the wrong direction.

We had originally been aiming for a place called Kermilin. We turned a corner to be confronted by another supplementary squiggle map and Kermilin was only a single turn away. We would make it! We cycled triumphantly straight on and turned left to be confronted not by the village of Kermilin, but by a farm called Kermilin. It suddenly all made sense. The items on the map were not villages at all. They were farms. And although we now knew how the system worked, it didn't really help us. An hour later, by sheer luck, we saw a busy road ahead and aimed for it. I'd never been happier to see traffic. We had escaped the Ker-Zone but feared for the thousands of others still trapped inside.

We were now in Guingamp, and it's a little bit special. It

has less than 10,000 inhabitants and yet it has a team in the top division of French football. They also won the equivalent of the FA Cup in 2014 and qualified for Europe as a result. As a comparison, in England, with most of the big clubs coming from the huge conurbations of London, Manchester, Liverpool and Birmingham, the smallest town currently represented in the Premier League is Sunderland with 180,000 inhabitants. Guingamp in the top tier of French football is like the Premier League featuring Henley-on-Thames United.

We had been on the road for four weeks now and it seemed like a good time to assess how we were progressing in the silly beard competition. Youthful Joe was still mostly unwhiskered, looking like he'd shaved a couple of days ago, but Dave was clearly winning with his ridiculous goblin effort.

"I've never had a beard this long," I said. "I think it's starting to look a bit daft."

"I don't know," said Dave. "It suits you."

Knowing Dave's attraction to deceased bucks, this wasn't such a ringing endorsement.

Our route took us through Morlaix, beneath its massive viaduct and besides its lovely tidal river. We sat for a while beside the water, our bikes leaning against the wall running parallel to the flow. We watched Dave's bike wobble and smash to the ground. Even though I won't mention Dave's bike falling over again, just assume it happens on a daily basis until the end of our ride.

It was time to start searching for a field. A few miles the other side of town we saw the brown sign of a tourist attraction.

"Places like these can be good to camp," said Joe

"Really?"

"Yes, everyone's gone by six. The place will be empty."

We followed the sign and ended up at Penhoat Chateau, a crumbling ruin built between the thirteenth and fifteenth centuries. The ancient building itself was fenced off but it was surrounded by woods and a small lawn that at some point had been levelled in a way that invited camping.

It started to rain and we hid beneath the trees at the far end of the lawn and started to cook up some very familiar food. Our camp was quiet tonight, as it had been most nights since Mark had left. Joe listened to music and Dave played *Snake*. No one talked. I enjoyed our days of cycling and fruit-collecting but these evenings had started to bore the arse off me. Nina called. It was lovely to hear her voice again. Hell, it was great to hear any voice. If this story was ever made into a film, it could be a silent movie.

Since arriving in France, we'd been cycling farther each day, averaging 60 miles rather than the planned 40. And because we were travelling slightly inland we'd reduced the total mileage by not having to negotiate every cove. We were already four days ahead of schedule.

The next morning's breakfast routine was a repeat of the previous day's. Before we'd eaten, Dave had once again packed up everything into his panniers.

"I need the pan, Dave."

"Yeah, I thought so."

Little things like this were beginning to niggle me. Sometimes I felt like I wanted to shake him, but then I might have been splattered with whatever was in his beard at the time. When I finally had access to the cooking implements, another layer of enjoyment was peeled from the breakfast experience. The cocoa powder we'd added to our porridge had gone the same way as the raisins. It was too expensive to replace. Tiny joys, once so insignificant as hardly to be noticeable as such, were being stripped from our existence and their impact was adding up.

Despite an *AccuWeather* forecast for sunny weather, we set off from the château under a grey sky and cycled through fields of potatoes, cabbages and huge, alien artichokes. We turned back to the coast, past hundreds of restaurant signs for *moules-frites* and oysters, and found the greatest field of samphire yet. Rather than the small clumps we'd found in Britain, here we had access to a luxurious carpet of the salty, little plant.

With a strong headwind we stopped for a rest by some poky sand dunes. Joe had been lagging behind this morning and when he caught us up he said he was tired and hungry, especially with the additional work caused by the wind. He'd gone from perpetually leading the group in England and Wales to bringing up the rear most days. At times he was miles behind.

I was surprised at Joe. He was 21, slim and athletic-looking whereas I was still a blobby old duffer. That said, I felt fitter than I'd ever done and was around a stone and a half lighter than when I'd started. I wanted to go farther and faster each day. Yes, I was frequently hungry but it was hard to explain why this wasn't affecting my performance. On previous trips, I would've eaten two or three times the amount I'd done on this one. Some power beyond food was keeping me going. I wanted to get back to Nina. I wanted to celebrate finishing my degree, and celebrate finishing this ride, but I had to get there first.

There was something about the asceticism of it all. In the early days, shopping in supermarkets had been painful, looking at what was available and knowing that all the fun stuff was off-limits. Nowadays, I simply didn't see it. We headed straight to the aisles that sold the things we wanted and then got out of there as quickly as possible. Whenever I now inadvertently glanced at a chocolate bar or a bag of sweets, what hit me was how ridiculously and unnecessarily expensive they were. It reminded me of a story my dad told me. He was doing some work at the *KitKat* factory and he asked an engineer how many pence it cost to make this two-fingered snack.

"You're asking the wrong question," the engineer said. "You should be asking how many *KitKats* can be made for a penny."

I was enjoying the liberation from the consumerism of modern life, and realising just how little I needed to survive. Yes, a lot of our diet was unvaried but it wasn't unhealthy and the supermarket staples were supplemented by plenty of free, presumably organic fruit. Joe, though, wanted more and I had no idea what Dave wanted because he never offered an opinion. Physically though, Dave seemed to be handling it well. He never complained about being hungry or tired. I suppose if he ever got desperate, he could've peeled that giant lump of congealed matter from the centre of his Tigger bowl and eaten that.

"If we're cycling twice as far as we planned each day, then we should get twice the daily budget," said Joe.

"The idea was to see if we could do it on a pound a day," I replied, "regardless of how far we go."

"Yes, but if we go twice as far, we use twice as many calories."

"True. But I could've said the trip was going to take 5,000 days, done it in 100 and spent 50 quid each day. What would that have demonstrated?"

He seemed to accept this argument. Besides, because of the low cost British supermarkets, we each had a little in the bank. He could always use his surplus to buy extras if he needed to.

"Anyway," I continued, "we aren't cycling twice as far

each day. It's about 50 per cent more."

There was an air of tetchiness between us. Maybe he was planning my murder.

After the sand dunes, with a round of peanut butter and marmalade sandwiches inside him, Joe perked up, keeping up with Dave and me for the rest of the day.

In the afternoon we stopped at a church to get some water. I noticed a half-empty *Coke* bottle and a shiny apple on the wall near the tap. I assumed it belonged to the gardener who'd probably wandered off for a moment. I returned to my bike. I looked up and saw Dave approaching. He was munching on an apple.

"Where did you get that apple?" I asked.

"From the wall."

"I can't believe you took it."

"What?"

"Who leaves an apple like that? It's probably a workman's."

"Oh," he said, finishing it off.

Why was I having a go at him? I didn't know for sure it belonged to anyone. Cabin fever was setting in. We'd been too long in each other's, and only each other's, company and we had so much longer to go. Was this really going to turn out like the Donner Party? Was I going to kill and eat them both? I wasn't ruling anything out.

Today, out in front as usual now, I'd set the pace. I'd hoped we'd reach Saint-Pabu, as that would take us five days ahead of schedule. We were there for early evening. We found a field of long grass that hid our tents from the road.

We had some fishing to do. High tide was just an hour away. Our timing was perfect. We cycled down a small hill to the large jetty near Saint-Pabu's marina. There were a few others already fishing, which we took to be a good sign. Some of those people were dads with their kids. Surely these fathers wouldn't be here to introduce a boring, fish-less hobby to their beloved offspring, would they? We fished for an hour without a bite.

"I'm disillusioned with fishing," I said grumpily. "I reckon there are only three fish in the entire sea."

No one else was catching either.

"Y'know those two fish I caught in Wales? I bet it was an accident," I continued. "That water was flowing so quickly. I bet they were just floating merrily downstream and suddenly they were like – Jesus! – why've I got a massive hook stuck in my head?"

At least we didn't lose any fishing tackle this time.

"I wonder how much is spent on fishing tackle each year compared to the value of the fish caught," said Joe.

"I don't think it's about that," I replied. "It's just a way to get out of the house and get some fresh air."

"I suppose."

"Well, I've got all the fresh air I can handle. I hate fishing!"

A fish or two would've been lovely, especially considering our standard evening meal would now be substandard as we'd used up all the cheap *Lidl* faux-soy sauce. At least the addition of today's samphire to the scrambled egg component of dinner gave it a little variation. We'd finished eating by half past seven. Dave took out his phone and played *Snake* and Joe disappeared into his tent. Silence reigned once again.

I lay on my sleeping mat, thinking. I felt like I was engineering ways to get this whole thing over with as quickly as possible. I wanted a good laugh. I wanted the freedom to eat and drink what I liked. But all those things were far in the distance. If we stuck to the schedule, they would still be two months away. And, right now, two months felt like two years. Yes, I could've given up – these limitations were, after all, entirely self-imposed – but I could hear the negativity that'd been voiced before the trip had started: "You'll never complete it." "You'll give up halfway." "It's a silly idea." Well, you know what? It was a silly bloody idea. But I wasn't about to give up that easily. No way. But I was buggered if it was going to take another two months.

Days Completed: 29
Ride and Seek: **Total spend £15.65, per day £0.54**
Live below the Line: **Total spend £23.31, per day £0.80**

Chapter 9: Naked in the Cemetery

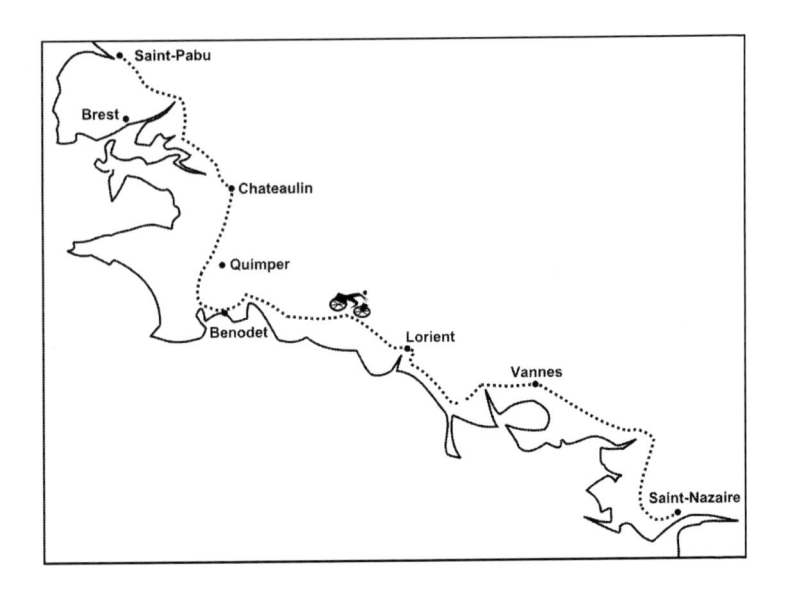

I woke up to rain pitter-pattering on the outside of my tent. *AccuWeather* had got it wrong once again. I climbed out on to the damp grass. Dave presented me with the breakfast pan, full of water. I looked up at the grey sky.

"Thanks, Dave," I said, "but it's too wet. We'll have to have breakfast later."

"Yeah, I thought so," he replied.

At least he was trying.

"Anyway," I said, "I'm sick of porridge. We could have something else."

"Like what?" asked Joe.

"We're in France. Let's get a baguette."

"It won't give us as many calories," said Joe.

"I don't care. I need a change. Just once."

We cycled to the next town, Ploudalmézeau, and found a *Casino* supermarket. We got a baguette and a cheap jar of apricot jam. Joe sliced the baguette into three exactly equal pieces. The bread may not have provided as many calories as porridge, and it ate a little more deeply into our daily budget – my one third of a baguette came to 25p instead of less than 10p for porridge – but smeared in thick apricot jam it was a delicious treat. On that damp morning, it's difficult to express how amazing it tasted without sounding like a weirdo.

The rain continued. I'd finally worked out why this area has the name it does. I think it's because the weather was very Britain-y. We cut off the tip of the Breton peninsula and headed south-east to Landerneau. Despite turning 135 degrees, we still had a headwind. The weather wasn't playing fair.

Once again, Joe was at the back of the pack. We stopped for our daily handful of peanuts to let him catch up, and then again at lunchtime for sandwiches. Unfortunately, we'd run out of peanut butter now and it was too expensive to replace, being three times the price in England. After the beautifully textured baguette of the morning, the lunchtime's cheap sliced loaf was a spongy, air-filled disappointment. I had to keep its bag closed to stop the slices floating away.

Towards the end of an uneventful day, we hit the town of Châteaulin. France has certain family names that might cause a few raised eyebrows in the English speaking world. This would no doubt be the case with the local minicab firm delightfully called *Bastard Taxi*. Or perhaps it was just an honest description of their company, their drivers dumping you in the middle of nowhere and then driving off over your foot.

We climbed a large hill on the other side of town. Joe was lagging behind again. It was clearly time for him to stop.

Besides, by the route we'd taken today, we'd already brought our completion date a day further forward.

I found a field with a protective hedge that overlooked Châteaulin. Anyone in town with a decent telescope could've seen our tents but we doubted they'd be looking. After another soy sauce-less dinner, and under a drizzling sky, we climbed into our tents at half past eight, like the party animals we weren't.

Despite our best efforts we'd been unable to find a public toilet today, which may have explained the gaseous output that evening. It was like the campfire scene in *Blazing Saddles*. But at least, hidden by canvas, each emission was anonymous.

"More tea, vicar!"

Well, most of them were anonymous.

Had those same telescopes been trained on our position the next morning, the eye behind the lens would've seen nothing at all. We woke to a thick mist. Joe had been taking longer and longer to get ready in the mornings. He said he couldn't use the alarm clock on his phone to wake him up because it wore the battery down if he left it on all night. As a result, Dave had become Joe's alarm clock, giving him a shout at the allotted hour. Still, it'd be another fifteen minutes before Joe would emerge from his tent. Perhaps it was his sly way of reducing the distance he'd eventually cycle each day.

Yesterday's breakfast baguette experiment had been an unqualified success and unanimously we wanted to extend it. We decided from now on we'd set off unbreakfasted and if we hadn't found a source of bread within an hour we'd fall back on the four days' worth of porridge we had remaining. I was praying we'd never have to use this option. It had been dull enough when full of raisins and chocolate powder. Without them, it was like eating putty.

As the morning sun burnt away the mist, we cycled down the other side of the large hill we'd climbed the evening before. We were close to our one hour breadline when we stumbled upon the entrance to the village of Locronan. Noting it was one of *Les Plus Beaux Villages de France*, we decided to have a look.

Locronan was built around the burial place of Saint Ronan, some time in the sixth century. His remains were later moved to Quimper, where they were apparently used with miraculous effect to extinguish a large fire in the town. Don't mention this to the Tories or they'll dismantle the UK's fire service and give each county council a bit of old dead saint to work with.

The approach to the village is lovely, a corridor of purples, blues and whites, with huge bushes of hydrangeas lining the road. The medieval buildings inside the village, constructed of blue-grey granite, are no less attractive. Before we started this journey, it was a village like Locronan that I'd pictured whenever I'd imagined what Brittany would be like. It'd taken nearly a week of cycling here before we'd finally found such a place. Maybe there's only one village that looks like this but it's the one they always use in their adverts.

In keeping with its ancient surroundings, Locronan seemed to lack a supermarket and so we hit the *boulangerie* in the village square. The *grand moulé* loaf, a large house brick of bread, was hardly a bargain, but spread with apricot jam and devoured while sitting at a picnic bench in the sun, our smiles were beginning to return.

We continued southwards and aimed for the coast at Benodet. Along the way we found an ancient orchard that'd fallen into disrepair. Nettles and brambles grew between and around the apple trees. It hadn't adversely affected their fruit production. We collected a bagful of tasty Granny Smith-like apples.

The treats kept on coming. In Concarneau, we found another *Lidl* offering the same 25 cent deal on that pretend soy-sauce-a-like we loved so much. We bought two bottles, which excited us in a way that now, writing this, I find difficult to understand. After two meals without it, we were actually giddy. Were we becoming slightly mad?

We cycled along the coast, passing the pretty yet heavily touristed village of Pont-Aven. A biscuit shop had set up a dish of free samples on a table outside its front door. As I whizzed past, I decided against taking a handful, especially given we'd no intention of buying any, but mostly because all the good ones had gone.

It had turned into a hot day, close to 30 degrees, the perfect weather for a laundry session. At a cemetery, I part-filled my placky bag-based washing machine with water and did some laundry.

Joe decided to go one better and have a wash by the cemetery wall. A woman came up to him and said he should also do his hair. They clearly expected better from their tramps in France.

While he had command of the tap, and with his beauty adviser long gone, Joe also decided to wash some clothes. He stood on the inside of the cemetery with a waist high wall separating him from Dave and me. He removed his shorts to wash them, basically standing half-naked – and that half being the most dangerous half – in a cemetery. I'm not religious in the slightest, but something felt, well, inappropriate.

While he washed, I looked over to the other side of the cemetery and noticed a burial was taking place. Dozens of soberly attired mourners lined the grave. Had this been a seventies sitcom, hilarity would have ensued. A startled groundskeeper would spy a semi-nude Joe, shriek in horror and chase him, tackle flapping, around the cemetery to the dismay of the friends and family of the deceased before Joe would trip and fall into the hole, landing awkwardly on top of the coffin. But this wasn't a seventies sitcom and hilarity didn't ensue, which was probably just as well in this case.

"Oh no!" said Dave.

He stopped searching his bike and hurriedly looked back down the road in the direction we'd cycled in on.

"What's up?"

"My ground mat. It's gone!"

"Were you still balancing it on your bike?"

"No, I bungeed it on for the first time today."

"Ah, that's ironic."

We all looked for it but it was nowhere to be found.

"The good news is, Dave, with the direction the wind's blowing it might be waiting for you in Gibraltar."

As always, Dave took his misfortune in his stride. On my first ever camping trip back in the fourteenth century, before I knew about the existence of ground mats, I spent three nights in Scotland shivering to death on uninsulated ground that sucked the heat right out of my body. If I'd lost my own mat I would have started to cry. Dave just kept smiling.

We weren't far out of Moëlan-sur-mer when we began our hunt for somewhere to stay. I found a lane but it didn't seem too promising and was about to look elsewhere. Joe persisted. He clearly didn't want to cycle any further today.

"This'll do," he said.

True, there was enough space and it was well-hidden from the road, but it was beneath a couple of large chestnut trees, last season's spiky husks still carpeting the floor, hardly the ideal first night for a man without a sleeping mat. Simon Calder, the *Independent*'s Travel Editor, once said the authenticity of your travel experience is inversely proportional to the thickness of your hotel's mattress. If that's true, Dave's experience was about to get painfully authentic.

What with the sunshine and the soy sauce, the mood was better than it'd been since the last cider piss-up. We even talked, except while we were eating. Nothing ever got in the way of eating. The meal time ritual was identical every day. The food would be cooked and everyone would watch the dishing out process like it was the Observation Round on *The Krypton Factor* to ensure no one got a piece of sausage more than anyone else. At this point, even if there'd been constant chatter before, silence would kick in as the realisation fell upon us that we'd once again get something to eat. Dishes would be handed out and the food would be devoured in seconds.

We'd once again knocked off another day from our schedule. Dave saw this as a positive.

"If we finish early, I'll be home in time for this year's garlic-eating event."

"Do you do training for it?"

"No."

"Do you wear a tracksuit and do stretches before it begins?"

"No."

Dave was immune to piss-taking.

"It should be good for you," said Joe. "Garlic's an aphrodisiac."

"What? Smelly breath is sexy?" I asked.

"If you've both been eating it, like in an Italian restaurant."

"I'm not sure it's the garlic that's the aphrodisiac. It's more likely the three bottles of wine."

Finishing our journey early wouldn't be quite so useful for Joe. He'd already booked a flight home a week after the planned finish date of the 23rd of September. Dave's plans were more fluid.

"It's only going to cost me 100 pounds to get back from Gib."

"Are you sure about that?" I asked. That seemed very cheap. "How much is the ferry from Santander?"

"About 85 quid."

"Well, you're not going to get a train or a bus from Gibraltar to Santander for fifteen quid."

"OK, it'll be something like 25."

"The last time I got the bus from Malaga to Madrid it cost nearly 50 quid. And that's only halfway."

"No, it's 25," he repeated. "I checked."

"When was that? 1960?"

Another day, another inaccurate *AccuWeather* forecast. After the sun has seeped into our veins and raised spirits yesterday, we were looking forward to a second day of sunshine from the weather website's predicted five day heatwave. Instead, the sky was leaking a grey drizzle. We packed up and waited under the chestnut trees for the rain to subside. We were in danger of losing the previous day's good mood.

"How was your night without a ground mat, Dave?"

"Alright, wasn't too bad."

"Good, 'cos tonight we take away your tent as well."

After twenty minutes, it showed no signs of stopping.

"We may as well go for it," I said.

It was just as well we did. It didn't stop raining until mid-afternoon.

Around two o'clock, with the rain easing, we found a bus shelter and had a round of sandwiches. Looking at the map, we discovered we were sitting on the edge of a village called Belz. The place warranted two stars out of three on Joe's *Michelin* map, one that highlighted places of interest. By the time we'd finished our butties, the sun had made a welcome reappearance and so we decided to explore the town.

Just across the river Etel, there's a tiny island, once the

home to the hermit Saint Cado. This island is linked to Belz by a stone bridge supposedly built, at least partially, by the saint himself. Obviously, he didn't like the hermit lifestyle 24/7 and liked to pop into town for an occasional pint. Legend has it that Saint Cado's first attempt to build the bridge ended miserably in its instant collapse. Just as always happens in real life, the Devil offered to lend a hand and build a more stable structure as long as His Nastiness could take the life of the bridge's first user. Despite what he'd probably been taught at Saint School, Cado struck a deal with Beelzebub, who, true to his word, constructed the beautiful stone bridge we see today. However, Cado was a conniving, little sod and sent a cat across the bridge first. Joe said there's a similar story in Aberystwyth regarding a bridge and a deal with Satan but on that occasion the first thing sent across was a dog. Credit where credit's due. The Devil may be an easily duped idiot, but he's a fine structural engineer.

If you're in the area, the island is well worth a visit. It's a tranquil, little spot with a tiny church and a gift shop that plays heavily on the Cado/*cadeaux* pun. If you've no idea what I'm on about, don't worry. It's honestly not worth explaining.

We continued eastwards through Auray and on to a village called Bono. There, we crossed an old suspension bridge. We decided not to look over the side because we didn't want to get too close to The Edge. Or some other crap, U2-based joke.

Our tents were still wet from this morning's soaking and so we found a large, sunny field to allow them to dry out for a while before we needed to climb inside. Joe and I made the usual dinner.

"That was good," said Dave after he'd licked his bowl clean. "But I suppose anything's good when you're starving."

"Cheers, Dave."

"Yeah, I'll eat any old shite."

"Thank you."

Alcohol deprivation was turning my mind. Whenever we cooked a meal, I noticed that French meths didn't smell like the British stuff. Things are added in the UK to make it less palatable. In France, it smells wonderful, like schnapps. It reminded me of Sabby's pálinka. Alas, I checked, but French meths is still poisonous.

It reminded me of a bit Alexei Sayle used to do as Bobby Chariot, his bucked tooth, alcoholic warm-up man. He goes into a chemist and asks for a bottle of meths.

"Sorry, Bobby, because of your drink problem we've been told we can't sell it to you," says the chemist.

"Ah, go on. I only need it to clean my photographic lenses."

"Ah, is that so? Well, in that case, here you go," she says, handing him a bottle.

Bobby pulls his face.

"Have you got a cold one?"

I got up at eight on a beautiful day, said good morning to Dave and packed away quickly. I'd only grown marginally more comfortable with wild camping. I didn't mind being there as evening descended and the day was slowing down, but if it was a working field, and today's definitely was, I wanted to be out of there as quickly as possible in the morning. And getting up at eight was too late. Most farmers have already put in a shift by then. I was wheeling my bike out of the field by the time Joe crawled out of his tent.

At the entrance to the field, a huge dog stood, snarling at me. We'd been rumbled!

A female voice called to Kujo and he trotted back to her.

"Bonjour!" she said happily as she continued walking past the field.

I waited on the road. Fifteen minutes later, Dave and Joe appeared.

"I'm not doing that again," I said.

"What?" asked Joe.

"Getting up so late. Fine if we're on a bit of wasteland. But if it's a working field I'm getting up at seven at the latest. Especially now we don't need to hang around making porridge."

Right from the off I'd said I wanted us to make decisions collectively, and if someone didn't like a particular group decision he could do what he wanted to do instead. But I felt I had to say something here. If an angry farmer came calling, it would be me who'd have to sort it out. Dave had no French at all and, though Joe knew some, a seeming lack of confidence meant he hadn't spoken any yet. My French was awful but it was all we had. I didn't particularly want to negotiate at gunpoint in a foreign language because of someone else's inability to get his arse out of bed.

We rolled slowly into the *Michelin*-recommended town of Vannes. There was a twang from the back of my bike and then suddenly the pedals locked. One of the bungees holding my tent on to my rear rack had snapped, setting its large hook free. Luckily, it had snagged in my gears and was easy to untangle. Had it snapped on a fast downhill and fallen into my back wheel, it could've ripped out my spokes and sent me sprawling again.

Vannes was beautiful, with its lovely Saint-Pierre cathedral, constructed between the twelve and fourteenth centuries, and old streets full of houses that looked like they were made of cake. Outside the town hall were huge oversized flowerpots. We got Dave to pose beside one of them. With his comedy beard, he looked like a garden gnome.

We continued to Muzillac under a sunny sky – perhaps

summer was here at last – and arrived at the Barrage D'Arzal, which, according to its information boards, bills itself as "the most important estuary barrage in Europe", a bold and thoroughly unverifiable claim. Nearby was a huge tangle of brambles and, ahead of its brethren in the rest of France, it was dripping with black fruit. We started collecting, one for the bag, one for the mouth, repeat. With fingers stained purple, we set off again, finally waving goodbye to Brittany, but not long afterwards Joe called out.

"Shouldn't we start looking for somewhere?"

"Isn't half past five a bit early?" I asked.

He thought for a minute.

"What do you think, Dave?" he asked.

Dave proved as non-committal as ever.

"I'm easy either way. I could do a couple more hours or stop now."

If Dave had a preference, he wasn't sharing it.

"If I go on past six, I'll be knackered," said Joe. "And knackered's no fun."

And in that statement lay the difference between Joe and me and the reason for this very English and restrained conflict bubbling up between us. I didn't say anything at the time, but I think he's wrong about this. Getting knackered is tons of fun. Getting knackered is how you get fitter and faster. It's how you know you've pushed yourself to your limit, and how you can later exceed that limit. And it's how you can fall asleep at night knowing you've given something your best.

"Alright then," I said. "Let's find a field."

It wasn't long before we found one down a nearby lane. The field was full of wheat but in its far corner there was long, unruly grass and enough room for three tents. The ground was slightly moist, which probably wasn't going to be very Dave-friendly without his ground mat but, as always, he said nothing. As we waded through the grass, a dense cloud of grasshoppers leapt through the air.

I rolled out my mat and, in the absence of anything else to do, snoozed for a bit. I held my hand over my mouth to prevent the grasshoppers from leaping inside.

We made dinner – the usual – but even the presence of soy sauce didn't lift the mood. Afterwards, Joe and Dave both returned to their phones. I was low on credit and wasn't prepared to give *Three* any more money, especially as their supposed No Roaming Charges spiel was a massive pile of bollocks and to use my phone in France actually cost ten times what it did in England. At half past nine, it was dark enough to put our tents up. The grasshoppers weren't happy about this and went slightly mental, attacking us ineffectively like tiny biplanes around *King Kong*.

"What time are we getting up?" asked Joe.

"Since it's a working field, I say seven," I replied.

"What do you think, Dave?" continued Joe.

Didn't he know this strategy was never going to work?

"I'm easy," Dave said.

Joe gave out a sigh.

"Seven it is then," he said resignedly.

I didn't like this. It felt like we were locked in a power struggle, but power I didn't particularly want. If Joe didn't want to get up at seven then he didn't have to. But I would. I could meet him, or the both of them, down the road later. It wasn't like he was being deprived of sleep. Getting up at seven would still mean nine and a half hours' sleep. Even toddlers don't need that much.

Fortunately, we were eight days ahead of schedule and we were steadily chipping away at the date this would all end.

Days Completed: 33
***Ride and Seek*: Total spend £20.89, per day £0.63**
***Live below the Line*: Total spend £28.10, per day £0.85**

Chapter 10: Farmers with Guns

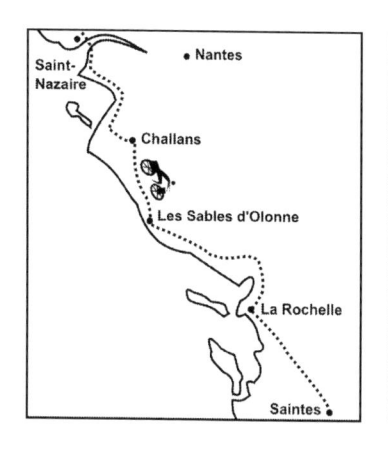

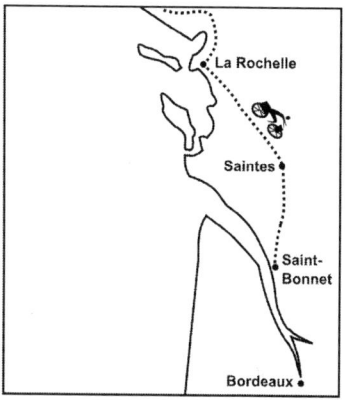

The next morning was a repeat of the previous one. I wheeled my bike out of the field just as Joe climbed out of his tent. It was Sunday. We always had our porridge to fall back on but since we'd started having baguettes for breakfast the porridge appealed less and less to everyone. Unfortunately, all the supermarkets we passed were closed. We needed a shop for other ingredients too. Last night we'd finished the pasta and there was hardly any jam left.

Today I felt like I'd worked out why Joe was always so tired. Whereas Dave always seemed to be in too high a gear and had to force the pedals around with great effort, Joe was the opposite, his feet spinning rapidly even on flat ground. I watched his pedals and mine. He did about six or seven revolutions to my three.

Late morning we arrived in Saint-Nazaire and fell upon a conveniently open indoor market. The arresting aromas of the charcuterie and cheeses were enough to drive us out of the place but not before we purchased a couple of expensive baguettes. The jams for sale, high quality ones that, unlike ours, probably contained fruit, sadly belonged to the taking-the-piss price range. We had to ration what was left of our apricot jam, a thin smear each, and hope we could find some more before lunchtime.

In Saint-Nazaire, there's a massive concrete monstrosity, a U-boat base built by the Nazis in World War Two. This carbuncle was more like a self-contained city than a military base, with bays for fourteen subs but also 62 workshops, 150 offices, kitchens, bakeries, restaurants and a hospital. It seemed a little underutilised now it was merely the world's ugliest tourist office.

Saint-Nazaire sits at the mouth of the Loire, France's longest river, and hosts a bridge across it. It is humongous. Its total length is well over three kilometres and is high enough to enable even the tallest ships to slip beneath it.

"I'm going to video this," said Dave, securing his Go-Pro to his handlebars, the first time he'd attempted to use it.

It hadn't seemed like a particularly breezy day but, as we crossed the bridge, it suddenly felt dangerously windy. Bikes aren't allowed across if the wind speed exceeds 50 miles an hour. If it was 50 miles an hour at the base of the bridge, on top it would've felt like the end of the world. I cycled at a weird angle to counter the wind's effect. As I passed each thick supporting strut, the wind would disappear and I'd be yanked to the right, tipping me sideways. Once through the windy ordeal, we reassembled at its far side.

"That wasn't much fun," I said. "But at least you've got a video of it. That should be pretty impressive."

"Nah," Dave replied. "It didn't work."

Oh well. It wouldn't be the first or last thing on Dave's bike to pack in.

We approached Saint-Michel-Chef-Chef, the double Chef being a corruption of Cheveché rather than the result of a naming ceremony performed by someone with a stutter.

All through France we'd seen posters advertising various circuses. They were always named after a bloke with an Italian or eastern European name that contained at least one high-scoring *Scrabble* letter. I don't think these fellas actually existed. It was simply Rule One of How To Make Your Circus Sound Exotic in the *Shit Circuses Marketing Handbook*. In Chef-Chef, the poster advertised the ringmaster as Sebastien Zavatta, or Trevor Ainsworth as he's probably really called. The poster contained an evil clown's face painted in garish colours. Is there anyone on Earth who likes clowns?

Once in the centre of town, the circus's advertising was upped considerably. A large truck pulled an even larger cage containing a terrified-looking lion and tiger. They paced about nervously as the truck blared a cacophonous medley of distorted music and sales pitch. I was hoping Sebastien Zavatta was going to get bitten in the ring this evening, or on any part of his body really.

If a French supermarket is going to open on a Sunday, it's only going to stay open until lunchtime. We saw a sign for a large *Super U*. We had no idea if it was open today but we thought we'd give it a go. We looked at our watches. It was ten past twelve.

We followed the signs out to the edge of town for a few minutes and, as we approached the supermarket, noticed a car park full of cars. Wonderful! We would eat later and we'd have jam too.

"Quick!" said Joe. "It closes at twelve-fifteen," he joked.

Ha, ha, we thought, what a stupidly illogical time for a supermarket to close. As if it would close at twelve-fifteen. We looked at our watches again. It was twelve-fifteen. We rolled up to the front doors and looked at the shop's opening hours. What? It *did* close at twelve-fifteen. Who the frig closes a business at twelve-fifteen? Joe threw his bike against the wall and rushed inside, only to reappear twenty seconds later.

"They won't let me in."

"I'll have a go," I said.

I went inside but a big bouncer type blocked my way. We huddled outside, cursing ridiculous closing times.

"Are you OK? Do you need some food?"

A French cyclist, a women in her twenties, stood beside us. What a lovely offer. We might've been hungry but we weren't going to nick her food.

We stopped for lunch. We had bread left over but nothing to put on it. Joe got resourceful. Using the empty apricot *confiture* jar, he conjured up an instant blackberry jam made with fruit, sugar and a splash of water. The results were surprisingly good.

Near the unfortunately named town of Pornic, Dave suffered further damage to his gear. With all the weight of his overloaded bike, his front rack snapped. Joe improvised a repair using cable ties. Dave's bike was a nightmare.

The landscape changed. It became flatter but was riddled with man-made water channels, rather than hedges, dividing the fields. There was nothing to hide us from the wind and its strength was increasing. We fought a horrible, five-mile stretch of gales head on until we reached Bouin.

"I need water," said Joe.

"There's a *boulangerie* there. Go in and ask for some."

He looked at the shop and thought for a minute.

"No, it's alright."

We continued. We still had a section of flat, hedgeless fields but at least it was nice to see an otter fishing in one of the water channels. Up ahead, I could see a small forest and I cycled towards it with Dave and Joe lagging a little way behind. Once inside the woods I stopped, knowing that after the hurricane battering he'd just received, Joe would soon want to finish. Dave was the first to appear. He slowed up and stopped beside me, looking a little guilty.

"Are you alright?" I asked.

"Yeah."

"What's the matter?"

"Did you see that motorbike?"

"The one that went past a few minutes ago?"

"Yeah."

"So what?"

"They fell off going around a corner."

"Did they? Did you see it?"

"Yeah."

"Did you stop?"

"No."

"What? You didn't stop?"

"I didn't know what to say."

Joe arrived. By the time he'd come across the motorcyclists, they were picking themselves up off the ground.

"Just cuts and bruises. They looked a bit disorientated," he said. "I asked if they needed anything but they said they were alright."

Joe may have been too chicken to ask for water at the boulangerie but at least he'd used his French when it mattered.

We quickly found a camping spot in a forest. It was difficult to wheel the bikes through the dense undergrowth. We set up our tents and had an insubstantial meal, with double eggs as an unsuccessful attempt to overcome our lack of pasta, and went to bed feeling hungrier than usual. This being a wood rather than a working field, at least there was no tension about what time we'd start in the morning.

The young French woman who'd offered us food yesterday had said how rain was on its way. *AccuWeather* disagreed, predicting a zero probability of precipitation. Have a guess who was correct? I was now checking out *AccuWeather* for its comedy value. How could such a massive weather forecasting service be so frequently off the mark?

After a supermarket stop in Challans to refill our panniers with pasta and our bellies with bread, a two-and-a-half-hour slog brought us close to Les Sables-d'Olonne. In all that time, one car, and one car only, had driven dangerously close to me and, from past experience, it was little surprise that it was British.

We arrived in Les Sables-d'Olonne, stopped outside a shop with a canopy and hid from the rain. We had lunch while sitting there. People walking past looked at us like we were wrong in the head.

Eventually the rain eased and we cycled into the old town. We got off our bikes to push them through its pedestrianised centre. After a minute or two, we came to a square in which four streets met. I stopped dead.

"Right then, where should we go, Dave?" I asked.

"I'm easy," he replied dismissively.

"No, it's your choice. We always go where me and Joe want to go. It's your turn."

He shrugged his shoulders. I didn't move.

"Go on."

He looked a little uncomfortable, laughed as though I were joking and then searched Joe's face and mine for clues. Joe wasn't going to help him out either.

"We can't help you, Dave. Today you decide what we do in Les Sables-d'Olonne."

Realising I was serious, he studied the streets around us, carefully assessing what he could see at the end of each one.

"This one," he said finally.

"Good choice."

He beamed widely. Any choice would've been a good one.

He'd finally made a decision. Les Sables-d'Olonne turned out to be a bit of a disappointment, but that wasn't Dave's fault.

We cycled down the coast, classier than Paignton but still uninspiring. The scenery improved slightly when the endless fields of corn were replaced by bright yellow sunflowers.

We got to five-fifteen before Joe first expressed a desire to stop. It was getting earlier each day. We found a rough field and pushed our bikes through its long grass to the far corner beside a tall, dense hedge. At this rate, it wouldn't be long before we would be finishing our day before we'd set off.

Only once we'd started to prepare food did we begin to hear noises coming from the opposite side of the huge bush. Either there was a house or, given the vehicle sounds we could hear, a farm, possibly the farm to which this field belonged. We'd have to stay quiet for the rest of the evening or risk discovery. This wasn't a problem since no one was speaking.

After dinner Joe had an attempt at a second variety of jam using some elderberries he'd collected today. He mashed them up with sugar and then tasted his creation. He quickly realised why elderberries are commercially turned into a jelly rather than jam. His mixture was seedier than Jimmy Savile.

Today had felt like a nothing sort of day, with long, uninteresting stretches of road, a nondescript town to break the tedium and the continuing rubbish weather. We were all looking forward to the glorious sunshine that could only just be around the corner and to Spain, less than a week away.

We'd agreed on a seven o'clock start and I was surprised that Joe was all ready to go by the time I climbed out of my tent. He was lying on his ground mat, dozing. Everyone seemed to be in a bad mood. We could still hear noises from over the hedge and so we silently pushed our bikes out of the field.

This morning, Joe was at the back as usual. Cycling beside me, Dave and I chatted.

"I'm sick of eating the same thing every night, Dave," I said.

"Yeah. I'm happy to have a change."

I should've expected that.

I don't know if it was just in my head but we seemed to be slowly falling apart. The camaraderie of the first few weeks had been replaced by, at best, a grudging tolerance or, more likely, a seething, unvoiced resentment.

Somewhere beyond Triaize, on a sparsely populated road, we found a small supermarket. Dave and I went inside to get our breakfast baguettes but they were too expensive for our meagre budget and we left empty-handed. In the car park, Joe was talking to a woman. Wow, I thought, he's using his French. When I approached them, I discovered she was English. Susie and her husband Mark were on holiday here and invited us to breakfast at the house they'd rented just down the road. We cycled alongside them.

"Does this place have some hidden depths?" I said to Mark. "I mean, it seems an odd place to spend a holiday."

"Tell me about it. It was last minute, the only place we could find. It's the arse-end of nowhere but Rochelle's not too far away."

Still, the house they'd rented was nice enough, a small, rustic cottage. We sat around their kitchen table, which Susie loaded with breakfast goodies, including a jug of iced watermelon juice. I'd forgotten just how lovely refrigerated drinks were. Water from French cemeteries was cool at best, usually tepid and occasionally hot enough to make tea.

I was genuinely excited about having someone to talk to, someone new. I suspect I probably yabbered on a bit.

Mark and Susie had come to France with their two teenage children.

"It was their idea actually," said Mark, "to come away all together."

"Yeah, I think the novelty's worn off a bit now," said Susie.

Their daughter had been finding her own outdoor food.

"She foraged a melon yesterday," said Mark.

"Where from?"

"A field."

"Isn't that just stealing rather than foraging," I said with a grin.

"Nah," smiled Mark, "it's scrumping."

"Of course." I turned to Joe. "Perhaps we should go to the supermarket and scrump a chicken."

We finished up our cheese, salami and bread, and fromage frais, juice and a couple of coffees. It was all wonderful. Susie and Mark were lovely, smart people.

Mark followed us outside as the cottage's landlord, a bloke from Warrington who lived in his own place across the gravel car park, came out for a chat. He offered us some foraging advice.

"You should catch a mullet and a tawny owl."

"Why?"

"So you can make mullet-a-tawny soup."

"Yeah, mullets are very popular in Germany," said Mark.

"Are they?"

"Yeah, if you go to a barber's."

Who'd have thought this region would be so popular with the Chuckle Brothers?

We cycled away. At our first stop, Dave turned to me.

"It was nice to have someone new to talk to, wasn't it?" he said.

"Yes," I replied. "Yes, it was."

Dave had clearly shared my feeling of cabin fever. The mood between us was suddenly lighter. This morning's grumpiness had been lifted by a great, varied breakfast and the lively conversation of a couple of generous strangers. They'd even told us that a high pressure system was stuck just south of La Rochelle. Sunshine was finally on its way as we crossed into the southern half of France. Thank you, Mark and Susie. You may just have saved our trip.

With lifted spirits, we continued down the Atlantic coast. The ancient sleepy town of Esnandes seemed like a worthwhile place to stop.

Before entering the town proper we visited La Pointe St Clément, a rocky headland invading the Bay of Aiguillon. A long walkway, constructed of wide, dilapidated wooden planks, stretched out into the misty sea. Mounds of empty oyster shells were piled either side of it. With the wisps of cloud obscuring the opposite shore, it felt like we were gazing out upon the River Styx. We waited for a skeletal boatman to appear but he never did. The mood-improving breakfast had spared us a visit to Hades.

The priory of Saint-Martin in Esnandes itself provided its own weirdness. Looking more like a castle owned by a king with a gargoyle fetish than a church, it beckoned us inside. To accompany loud Gregorian chanting, models of galleons hung on long cables from the ceiling. Why were they there? St Martin was the patron saint of the poor, which must be a much more demanding job than being patron saint of, I don't know, window cleaners or whatever, and so there's no connection with shipping there. The church's website didn't even mention them. The only link with St Martin and seafaring came from *Wikipedia*: "Martin introduced a rudimentary parish system. Once a year, the bishop visited each of his parishes, travelling on foot, or by donkey or boat." Could that be the reason for the dangling ships? In any case, it was better than hanging a live donkey from the rafters.

We continued to the gorgeous old sea port of La Rochelle,

choked with tourists and pretty towers. Sure enough, we found the promised high pressure system and perfect sunny weather.

"Dave, we're now in the south of France," I said, looking at the sky. "It's all going to be alright."

Dave smiled widely.

We stopped at a *Lidl* supermarket and everyone agreed we should try something different for dinner. Our options were limited because the large tins we needed to feed all three of us only came in a few different flavours. It was my turn to shop and so I chose one tin of ravioli and one of dauphinois potatoes. I was looking forward to the change.

It was not long after six when Joe suggested that we stop. We began our hunt for a pitch. The roads south of La Rochelle started to undulate, adding to Joe's tiredness. To make matters worse, that bloody high pressure system had realised we were on to it and had sodded off somewhere else. It started to drizzle.

It took us another two hours before we found somewhere to sleep, and even that wasn't entirely suitable. It was a field the size of several football pitches with a track running along the nearside edge of it. We decided to push our bikes to the very far corner. Even if someone came along the track and saw us, they probably wouldn't be arsed to come so far over and have a word. We set up our tents and waited inside for the rain to stop.

Half an hour later we cooked our dinner. My excitement quickly turned to disappointment when I realised that the tin of dauphinois potatoes was high on dauphinois and light on potatoes. We cooked up both tins, spooned them together into our bowls and added soy sauce. It was an odd combination that didn't even nearly fill our stomachs. It'd be back to the more reliable lentils, pasta and egg tomorrow.

Despite the food, everyone remained happy, invigorated

by this morning's events. Joe talked at length about his experience of the Spanish north coast. He wasn't looking forward to it. It had been full of motorways and busy roads and so he'd headed inland to avoid them. If we were going to carry on fishing, and no one seemed particularly motivated to do so, we'd have to fight the roads. But that was a problem for another day.

We got up and packed away. We hadn't heard any cars on the track last night. Maybe no one used it. Just as we were about to leave, we saw a man walking along it.

"Don't move," I said to the others, mistaking the man for a Tyrannosaurus Rex or another creature whose vision is based on motion. "It looks like he's got a gun."

"Nah," said Joe casually. "It's a fishing rod. He's going to fish in that stream over there."

We started to push the bikes out of the field, Joe a little ahead of Dave and me. The man changed direction and started to walk towards us. As we got closer, we could clearly see he was carrying a big rifle.

He reached Joe first, who opened the conversation by asking him in French if he was the farmer.

"I live here," replied the man vaguely. Maybe the title of farmer was beneath him for some reason.

I tried to explain that it had started to rain last night and so we'd put up our tents in the field. I figured this was a better approach than trying to explain the concept of usufruct.

"Mmm," he said, "but it didn't rain much yesterday."

"A little," I said.

He stood there in silence looking at us.

"Tout bien?" I asked, seeking his approval so we could be on our way.

"No," he replied.

Shit! I'd asked a man with a gun if everything was alright and it wasn't. Was he going to shoot us?

Then he started talking about the weather. He'd thought my "tout bien?" was related to the day's forecast rather than how he felt about us being in his field. He told us that some climatic misery was on its way but at least it wasn't as bad as England. If you're discussing the weather with someone, it's unlikely they're going to kill you. We thanked him for not murdering us and went on our way.

The daily morning requirements – The Three Bs – of bin (to dispose of last night's rubbish), bog and baguette were all provided by a supermarket in Saint-Savinien. It also offered a change from the usual baguette filler in the form of a remarkably cheap paté, whose ingredients were best left unpondered. It was odd how just a little variation in our diet could improve team morale.

We continued towards the small town of Saintes. We had a look at the cathedral and then climbed the hill looking down on the town, every roof seemingly constructed of dirty terracotta tiles. On this grey morning, Saintes was a world away from its exotic twin city of Timbuktu.

Moving south, we passed through a string of small villages. In one, a poster in a hairdresser's window displayed a head shot of an attractive young woman with the caption in screamingly large capitals that said "Blond Shag". I assume it's a hairstyle in France but you'd better check before asking for one.

And then we lost Dave. I'd been out in front – a long way in front, I thought – and was struggling to find the right turning out of a village. I went down one exit, decided against it, went down another, and returned to the junction to wait for everyone else since we didn't all want to be firing off in different directions. Eventually Joe arrived.

"Where's Dave?" he asked.

"I don't know. He was behind me."

"Yes, but he was in front of me."

This was potentially dangerous. Dave had no map, no compass and absolutely zero French. I checked my phone but the battery was dead. Joe had just enough juice left in his to call Dave. He had arrived at the junction while I must've been down one of the lanes and he'd chosen the other one. He was now five miles away in the next village. If Joe's phone had been down, we'd never have seen him again.

The uneven land was now being used to grow grapes and there were fewer and fewer fields for us to hide away in. It took us an hour of searching before, near St-Bonnet, we saw a hole in a hedge. We pushed our bikes over a large concrete obstacle into a piece of lumpy wasteland. At the far end were large bramble bushes. We suspected this spot may once have been a nuclear waste dump if the misshapen blackberries with fat, oversized drupelets were anything to go by. We were also suspicious of the twelve-legged spiders and two-headed sparrows.

It was still early. We lay around on the uncomfortable ground, mostly in silence. I looked at Dave. Rather than playing *Snake*, he was staring into space.

"What's on your mind, Dave?" I asked.

"Nothing. Sometimes I like to sit with an empty head."

I wish I could do that. Later, I heard Joe on the telephone speaking to someone. He was saying how it was fine for Dave and me to finish earlier than expected because our plans were open-ended, but he'd booked a flight.

"Why does it matter?" I asked. "You were planning a short tour of Andalusia after the ride. If you've got more time, why not just make it longer?"

"I haven't got the funds."

"You could continue on the one pound-a-day thing. I mean, if we slowed up you'd be living on a pound. Why not continue afterwards?"

"I don't want to. I'll have proved we can get to Gibraltar on a pound. I don't want to keep living like this afterwards."

I didn't know what to say to that.

"Besides," he continued, "the food we have doesn't give me enough energy to go as far as we do each day."

I still couldn't work out why this was. Both Dave and I were much heavier than Joe, and Dave's bike was the weight of a small car.

"How about we give you some of our food?" I said.

"No, that'd be cheating."

"Use some of your budget then to buy something just for yourself."

When I'd originally envisaged this trip I hadn't thought all the money would be used communally, as it had been so far. I imagined I'd buy my food, and Dave and everyone else theirs, and we'd cook it separately and eat what we needed. Perhaps if there was an expensive fresh item that'd go off quickly, like a packet of mince – not that we could ever actually afford mince – we'd club together and share it, but I didn't think this is how it'd work for all our meals. This probably started because Sabby took charge of the kitchen and it was more efficient to cook a large pot of something than four smaller, individual pots. But we were still under-budget and so if Joe wanted to buy something additional to provide the energy he so clearly needed then that was fine. It was certainly better than reducing our cycle day and sitting around in near silence just to prolong this adventure, or ordeal as it often appeared to be

"The other option is that we split up," said Joe. "You continue at the speed you're going and I go more slowly."

Wow. That'd force Dave to make an interesting decision, probably one that'd make his head explode. Although given how prone to falling apart his bike was – it was still making clanking noises – and my minimal mechanical skills, it'd be asking for trouble if Dave joined me. Also, Dave had no map and my phone was frequently without charge. If we ever got separated, Dave would be condemned to wander the French highways forever.

Joe had a big decision to make.

Days Completed: 37
Ride and Seek: **Total spend £24.73, per day £0.69**
Live below the Line: **Total spend £32.19, per day £0.87**

Chapter 11: The End of France

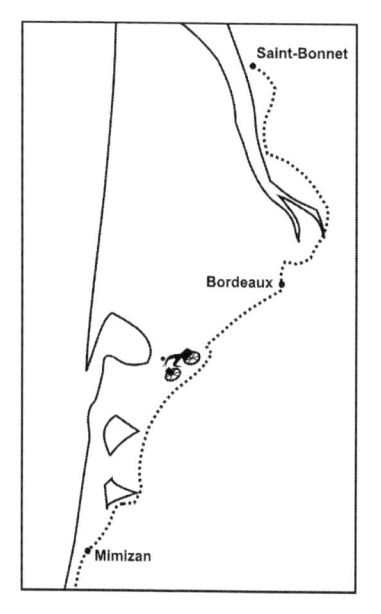

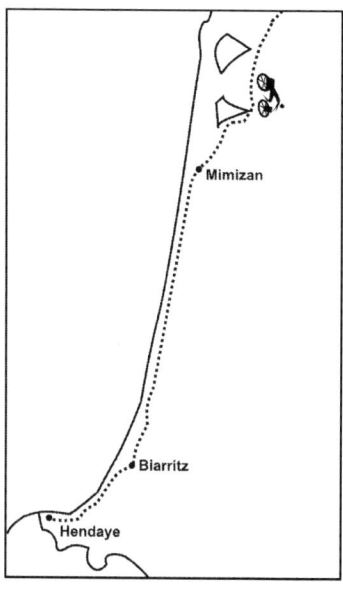

Joe awoke in a better mood and, with renewed energy from somewhere, was close behind us. We found a supermarket in Blaye and he bought himself a few extras. His plan was to make easily portable flatbreads and fill a plastic box with cooked pasta, both ways to refuel himself while on the road. He was staying with us, at least for the time being.

Our next stop was the town's stunning citadel, a seventeenth century walled city that included, surprisingly, the town's municipal camping ground. On a board outside the campsite was its price list. Despite only being a fiver to stay, there was a curious additional option. For 45 cents you could have a 'visitor for two hours'. Did they provide this 'visitor' or did you have to find your own and smuggle her inside? You couldn't argue with the prices though. Just think of the fun we could've had by blowing two days' budget on four hours with three 'visitors'.

We followed the bank of the Dordogne river and reached Bourg. I found a large ball bearing on the road.

"Give it to Dave," said Joe. "He's been collecting shiny things."

I presented it to our half-man half-magpie. His eyes lit up.

"Oh, I'll have some fun with this," said Dave a little worryingly.

"I don't want to think where you're going to put that," said Joe.

His collection wasn't limited to pretty metal objects. He'd also picked up a selection of stones. As if his bike wasn't heavy enough already. Maybe he thought his machine could use what we'd found.

"Have you heard it recently?" asked Joe. "That noise it makes?"

"What is it?"

"The bearings have gone on his front wheel. It'll fall apart soon, like his back one."

We fought our way into Bordeaux. It wasn't easy. For a long time, there were no signs for the town and then none for the centre, and the traffic was intense. Joe weaved his way through backstreets, paying close attention to a map much better suited to rural navigation. Eventually, after some dodgy roads and even dodgier roundabouts, we hit the river again and found the bridge we needed to cross. Of all the European capitals I'd cycled into, only Madrid had been more complicated to penetrate than Bordeaux, a town with only one twelfth of Madrid's population. Joe had done a great job.

Once in Bordeaux, we were drawn to St Michael's basilica and its associated church. Upon entering, someone was giving it large on the pipe organ, all *Phantom of the Opera*, like, with its clashing notes and discordant rumble. The stained glass windows were unusually modern-looking, with angular depictions of humans and particularly camp soldiers. One window gave a blow-by-blow account of the beheading of John the Baptist, the stained glass equivalent of an ISIS video.

We were twelve miles out of Bordeaux. For the last half an hour, we'd cycled beside a dense forest. It was around six and Joe wanted to stop. We set up our tents and cooked dinner. Spirits were higher than of late, possibly because Joe had a solution to his fatigue. As I packed away my stove, I heard three gunshots from not too far away. I quickly put them out of my head, the way stupid people do in horror films.

I was lying in my tent struggling to go asleep. At around eleven, even though we were miles from any town, I could hear a group of people talking. They were deeper in the woods than we were. Who'd be out at this time? Hunters? The voices grew louder. They couldn't have been more than 30 metres away.

Suddenly there was the sound of crashing trees, something forcing its way through dense shrubbery and a loud, high-pitched squeal. It was a wild boar and, spooked by the hunting team, it sounded like it was charging towards my tent. There was nothing I could do but stay put. Better if it didn't know I was there. And I didn't want to attempt to chase it away. The hunters might have mistaken me for something worth shooting. I didn't want to end up on their dining table with an apple in my mouth.

The boar hung around my tent for twenty minutes, snuffling in the undergrowth and hiding from the guns. Eventually, around midnight, the voices grew quiet and my pig wandered off. None of this, by the way, is very helpful when you're trying to go asleep.

I woke up to find Dave and Joe's bikes upside down, in repair stance. This wasn't good. Joe was mending yet another broken spoke on his own bike while Dave span his front wheel and watched it wobble as it revolved. Joe finished his own job and then carefully explained to Dave exactly what the problem was with his wheel. This wasn't the first time Joe had acted as a patient teacher to Dave.

"But it's not going to last long," said Joe.

I looked at Dave. He smiled, his usual response to good news or bad.

They righted their bikes and we set off down the country road. Dave's bike sounded like he was balancing a steel band on his front mudguard.

After Joe had his first supplementary flatbreads, our route took us through the amusingly named village of Le Barp, the French word for a gaseous emission from an unspecified end of the body. Probably. The road was long, straight and dull, lined with tall trees and dense shrubbery. It was like Belarus without the excitement of knowing the forests were full of radioactive wolves. The only thrill came when another car came too close and, no surprise, it was UK registered again.

The trees that we passed now were changing. We'd clearly moved into the sunnier half of France, even if the weather wasn't always confirming that. The leafy, green plum trees had disappeared and had been replaced by useless, spiky pines. Our fruit-collecting was limited to blackberries.

I found my head in a strange place. On a long, flat road, blasting away at fifteen miles an hour, I was far ahead of Dave and Joe as usual. With my phone dead, I found myself fantasising about taking an unusual turning and getting myself purposely lost. With no way of being contacted until I could recharge the phone, I'd continue alone, with no need to wait around constantly for the others to catch up. By the time I was reachable again, I'd be hundreds of miles into Spain.

Mimizan was a town in two pieces, the town itself and a separate beach resort. When you consider how much effort the council had put into the local environment and prettying up the place – it'd earned the top prize in the poncily-named *Flowery Towns and Villages* competition – it was surprising the town smelled so awful. Unlike the constant petroleum fume aroma of Port Talbot, Mimizan offered an ever-changing hum. As I cycled along, I first noticed the whiff of rotting crab sticks. Within a short distance, this had been replaced by the sulphurous smell of fireworks, an improvement at least. Finally, after another quarter of a mile, the overriding stench was that of urinals. I looked to my left. Up on the hill were the belching chimneys of an ugly factory, which I assumed was responsible for this nasal assault. Maybe the council had brought in all the flowers to mask the smell of the place.

The cycle path entered the forest. The 25 miles of track were close to the sea, at times only a couple of hundred metres away, but separated from the beach by trees. The tarmacked road was only the width of a car and consisted of a series of gentle humps joined by the occasional flat. In the evening sunshine, the forest's canopy dappled the light, making it feel like a fairy's grotto. Dave's wizard beard had never felt more at home.

Every now and again, we'd emerge from the trees into a beach resort. The first was Conti. It had the feel of a skiing village, a collection of wooden buildings erected quickly to cash in on the rising popularity of the place.

It was six o'clock and the hoards were leaving the beach in search of beer and wine, walking along the road in bikinis and swimming shorts. This crowd looked a lot healthier than their Paignton counterparts. We turned a corner and were confronted with the overpowering funk of hamburgers. My stomach spasmed at the possibility, but then my brain quickly took over and closed down the fantasy.

We'd half-planned to go fishing, or at least check out the opportunities. However, when we saw how far away the sea was, and how much soft sand we would've had to push the bikes through, and then actually not be able to catch anything because we didn't have beach rods or any fishing talent whatsoever, we abandoned the attempt and returned to the woods.

Clouds suddenly rolled in. By seven, the sky was completely grey. The God of Minging Weather had discovered our position and was taking action accordingly. In this huge, sprawling forest, it wasn't difficult to find somewhere to camp. We found a clearing and set up the tents just as the first raindrops fell.

By tomorrow, we'd be within touching distance of Spain. We discussed how we were going to tackle the Iberian Peninsula. Everyone had decided against the coast. We were totally useless at fishing. We were to angling what Michael Barrymore is to swimming pool advertising campaigns. Instead, we would cycle slightly inland but, to add an additional element to the ride, we'd also undertake our own pilgrimage to the city of Santiago de Compostela.

During the night, something large emitted a long and mournful bark. From inside my tent, I considered all the possibilities before finally concluding it must've been a werewolf.

"Did you hear that deer last night?" asked Joe the next morning.

"Ah. Is that what it was?"

I'm still fairly certain it was a werewolf. Surely Bambis can't make a noise like that. *An American Deer in London* would have been a very different film.

With no need for an early start, we left around half past nine and continued along the forest track occasionally passing a cyclist coming in the opposite direction. The number of riders would increase as we approached each resort. The next one was St-Girons Plage, a popular surfing spot.

Looking for our breakfast, we found a small *Casino* supermarket but, geared up for tourists, the prices were massively inflated. One euro for a tiny baguette was way out of our league. We left empty-handed and empty-bellied. Well, Joe wasn't empty-bellied because he had another flatbread. His additional food might have been helping his energy levels but at times like these it wasn't doing much for my morale.

While in town we took advantage of some other tourist facilities. There was a public toilet with a warm water tap and a large sink. We each washed some clothes using our portable washing machines. Suddenly, a panicked young French girl approached us and spoke hurriedly in English.

"I need to contact my friend," she said. "She was supposed to pick me up, but she's not here and my phone is dead."

"You can use mine if you like," said Joe.

"Thank you," said the girl, taking Joe's phone. She looked at it for a moment and then scrolled down Joe's list of contacts. It took her a moment to discover an obvious truth. "You haven't got her number."

"No," said Joe, amused. "Do you?"

"No."

"Ah."

She handed the phone back to Joe and walked away.

We continued on our way. Riding the cycle path wasn't always easy. Approaching Moliets-et-Maa, two young lovers were riding a tandem in a manner suggesting they'd never ridden one before, or even any sort of bike. They lurched drunkenly from side by side, yelping at each unplanned lunge and nearly crashing into a fence. I kept my distance.

In town we found a supermarket, one that didn't expect payment in gold bullion, and stocked up for the weekend. We returned to the track and quickly found a sign for the *EuroVelo 1*, which, after switching to the *EuroVelo 3* later, would guide us all the way to Santiago. Unless of course it constantly took us on silly bloody routes through housing estates as it'd done in Saint-Nazaire. At the very least, it'd guide us painlessly over, or rather around, the mountainous barrier separating France and Spain.

In Vieux-Boucau I sat waiting for Dave and Joe. They couldn't be so far behind to take this long. I thought, perhaps hoped, we'd become separated. Just as I was about to continue alone, they appeared. Dave had spotted a bike shop and had bought himself a new front wheel. No longer would his bike sound like a biscuit tin full of bolts in a tumble dryer.

It happened again ten miles later in Capbreton. We'd only met in Hossegor, about two miles earlier, but here I was, waiting for them again, this time for half an hour. I found somewhere to sit down, a bench looking upon a skate park. It was full of kids jumping from ramps and falling awkwardly on to their faces. Suddenly a police car turned up. Maybe I shouldn't be sitting here, I thought. Maybe they were the paedo police.

Where were Dave and Joe? They must've taken a different route through town. One of the road signs earlier had been a little vague. We were separated. We'd never find each other. I had my freedom. Finally!

I felt instantly liberated, free to travel at my own speed, to get up whenever I wanted to. But maybe freedom would come at a price. We were each carrying different components of our communal kitchen. I had the soy sauce and flour, but Dave and Joe had the tins of cassoulet and lentils. They also had the fuel. I'd have to spend heftily to make a meal worth eating. And without their watchful eye, would I give up or cheat? With an unspoken authority, we'd each acted as the others' policeman. Two of us always went into the supermarket together while the third guarded the bikes outside. There was no opportunity for a sneaky *Mars Bar* while waiting in line at the checkout. And knowing two other people were going through what I was going through, and in Joe's case finding it more difficult, spurred me on. If they could do it, so could I. Alone, my will might crumble. They'd still have each other. They didn't need me to police them. And Joe would probably be happier without me getting him up before mid-afternoon. He could slow down and Dave would surely agree to it, as he would've agreed to speeding up or cycling headlong into an active volcano. I kept looking back down the road in the direction I'd come but they never appeared. How long would it be before I'd set off, thereby splitting us into two groups for the rest of the journey?

"Ah, that's where you are," said Joe, appearing over my shoulder.

"Eh? Why are you coming from this way?"

"We went through town and thought you must've waited for us by now. When we didn't find you, I figured you must have gone a different way."

That was nice. They'd come looking for me. But maybe they only wanted me for the soy sauce.

We cycled back to where Joe had left Dave.

"Dave ran over a little girl," said Joe.

"What? That's terrible. Is she alright?"

"Dunno. I suppose."

"What, he didn't stop?"

"No."

"Isn't that a hit and run?"

Perhaps it was a good job we were leaving France. The story, as it turned out, had been slightly exaggerated. She'd been toddling along the cycle path and had turned quickly and walked into Dave's pannier at low speed.

"She was fine," said Dave.

I hope so. There were times when he was so focussed on cycling he could've crashed through an orphanage without realising.

We reached Bayonne, the pleasant city at the confluence of the Adour and Nive rivers. We sat by the water and had some sandwiches. Growing there was rock samphire, not to be confused with the marsh samphire we'd already found bagloads of. Rock samphire is also edible but unfortunately it tastes like kerosene.

While Dave attached his new wheel, an Australian on a bike came up and introduced himself to us. He'd lived here a while. We'd heard rumours that the flatter route around the Pyrenees through Biarritz, the next town along, was difficult to find and so we probed him for his local knowledge.

"Nah, mate, you go across this bridge, turn left at the lights..." and then that thing happened when you start to drift away from the directions you're being given. He continued speaking for another five full minutes. His instructions eventually included approximately 40 turns, straight ons or hills to climb and the route he described actually finished 30 miles away over the border in San Sebastián.

"Did you get all that?" I asked Joe.

His instructions had mentioned a 455 metre hill that we had no choice but to climb close to the border.

"So there's no way to get to Spain without going over a large hill?"

"Nah, mate."

We continued on to Biarritz. Having now seen much of France by bike, I know a lot of it looks very similar. It's difficult to distinguish one pretty village from another, or one sumptuous cathedral city from its neighbour. But Biarritz is genuinely different. If you want to picture it, imagine how a town would look if five thousand Cruella de Vils suddenly appeared in a Cornish village and ordered the town council to build them each a home. Architecturally, the Art Deco buildings look like someone went on to *Grand Designs* with a haunted house and tried to convert it into a large, fourteen-bedroomed wedding cake.

This being the end of July in one of France's glitzier resorts, the place was stuffed with tourists. We cycled slowly through town, dodging traffic and getting off at strategic points to look down on to the beach with its waves and surfers. Well, I say surfers, but in all the time we were there, I didn't see anyone manage to stand up. It's not such a glamorous sport when everyone's just paddling around like a fat kid on a lilo.

We left town heading south, sticking to the *EuroVelo 1*. It had, after all, seen us safely through Biarritz. The cycle path signs took us from the main road on a downhill excursion to the tiny village of Bidart. Here we go, I thought, another stupid diversion. Down we went, losing height, until we nearly touched the coast, and then turned left. Up we climbed back on to a very similar main road to the one on which we'd started. Obviously we still needed to go south, the direction of Spain, and yet the *EuroVelo 1* sign at the junction was pointing north. We followed the sign but arrived at the signpost for Bidart again. We'd ridden in a large, utterly pointless circle. Either Dick Dastardly and Muttley had been pissing around with the signs or whoever created the *EuroVelo 1* was a pillock. We abandoned the path and stuck to the coast road, which meant an unpleasant ride on a busy dual carriageway for a few miles but at least we were nearing Spain.

We decided to keep the excitement of a new country for tomorrow and found a place to camp on the cliffs a mile or so short of the border town of Hendaye. We could see the town in the distance and there was definitely no hill between us. So much for the Australian. It was a good job no one could remember his directions.

As on our first night in France seventeen days ago, we were joined in our lonely spot by a team of barbecuers, but at least this lot didn't tear up the grass or hoof a plastic bottle to one another. They simply cooked a load of meat, drank tons of beer and then fell over repeatedly as they struggled back to their cars in the dark. Tomorrow, España!

Days Completed: 40
Ride and Seek: **Total spend £28.60, per day £0.72**
Live below the Line: **Total spend £35.52, per day £0.89**

Chapter 12: The Way of St James

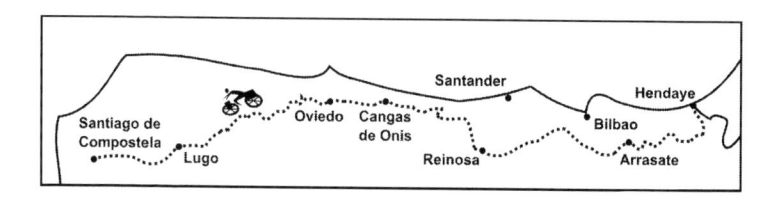

We woke up at seven, excited at the prospect of entering a new country and continued to the border town of Hendaye, the most south-westerly in France. As we approached we saw a public toilet, the extremely modern type France offers every now and again. It had large, silver sliding doors with enormous electronic buttons on the outside, the sort of crapper an astronaut would use. To access it, you press the green button and wait a few seconds for the doors to swoosh open like those off Star Trek. Then you go inside and notice it's a squat toilet.

We were, without knowing how, back on the *EuroVelo 1*. We lost further confidence in it when, near the centre of town, it wanted to take us down a long flight of stone steps.

Hendaye is separated from Spain by the river Bidassoa. Lying in this river is the fortified Pheasant Island. France and Spain once fought over this tiny rock but, back in 1659, they signed an innovative treaty agreeing to share ownership of it, with each country governing it for six months at a time. You might think it'd be confusing for the visitor, turning up and expecting tapas only to be greeted by wall-to-wall crêpe, or vice versa, except no visitors are allowed. Still, it's a political solution that could work in other nations too. Just imagine how much more fun it'd be to visit the USA if, after every six months of White House rule, it reverted to control by the

Navajos.

We followed the river and after another brain fart by the *EuroVelo* designers we rolled into Spain, except that, this being Basque Country, they don't tell you that. The change is announced by the fact that suddenly every word you see printed anywhere contains an X or a Z.

The Spanish border town is Irun, which appears to be one large off licence. Despite being a Sunday, we found an open supermarket and immediately saw that prices in Spain were different again. A baguette here cost €1.15, over 80% of our daily budget. The good news was that we could've bought a litre of wine for 69 cents.

We headed a little south to avoid the coast and instantly found a petrol station. It was closed but we quickly realised this is where our drinks would come from while in Spain. Nearly every petrol station in the country offers free water, and many also have public toilets. Two of our daily requirements had been solved within an hour of arriving. If petrol stations had also given away free breakfasts we'd have been sorted. This one did offer the additional bonus of a small apple tree but only a few garages offered free fruit.

We cycled beside the Bidassoa river on a rough forest track and came to a long, very dark tunnel. Its gaping mouth seemed to suck in light like a black hole. Joe fumbled in a bag for his lights but I'd already spied something.

"Are you ready for a magic trick?" I said.

"What are you talking about?"

"Abracadabra!"

I leant against the inside wall of the tunnel and pressed the almost invisible grey button set within it. A series of lights flickered within the tunnel and pinged into power.

"Nice," said Joe.

We cycled through. As we approached the bright, white hole of the exit, Joe started to whistle the theme music from

The Great Escape.

"If we're doing a pilgrimage," I said, "shouldn't we have some deep question that needs to be answered?"

"I know my question," replied Joe. "Why the hell am I doing a pilgrimage when I don't believe in God?"

The bright sunshine percolated through the forest's canopy creating a strobe effect. It wouldn't have been a good time to be epileptic, although I doubt there's ever a good time to be epileptic. I cycled ahead and – joy of joys! – discovered the first ripe fig tree of the trip. I waited there for Dave and Joe to catch up. Once again, they were ages and on this occasion there was no possibility of any of us taking a different route. I turned my bike around and found them. Joe had cycled over a nail.

"I want to show you something," I said, as we approached the tree I'd found earlier.

"Figs!" said Joe.

I'd already told him how wonderful it would be to find this fresh fruit but I thought they were only in season after the end of our ride. We were excited to find this anomaly. I plucked a fig and bit into it.

"Bleurgh!"

Despite being purple on the outside, the sign of ripeness, its insides were full of sawdust.

We may not have found any figs but apple trees were aplenty. This shouldn't have been much of a surprise. Northern Spain loves its cider. We found green ones and brown ones and ones that looked like little cherries.

Trundling down the lane, we came to a field full of cute baby goats.

"Pick one, Dave, and I'll have a word with the farmer."

We cycled through the pleasant town of Doneztebe and up the large hill to Leitza. This was the first real climb we'd experienced in days. Unlike his speedy ascents over the hills of Wales and England, Joe huffed and puffed his way to the top. From lycra-clad *Tour de France* types we received a *"Bon Camino!"* or two, the standard greeting offered to pilgrims in these parts, and one even took his hands from his handlebars to applaud us crawling up the hill with our heavy bags. We were two opposite ends of the cycling spectrum: They attempt to shed every unnecessary microgram from their machines while we load ours up with all sorts of crap. Just looking at Dave's overloaded shitheap would cause most sports cyclists to vomit. Something else nearly caused Dave to vomit.

"Oo, oo, oo, look!" said Dave excitedly, pointing at a tree. "Cherries!"

I looked closely.

"They're not cherries, Dave. They're poisonous berries."

"Ah, I thought so."

After Tolosa and another climb, we decided it was time to look for the location of our first night on Spanish soil. Unlike a lot of French fields, Spanish ones were always gated and so it looked like I'd be using my basic Spanish to negotiate with a farmer.

We passed an old house with a large, flat piece of unused land beside it. I knocked on the door and Methuselah's grandmother answered. Conversation was difficult what with her being almost completely deaf and my speaking Spanish in a Lancashire accent. Her accent was odd too. She understood what I was asking but I couldn't understand her response.

"Is that a yes or a no?" I asked gently.

Again I couldn't understand what she was saying and so I repeated my question. She nodded, which I took to be a yes but when I began to wheel my bike on to her field she shouted "No, no, no!", which would've saved us a lot of time earlier.

We cycled for miles without finding anywhere suitable. We stopped to look at our map. A couple walked past and asked if we needed help.

"Yes, we're looking for somewhere to camp," I said.

They had a pow-wow and seemed to provide a solution.

"There's a chapel two kilometres from here. I'm sure you can camp there. You cycle ahead and we'll meet you there in twenty minutes."

We found the chapel and beside it was a small garden, but this wasn't where the couple meant.

"No," said the man, "but you can camp here."

He pointed to a large expanse of lawn directly overlooked by a couple of tower blocks. It was hardly our usual hidden approach. Just then a police car rolled past. The man hailed the coppers and had a discussion with them that sometimes got a little heated.

"No, you can't camp there either," he said. "It's residential. But the police said you can camp at the recreation area up the road. You just need to be out of sight."

We found the area and realised that to be entirely hidden would be impossible, but in one corner some trees provided a little darkness. A bloke approached us and asked about the trip. We mentioned how disappointed we'd been by all the rain, even in the south of France.

"Not here," he said. "There's been no rain. But it's been hot. Too hot."

At last!

We set up camp beneath the trees, beside a busy main road but, importantly, with the approval of the police in a country where, it must be said, wild camping is completely illegal. You've got to love Spanish flexibility.

Here's a tip: Pay close attention to where you decide to

sleep. Not only was our pitch next to a main road but on the other side of the recreation area was a wall behind which, unknown to us, were both a motorway and a railway. As we approached midnight and traffic on the main road eased, the motorway became very audible. Just when I'd become used to the distant rumble of speeding trucks, a train would scream past and shake out my fillings. I would have slept better at a Mötorhead gig.

After last night's promise of an arid Iberia, we were more than a little annoyed to wake up to yet more rain. Remember, this was Spain at the end of July, a time and place when it's possible to die in the streets from sunstroke. We were more worried about drowning.

We cycled through Ordizia and then up a long, slow hill. As yesterday it was lined with fruit trees, mostly apples and purple damsons. We were still without breakfast, although the fruit was filling a gap. We'd found a couple of small supermarkets but bread was too expensive. If Spain continued like this, we'd soon eat through our budget surplus or get very hungry indeed. And we didn't need that. Even with his additional meals, Joe was still lagging behind.

Eventually in Arrasate we found what I suspect is the largest supermarket in Spain. In fact, this *Eroski* store was so large the owners couldn't think of enough things to sell. The aisles were so far apart you could easily have driven a lorry between them. One part of the supermarket had no aisles at all. The space was comfortably big enough to host a decent bout of *Robot Wars*. At last, however, we found baguettes and jam we could afford, despite it taking nearly three weeks to walk from the bread counter to the checkout.

The day continued through slate grey villages with sturdy houses built of stone. This was very different from the whitewashed walls of the Costas. And the fruit kept on coming, more apples and juicy, fat green plums.

Near Oxtandio, a quaint village with oddly incongruous tenement blocks, we decided to stop. We wanted a little more peace this evening and found a large picnic site a mile out of town that, on closer inspection, had been abandoned. There was a block of filthy toilets in the centre of it. Soiled knickers lay in the doorway and used toilet paper was scattered far and wide. We pushed our bikes to one edge of the field and down a banking that hid us from the road. With the squalor of the rest of the picnic area concealed from us, it was a pleasant place to stay.

We had imported our lack of culinary imagination into Spain but were still struggling to find food for dinner that was cheap enough and yet filling. The tinned lentils and sausage delight we'd eaten each alternate day in France wasn't available in Spain and so we recreated it by buying a jar of precooked lentils and a packet of cheap, don't-ask-don't-tell-meat-variety sausages.

"So we're definitely not doing any more fishing?" asked Joe.

"Well, I'm not," I said. "I've had enough of it."

"But you're still going to carry all your tackle?"

"Dunno. I'd leave it somewhere but then it might be found by a small child and I'd feel bad about setting him up for a lifetime of disappointment."

The topic of conversation moved on to one that occurred more frequently the closer to Gibraltar we edged: What would we buy at the *Morrisons* supermarket in Gibraltar once all this was over? Joe's obsession was currently *Haribo* and biscuits while Dave's was once again fixating on *Sherbet Dib Dabs*. And after a fortnight of inhaling French meths each dinnertime, I had a craving for schnapps. Despite the continuing rubbish weather, the limited diet and the reintroduction of hilly terrain, we were getting on better. I don't know what was inducing a better mood in Dave and Joe but for me it was the knowledge we were nearly two weeks ahead of schedule.

If you restrict your camping to campsites, then there's usually a light on somewhere outside your tent. If you don't choose your spot carefully, you can find yourself directly beneath a sun-like lamp that keeps you up all night. It's not like that with wild camping. Last night it was so dark I woke up in the middle of the night convinced I'd gone blind. I fumbled for my phone and switched on its display just to prove to myself I wouldn't have to finish this ride towed by a guide dog.

During the night I'd also made a decision. I wanted out of the communal eating arrangement. I wanted to go it alone. There were two reasons for this. The first was that I was utterly bored of eating lentils, pasta and something approaching an egg dumpling every night. Yes, it tasted great whenever we had soy sauce to accompany it, and it gave me the necessary calories, but I wanted something else. I needed variety. The second reason was that I didn't want to have the amount I ate each day dictated by a group decision. If I wanted a handful more pasta then I'd bloody well have it. I announced my decision over breakfast. Dave and Joe would continue eating jointly, possibly because if Dave ever had to choose his own dinner he would've starved to death. I instantly felt a little freer.

We set off under a sunny sky, riding through northern Spain's green lushness. There was no way this year had been back-to-back sunshine. At times it looked like a rainforest. Dave was a little ahead of me and, as I rounded a corner, I saw him talking at an old Spanish fella sitting on a bench.

"My mate's here," Dave said to the man. "He speaks Spanish."

The man looked at him blankly, unable to understand a

single word that had escaped his lips. I wonder how long Dave had been chatting to him.

I nattered to the old guy while Dave made a move on the huge apple tree overhanging the fence on the other side of the lane.

"A couple of English people live in the village," the man said.

"Yes, we're everywhere," I replied.

He pointed to the house whose garden hosted the massive tree.

"And the people who live in that house are cyclists."

He looked at Dave picking fruit.

"You're only supposed to take an apple or two. No one minds that. You're not supposed to strip the entire tree," he said, as Dave continued to strip the entire tree.

On a busier road with a small, gritty hard shoulder, both Dave and Joe got punctures. While they fixed them, I spread my tent out in the sun to evaporate the overnight dew. I also downloaded a *Kindle* app to provide me with some evening entertainment. If no one spoke from now on, so be it.

After being banned from a dual carriageway a couple of miles down it – why not just put the sign at the beginning of the road? – we had to find another way. I asked a bloke serving in a petrol station shop how to get to the next village, whose name I read from my map. He looked unsure. I laid the map on his counter and he looked at it, open mouthed, as though it were a bit of old parchment with an X to mark the spot of a hidden treasure chest. In the end it turned out we just had to go straight on. Around here a lot of towns have two names, one Castilian and one Basque. I was asking for the Castilian one from my map. He'd never heard of it.

It was time to start looking for somewhere to sleep. On a

long, flat road, we saw a house with a nice, unused field beside it. Sitting in the garden was a couple. I went up to them. It was only when I got closer that I discovered they were unlikely to be man and wife. The bloke was Spanish and in his eighties, the woman Asian and in her twenties. She turned out to be his carer. I asked about the field. She said it would be alright, but the old fella started ranting. With his accent and frothing mouth it was difficult to understand what he was saying, although I detected some anti-English sentiment. She tried to persuade him but he was having none of it.

"He doesn't know what's going on," she said dismissively, spinning her eyes as a comment on his mental state.

I vowed not to approach geriatric landowners in future. We continued looking but it wasn't easy.

"We'll find somewhere by midnight," I said as a joke. Two hours later, I regretted saying it. I'd given false hope. Eventually though, we found a large, slightly sloping field beside a busy main road with a French-style open entrance. A large, thick hedge blocked us from view of the traffic.

I'd survived so far today on two-thirds of a baguette and about four million apples. I had the remains of my baguette for dinner. I had hardly used my first day of culinary freedom to good effect but the liberty tasted great. Tomorrow would be different. Dave and Joe's first meal without me was, well, you've guessed it.

Oh the dogs! Last night, from around midnight, two dogs barked and howled. I thought they belonged to the farm on the other side of the main road but in the small hours they seemed to move around, their barks and yelps circling our tents. I got up at seven after less than an hour's sleep. Although the dogs were nowhere to be seen, Spain wasn't proving to be the most relaxing of night time locations.

Joe had flatbreads while Dave and I scoffed more apples. We packed up and set off, starting the day with a climb to 740 metres over the Puerto de El Cabrio. We hadn't been able to find a supermarket and so, after three hours of cycling, it was with some relief that we rolled into the small town of Espinoso de los Monteros, the place that gave the father of philosopher Espinoza his name. Joe, who'd been lagging behind again, wanted to have his say.

"If we're going to do three hours before breakfast, we should've had porridge."

"I thought you'd had your flatbreads," I said.

"I did. But they're not enough."

"You can have porridge whenever you like. But I'll save mine until a Sunday when the shops are closed."

The mood might have improved marginally since we'd hit Spain but an underlying tension remained.

We found a supermarket but they wanted a euro for a not particularly large baguette. We went elsewhere for it, to the *panadaria*, only to find this bakery had supplied its bread to the supermarket in this half-a-horse town and the price was exactly the same. I took the hit in order to eat. I could thankfully make this decision without a group discussion as I was now free. It was a refreshing feeling. But what would Dave and Joe do. Being now on the outside looking in, it'd become more amusing to watch how things panned out.

"Should we get a baguette, Dave," asked Joe, "and save our sliced bread for another meal, or should we just eat the bread we already have for breakfast?"

Dave looked at me and smiled.

"Nothing to do with me," I said.

"I'm easy," he said to Joe.

"No," continued Joe. "you must have a preference."

"I don't mind."

"Choose!"

As in the past, he seemed genuinely uncomfortable to make a decision. How had he ever decided to come on this trip?

He looked at Joe, possibly trying to read him.

"Let's get a baguette," he said, perhaps assuming Joe's own preference was the first option stated.

I returned to the supermarket and bought my own – my very own! – pot of plum jam from its barely stocked shelves thereby giving me yet more freedom and removing myself from what I'd long ago mentally christened *The Jam Issue*.

I can't write about this without feeling painfully petty, and even at the time I couldn't bring myself to mention it for the same reason but, when food is restricted, your mind goes to dark places you'd rather it didn't. *The Jam Issue* revolved around Joe's sandwich-making policy. John Montagu, the Earl of Sandwich, is claimed to have invented the famous snack that bears his name by requesting 'a piece of meat between two slices of bread'. The two slices part is important. The jam sandwiches constructed by both Dave and me conformed to Montagu's original specifications. Sadly, Joe's did not. He took a more Scandinavian approach and preferred the open sandwich. The problem with this method is that it takes twice as much jam to adequately coat four open sandwiches than it does two closed ones. I started to feel cheated. Joe was pilfering in excess of two pence-worth of extra jam per lunchtime. This had been going on since Day One and I wasn't happy, just one more taut string in a strained relationship. As a means to redress the imbalance, I'd taken to increasing the quantity of fruit preserve on my own, traditionally assembled sandwiches. Unfortunately, however, there's a limit to how much jam you can apply before it starts to leak from the bread when held at the appropriate angle for consumption. After each lunch, I would look to the ground beneath my feet and see the wastage resulting from my petty response. In an attempt to achieve equality, my actions were reducing the communal store cupboard for everyone. There's probably an important political or economical parallel here but I can't for the life of me work out what it is. Today though, I was the proud owner of my own jar of jam and I could now apply the ideal amount of fruitiness to my bread, enough for a tasty snack but not so much as to squander an already scarce resource. As William Wallace would've said about a similar issue: "Freeeeeedom!"

If you think my acrimony was directed solely at Joe, you're mistaken. I haven't mentioned *The Peanut Issue*. That was caused by Dave and his bloody great bears' paws. Mercifully, this problem too had been removed by my bid for liberty.

Full of breakfast and with *The Jam Issue* put to bed, at least as far as I was concerned, we continued. We saw lots of signs across the road saying "Fracking EZ!" At first I thought this was odd. Unlike absolutely everywhere else on the planet, here was a nation actually demanding shale gas extraction with their "Fracking – Easy!" posters, until I realised 'ez' is the Basque word for 'no'.

With the freedom of choice I now enjoyed, I spent the whole day fantasising about what I'd have for dinner. Food had become the only thing that mattered. I wanted to use more foraged ingredients and become less dependent on the supermarkets. This wasn't easy as we were only finding fruit at the moment. However, I dreamt up the perfect dinner utilising the remaining half of my breakfast baguette and consumed it mentally at least twenty times over the course of the day.

We stopped at the non-town of Soncillo and spread ourselves out on a large patch of grass near its entrance. Despite the overcast weather, we dried out our tents while Joe fell asleep. I was still owed a few pieces from the communal sliced loaf we'd bought two days earlier. Since Dave preferred to gift our bread to the squirrels, I'd been responsible for carrying it. The problem was my panniers were already quite full, and this meant the soft, airy loaf got a little squashed. Lunch today consisted of four tiny, dense parallelograms of bread.

Once again, I was out in front. Whenever I came to a junction I'd stop and let the others catch up. We didn't want to lose Dave again. The weather was closing in, and so we decided to stop early. At one such junction I waited. Across the road were two *hostals*, which in Spain are small hotels rather than dormitories. All previous rides across Spain had involved overnighting in them. They're cheap and basic but warm and comfortable. I sat on my saddle looking at them longingly. How nice it'd be not to have to spend ages hunting for a field hidden from the road. How lovely to have a shower. It'd been over three weeks since our last one. How amazing to lie on a soft mattress after a meal and a couple of pints and to drift away contentedly. Stop it! I gave myself an internal slap. I had to clear my head of such nonsense. Physically, this adventure, the moving from A to B part, wasn't too difficult for me and Dave, even if it was for Joe, but the mental side was much more challenging.

The route continued beside a large reservoir formed by the Ebro, Spain's second longest river. Joe had been entertaining fantasies of his own, about the ideal place to camp.

"I want a lakeside spot, no dogs, lapping waves. And a chocolate tree," he said with a smile.

There was very little access to the lake. The one path that would've taken us to its shores looked directly across at a farmhouse. We continued on and eventually found a forgotten lane somewhere in the dark, dank woods. There were no lakes with lapping waves and definitely no chocolate trees but at least there were also no dogs.

While Dave and Joe assembled yet another lentil and pasta dinner, I got to work on the meal that'd been on my mind all day. Given that I wanted to use more foraged ingredients, I decided to go for something sweet. I cubed an apple and fried it with oil and loads of sugar until it caramelised, and then I tipped into the mix an egg-and-flour batter and let it cook. When the aroma of toffee hit my nose, I flipped it over and frazzed the other side. The bottom was deliciously black and crispy. It looked burnt but, then again, it was supposed to be. Once done, I loaded the lot on to my half-baguette and smeared it with plum jam. There I had it: a caramelised apple omelette and jam sandwich and it tasted as good as the imaginary one had done all afternoon. It was without doubt the best thing in the entire world ever. You could stick your lentils up your arse!

After a late start, we hit grimly industrial Reinosa, supposedly Cantabria's coldest town, found a baguette and ate it in a bus shelter while the rain came down. It wasn't likely to stop and so we continued further into town. I was a little ahead when the clouds properly burst. I climbed the kerb and waited under a jeweller's awning. Dave was the next to pass. I called out to him to offer him similar protection.

"Dave...Dave!...DAVE!"

He sped right on by. Whenever he cycled, his eyes never left the tarmac. I could've been dressed as Mr Blobby and riding a penny farthing and he wouldn't have seen me.

Today we would reach the highest point on the ride so far, the Puerto de Palombera, at 1,260 metres. We'd no idea how severe a climb this would be. We didn't even know our starting altitude, and since we were stuck inside a cloud we couldn't even take a guess.

I remember a walk up Ben Nevis many years ago. We started at two in the morning with head torches. The clouds were low. We climbed higher and higher and all we could see was grey mist. And then, around five o'clock, just as the rising sun was beginning to illuminate the fog, we reached the summit and our heads popped out above the clouds. We looked down on what appeared to be Heaven, a carpet of cloud gently warmed by the sun, crystal blue skies above with the occasional peak puncturing the cotton wool in the distance. It was, perhaps, the most majestic sight of my life. I was hoping for something similar today.

I was therefore surprised and a little disappointed that only two and a half miles out of town, we reached the summit. It was still grey, misty and raining. It was also damn cold. We now had a fifteen mile descent, which would normally have been the highlight of the trip, except the sweat inside my jacket from the journey peakwards had chilled. My gloveless hands were frozen into a petrified claw by the cold, moist air and painful to move as we barrelled downhill. I'd been concerned that adventure sandals might be a daft idea in northern England in June, but it'd never occurred to me our coldest day would be in Spain at the end of July. My toes talked amongst themselves and the discussion focussed mostly on frostbite.

We stopped halfway down to make sure everyone was alright.

"Well, that was the best view I'll never see," I said.

Down we continued. We passed a bar I'd normally have entered to defrost my fingers with a cup of hot coffee and my lungs with a slug of brandy. No such option today. Next up was a contorted statue of a male, graffitied with anti-fracking slogans and the word 'Cancer' daubed in large, red letters. It seemed that today's theme was 'grim'.

We stopped at the bottom, in Cabuérnica, for a sandwich and I stomped some life back into my blackening toes.

Our descent had taken us down to 200 metres above sea

level and now the road climbed again, back up to another pass at 611 metres, the rugged Picos de Europa and their emerald meadows playing hide and seek in the mist. From high, we looked down on Carmona, a village of less than 200 inhabitants and seemingly the inspiration for Sleepy Hollow, all low, stone cottages with smoking chimneys.

"Oh, I forgot to ask," I said, "did you hear that snuffling sound outside our tents last night?"

"Nah," they said in unison.

They hadn't heard the wild boar a few days earlier nor what I thought might have been someone prowling around the tents back in that grasshopper field in France. Perhaps it was Dave dicking around in the middle of the night.

We fell back to 200 metres and climbed yet again, this time over the 556 metre pass at Collado de Ozalba. I stopped to allow the others to catch up. Three horses escaped from a nearby field, trotted on to the tarmac and then legged it down the winding road. Someone driving up the hill was going to get a surprise.

We descended again, to the village of La Fuente, and this time we'd had enough. Two farmer types leant against a fence. I asked them if there was anywhere to camp. They replied in a strong accent.

"Sorry, I don't understand," I said in Spanish.

"Of course you don't," replied the portlier one with a cocky smirk.

It's alright. Be as smug as you like, fat boy. I continued my questions. He said we could camp anywhere we wanted in the hills, that nobody cared. He gestured with a podgy arm to the mountains around us. None of us felt like doing any more climbing today.

Around the corner I saw a middle-aged Spaniard fussing over his runner beans in a large field. I stepped over his decrepit wooden gate and asked him if he'd let us camp on his land. He seemed to think we deserved better, that it wasn't flat enough. I said it was fine and so, slightly bemused, he agreed. It was a small victory for international relations and the first time since that grassy field half a day from Poole that we'd been given permission to sleep in a field. It was also the first time since then that I wouldn't have to sleep with half an ear listening for an angry farmer.

We made dinner. I made another caramelised apple omelette, this time with the piquant addition of chilli, with more sugar and more blackened, crispy bits. Dave and Joe had the usual, but finished with a small apple omelette of their own.

Once again we discussed cravings. Joe still wanted a massive bag of *Haribo* but everyone seemed more interested in taking this omelettey-pancakey thing we were all now making and adding new and currently out-of-reach ingredients like bacon and cheese. Yes, I know these sound like uninspired foodie options but, to us now, bacon and cheese felt like the stuff of myth.

It was Day 45 and I estimated we had only 24 more to go. From Santiago, our new route was to head due south through the centre of Portugal, turn south-east at Viseu, sneak around the edge of Seville and head for Gib. The Algarve, with its tourist over-development, would've been a miserable place to try to wild camp and so we'd omit it completely. Our target date to reach The Rock was now the 23rd of August, almost a month ahead of schedule.

There was a feeling Gibraltar wasn't too far away, as though we might actually manage to reach it. The only negative was my phone was once again dead and the shitty weather, due to continue for a couple more days, meant there was no way to recharge it.

"Don't worry, Dave. Once we get to southern Spain, I can guarantee sunshine."

He smiled but he no longer looked convinced.

When a man tells you his field is rubbish for camping, maybe you should listen to him rather than trying to prove to a couple of smug gits that we didn't need to climb into the hills again. It hadn't seemed so steep when I'd pitched the tent but I spent the night slowly sliding to the bottom. Maybe gravity worked differently around here.

A huge thunderstorm exploded around six in the morning and soaked our homes. We packed them away, wet and heavy. To vacate our field, we had to step over the crappy wooden fence, passing our bikes above it. In his attempt to do this, Dave broke the fence further, knocking a not-very-carefully-balanced wooden slat to the ground. He picked it up and was just about to replace it.

"Do that later, Dave," I said. "It'll make it easier for us to get out."

He smiled.

"Yeah, I thought so."

We escaped the field and he replaced the piece of wood, in doing so breaking off another piece. It wasn't entirely his fault. The fence looked like it'd been constructed by someone who'd spent too much time playing *Jenga*.

I climbed the steep road above our field and peaked at 658 metres at the Collado de Hoz. Dave and Joe were somewhere back down the hill. Normally I would've waited on top but it was raining and I preferred to stop somewhere drier. Just over the other side, the rain eased and the sun bashfully made a brief appearance and ripped apart the clouds over a stunning vista.

We were now in the Picos de Europa, one of the continent's most spectacular ranges, with mountains rising to 2,650 metres. This heavily folded landscape is home to some of the world's deepest caves. I'd wanted to come here ever since seeing Judith Chalmers visit the region on that holiday programme, which gives you some idea how long this place had been on my mind.

Halfway down the steep slope, I passed a five-a-side tarmacked football pitch clinging to the side of the hill. To prevent the ball tumbling into the ravine, it was surrounded by tall fences but they wouldn't have posed too much of a challenge to a clumsy oaf like me. I wonder how many hundreds of games had been interrupted.

"That's the last ball, Carlos, you moron. Now get on your moped and go fetch it!"

The rain returned but it wasn't as cold as yesterday. Both Dave and Joe screamed past me on the slope. I don't go fast downhill. I'm too aware of my own mortality. When I caught up with them, they were breakfasting on bread and jam at the bottom. I had a subject I needed to broach.

"I'm running out of toilet paper. Is anyone else? 'Cos if you are, maybe we could share a packet."

"Nah," said Joe. "I've still got some spare."

"And I'm still on the one I brought to France," said Dave. "And I reckon it'll last until Gibraltar."

I did a quick mental calculation.

"You can make one toilet roll last for six weeks? Is it the size of a tractor tyre?"

"No, it's only normal."

"Are you a one-sheet-a-go man?" Joe asked Dave, conjuring images I didn't want to contemplate. Even more unbelievably, and fully anticipating your cry of "Too much information!", Dave usually went for big jobs two or three times a day. In any case, it looked like I'd be forking out for more paper than I needed.

We followed the bubbling river down the hill to Panes, where I blew an entire full-fat euro on four toilet rolls when I'd much rather have spent it on a baguette or a tetrapack of cheap plonk.

Continuing eastwards, I was once again out in front. I came to a petrol station with a public toilet. I wondered how anyone less prepared than we were could use their facilities. The light inside didn't work. I had to use my head torch.

I came outside and waited for the others. Despite the fact that this petrol station was the only building on an otherwise featureless road, that we almost always went into such buildings to collect water, and that I was standing outside wearing a bright red t-shirt and holding my fully loaded bike, Dave didn't see me.

"Dave!"

He kept going, pedalling hard, head straight forward.

"DAVE!"

He passed me. Was he ultra-focussed on the road ahead or simply cycling with his brain switched off?

"DAAAAAAAVE!" I screamed.

He looked around, seemingly oblivious to the idea that humans might be present.

"Ah, right," he said and cycled over to me.

"There's a petrol station here. They've got water, and a toilet if you need it."

He always needed it. While Dave disappeared for ten minutes, I waited for Joe. He was another twenty minutes.

"Did you use your head torch?" I asked Dave a little later.

"Eh, where?" he replied.

"In the toilet. The light didn't work. It was pitch black."

"No, no head torch."

"What, you left the door open a bit?"

"No."

"Well then, how could you see what you were doing?"

"You just go, don't you?"

We hid out from the rain for a while and then cycled off, collecting apples and plums along the way and passing a little town called Poo. Dave and Joe were a long way behind again. Suddenly I was faced with a wall of plump blackberries and so decided to convert the remnants of my plum jam into plum and blackberry. I must have spent fifteen minutes picking them, and then another half an hour waiting before they turned up. I wondered if they stopped every so often for a nap.

We eventually arrived in Cangas de Onis, a pleasantly touristy town, full of shops selling cured hams and huge cheeses and mountains of dried black, shiny beans for ten euros a kilo, an amount we simply couldn't comprehend.

The rain had eased and evening sunshine made a welcome appearance. We found a field, half of which was an empty driving range. Our chosen spot was obscured from the road by six foot corn. We set up our tents. Surely if anyone had wanted to play golf, they'd be here by now.

"Dave," I said, "have you ever said no to anyone who asked you to do something?"

He thought about it for a minute.

"Yeah."

"Really? It's just you always agree with everything."

"I'm more assertive now than I used to be."

"You're kidding."

"I had an argument with my boss a while back."

"What happened?"

"I had to leave the job."

"Did they fire you?"

"No. It's just, well, you can't work for someone if you've argued with them, can you?"

Tonight was a full moon, a blue moon in fact. Maybe Dave would take this rare opportunity to disagree with one of us.

As we ate our dinner, some golfers appeared. They saw us but didn't seem bothered by our presence. Spanish people seemed very chilled at the idea of wild camping. I mean, it wasn't as if we were in their way. If we'd camped on the driving range, maybe it would've been a different story, or perhaps they'd have used us as target practice.

We woke up to a sun shrouded in mist. Dave was already up by the time I emerged.

"What time should we have breakfast, Dave?" I asked.

"I'm happy to have it any time."

"No, what time do *you* want it?"

Joe poked his head out of his tent.

"Yes, Dave, what time do *you* want it?" he said with a smile.

Dave couldn't *always* agree with our choices. It wasn't possible. We just wanted him to have his say. Once again, Dave looked ill at ease while making a decision, even one this simple.

"Now or later, Dave?"

"Either way."

"Now or later?"

He thought for a second.

"Let's ride for a bit and then have breakfast," he finally said.

"Good."

We set off and cycled on a long, straight road. We were now in bright green Asturias, the impressive lumps of the Picos behind us. We passed a restaurant by the side of the road, its name picked out in large, multi-coloured letters: *Titilandia*. Names like that amuse my tiny, puerile mind. If I'd had more money to throw around, I would've gone inside just to order a glass of milk.

It was close to eleven and I thought Dave had totally forgotten about breakfast. There was a road sign up ahead for the next village. Dave saw it.

"Let's have breakfast in Nava," he said firmly.

On the edge of town was a picnic table. The sun was out properly now. We set up our solar panels and charged our phones while we sat at the table and began our meal. I loaded my baguette with jam and started to eat. Joe extracted the sliced loaf that he and Dave were sharing.

"I think we should have five slices this morning," said Joe.

"I'd rather have four," replied Dave confidently.

"Bloody hell, Dave. Taking command," I said. "I like it."

Joe could hardly argue with him. We'd been willing Dave to make a decision for weeks. What other rulings would now spring forth from Dave's mouth? Maybe we'd created a monster.

Dave and Joe were in a supermarket in Pola de Siero while I waited outside. Joe was the first one out.

"You should see Dave," he said. "He's trying to decide if he should buy some wine or not. He's hovering over the shelf, picking it up and putting it back down again, stroking his beard."

Dave came out empty-handed.

"You didn't get any wine?" I asked.

"No. And it was only 60 cents (43p)."

"Yeah, I was tempted too," I said, "but I thought it'd be a bit mean on you two, drinking it alone."

"OK," said Dave decisively. "I'll get some!"

He rushed inside excitedly. Our assertiveness course seemed to be bearing fruit. And clearly Dave wouldn't feel mean drinking it alone.

"Do you want some?" I asked Joe.

"Nah, but don't let that stop you."

It didn't. Now I was the one mindlessly going along with Dave's decisions.

We continued and hit our largest Spanish town to date,

Oviedo. We cycled into its centre and found the fourteenth century cathedral but, unlike all the French ones, it demanded payment and so we had to decline. Instead, we headed towards the town park.

On the way, we passed a restaurant. A waiter was pouring a glass of cider from a great height. He didn't seem to be concentrating too carefully on the job at hand. At least a third of the drink splashed out of the vessel. That's apparently how they pour it around here. All over the floor.

We found the park and spread ourselves out for a while. It was a swelteringly hot day, the sort of weather I'd expected to become weary of in Spain. Today though, it made a welcome change.

My plum and blackberry jam was a little runny. I added more sugar to the jar. Although it didn't reduce the amount of liquid inside, it made the concoction deliciously sweet. I dripped chunks of baguette into it and stuffed them into my mouth before they dripped all over my legs. It was gorgeous. Dipping jam should definitely be a thing.

After an hour or so we decided to get moving again. Joe wheeled his bike out of the park. We heard a familiar cry.

"Oh no! It's the worst thing in the world!"

He'd had another puncture. I waited in the shade while he repaired it. He'd just completed the job when the tyre deflated yet again. The first patch had failed.

I walked around and looked at some nearby statues. Oviedo had over a hundred of them. An impressively solid one was of José Tartiere, a man who went to great lengths to create explosives and who would've been more aptly remembered by a sculpture featuring a pile of dead bodies. Directly opposite was his antithesis, a statue of a breast-feeding woman – La Encarna con Chiquilin – a tribute to motherhood. You know when you see a statue in a heroic pose and some tool of a tourist stands beside it in the same posture for a photo opportunity? Well, that also happened beside this statue. A woman walked up to it with a baby in her arms, whipped out a tit and got her husband to photograph her. Nigel Farage would've sent her to the corner of the city.

Leaving Oviedo, the lush, green landscape squeezed into the shape of mountains to our south. We soon realised we were back on the official Camino de Santiago trail. We passed an *albergue* with a mountain of walking boots outside. The weather had cooled slightly and we were in for a perfect evening, warm and dry.

We found a field hidden from the road by a line of trees and set ourselves up. Today we'd collected a barrel of apples and pears. Tonight's dinner was a variation of the earlier winner, a caramelised apple and pear omelette, this time smeared with beautifully sweet blackberry jam. Dave and Joe had lentils and sausage again.

After dinner we drank our cheap tramp's wine, a litre in a tetrapack, and got a little merry. It was our first taste of alcohol for four weeks. The conversation flowed more freely than normal. Joe, it turned out, had rearranged his flight so that he wouldn't have to kick around Andalusia for so long on a pound a day. Dave then decided to check out his own options for getting home. After telling us earlier he could do it for £100, he was horrified to discover that the trains alone would cost £140 and the ferry another £170. He could live for nearly a year on that total.

Even before the sun was up, I could hear the pilgrims from the nearby albergue tramping along the road. There was a time when to walk the Camino you would've been in a very select group. People have been walking this route for centuries. Only 30 years ago, the total number to complete the route in an entire year was only 690. In 2014, it was a whopping 237,886. The *refugios* and albergues that provide a cheap, or sometimes free, night's lodging are now swamped. Pilgrims have to get up extra early and race to the next budget option or else pay full price in one of the numerous hostals that have opened up to take advantage of the pilgrimage's popularity. As with sport and just about everything else, walking for God is big business.

Dave seemed a little hungover but shook his head to clear it and set off cycling. Today we'd climb again. We collected more apples and peaches and had our breakfast at a large picnic site on which a small team was setting up the paraphernalia for their village's summer fiesta. After weeks without a shower, we washed our legs in the on-site water fountain. It was only a token gesture but it made us look less grubby.

A few friends had worried out loud that our diet on this trip would suffer, but I felt incredibly fit. I'd lost lots of weight and I knew my blood pressure, high enough a few years ago to have caused a brain haemorrhage, had been reduced massively. Whenever I took my medication, I'd quickly become light-headed, a sign of low blood pressure. Long-time dry skin patches on my body had cleared up. The fruit and their vitamins must have played a large part. I'd eaten more apples on this trip than during the rest of my entire life. I must have been scoffing my way through twenty a day. They lined the roads wherever we went. If an apple a day keeps the doctor away, we had enough to close the NHS.

It was a Sunday and we needed a few things, but we were cycling in near wilderness. We hadn't passed a house for miles. It looked like we'd just have to go hungry, or eat what was left of the boring porridge. And then, in the middle of nowhere, with no other buildings around it, a small supermarket appeared at the side of the road. It closed at one o'clock and it was now five to.

I went inside and bought a large baguette for a euro and a small pack of frankfurters for 61 cents, more than the daily budget of €1.40 but there was little alternative. The shop assistant was in a sarcastic mood and, when she saw my meagre purchases, wished me the Spanish version of 'Bon appetit!'

We knew there was a big climb ahead, but we weren't sure when it would start. I stopped at what I believed to be the bottom and waited for Dave and Joe to appear. I was beside the Puente del Infierno, the Bridge of Hell. Maybe today's ascent was going to be a literal lungbuster.

It was around two in the afternoon and the temperature was well over 30. We climbed for twenty minutes and then, to everyone's dismay, the road fell away and we dropped twice as far as we'd just climbed. The descent provided a welcome and refreshing breeze but no one was enjoying the knowledge that we'd have to make up every metre before we could even return to our starting altitude.

But the climb wasn't coming yet. I cycled into Pola de Allande and drank heavily from a fountain spurting ice cold water. Dave turned up at the same time as a text from Joe. He'd suffered another puncture and hadn't manage to fix it properly and so was mending it again. He told us to carry on, find somewhere to camp and let him know where we were. On the other side of the village, the road suddenly began to climb. It was hot and sweaty but we made steady progress. Dense, thorny bushes lined the road. It was half past four. If Joe was an hour behind then we'd have to start looking for a spot soon. An occasional break would appear in the bushes but on closer inspection there'd be nowhere suitable for camping. We continued to climb. Around one thousand metres above sea level, the trees disappeared to leave bare hillsides, visible to all passing traffic. A man in pink lycra cycled beside me.

"Only two kilometres to the top," he said.

It looked like Joe would have to meet us on the other side of this 1,200 metre mountain pass. But at the summit I noticed a large electrical plant on the hill beside the road and went to investigate. The plant produced an annoying static hum, but there was a clear, flat patch of grass beside it. The building sheltered us from the wind and the views out over a hundred miles of mountains were spectacular.

I came back to the road and sat with Dave while waiting for Joe. A young Spanish bloke appeared from nowhere. He was carrying a large branch as a walking stick, which seemed to be the law if you're doing the Camino.

"Where's the nearest town?" he asked.

I showed him my map. Maybe he should've had one too.

"It looks like it's Grandas de Salime," I said. "But that's 25 kilometres away."

"No, that's too far," the pilgrim said.

He carried on walking, his head held low. I'd often thought it might be fun to do the Camino, but the more people I saw crawling slowly along, the less joyful it seemed. We could see the same scenery by bike and do four times the daily distance. We could also carry enough equipment that if we found ourselves stuck on top of a 1,200 metre mountain at seven in the evening with the nearest accommodation fifteen miles away then we could stick up a tent and at least be sheltered from the elements. I hope he found somewhere.

Joe eventually turned up in a very positive mood given the recent punctures. He was glad to have climbed the mountain in the cooler evening air rather than in the heat of the summer afternoon. This was a good argument for cycling later in the day, but I couldn't be arsed to make it. We were all getting on better now. There was no need to antagonise him.

I showed Joe to our power station campsite. Its hum was a

little disturbing.

"Do you think it'll make our hair stand on end?" asked Joe.

"No, but we'll probably wake up in the morning with loads of balloons sticking to us."

We had our dinner. As a cost-cutting exercise, Dave and Joe had removed sausages from their meal this evening and were simply having lentils, pasta and egg. I felt a bit mean rustling up a curried toad-in-the-hole. When dipped into soy sauce, it was lovely.

After our morning washlet, we discussed how badly we ponged. I couldn't smell either of them, or myself, and neither could they, but maybe we'd all gotten used to our stench. The odd thing was that, although Dave was the only one who'd brought a mirror with him, he was also the only one with an absolutely filthy face. He looked like a commando.

The gusty wind of the afternoon disappeared entirely as the sun set over the mountains. In the distance we could see a cloud of smoke from a forest fire merging with the dusk mist. The hills turned from orange to red to black. No hotel in the world, no matter how expensive, could top the views we'd seen all night long. Sometimes the best things in life really are free.

I was in a strange house and it was infested with monster insects. I tried to swat them, but they kept on coming towards me. A giant moth, the size of a pigeon, flapped at my face. I went to slap it away but it got tangled in my long hair. I tugged at the ugly bug to free it, but it was stuck and started making a horrible buzzing sound. I grew more alarmed as the sound became louder, so loud I woke up. The electrical plant hummed away contentedly.

The morning views may have been spectacular due to our

great height, but cycling down the hill the next morning with the road mostly in shadow was a chilly ride. We wrapped ourselves in fleeces, the first time I'd used mine while cycling on the entire trip. We rapidly lost height. We'd expected a gentle downhill all the way to Grandas, but then the road passed over a huge dam, with ancient abandoned workers' cottages in the hills around, and we started to climb again. Spain loves its hills.

We eventually arrived in Grandas. Despite this being a Monday morning, we were reminded that it was a *Spanish* Monday morning because its only supermarket was closed for the village fiesta. We were given directions to a tiny shop a couple of miles out of town but it had little choice and large prices. Smalltown Spain was buggering up our budget. While we sat outside the shop, an escargatoire of backpackers plodded past, heavy rucksacks on their backs. We'd reach Santiago in a couple of days. They had another week of this shit.

According to our map, we had three passes to climb today. The first was also the highest at 1,050 metres and tipped us into Galicia, Spain's north-west. Over the first one, I stopped at a supermarket in the town of Fonsagrada. Standing outside, I waited for Dave and Joe. It was 40 minutes later when Joe appeared. That was odd. I thought Dave had been ahead of Joe.

"Where's Dave?" Joe asked.

"Bloody hell."

We'd lost him again. Joe managed to get him on the phone. Despite being on the lookout for a supermarket, despite this shop having a large supermarket sign and despite my bike leaning against the wall outside, Dave's blinkered cycling style had taken him right past and into the countryside beyond. He never seemed comfortable being in front. The odd times he'd led us as a group, he seemed a bit nervous as he approached each junction. He decided to stop where he was and let us catch him up. Without someone to lead the way, Dave would probably have ended up on Uranus.

Over the next pass, I collected another load of blackberries. I'd now perfected the recipe for instant blackberry jam. Fill your empty jar to the top with blackberries and use a spoon to mash the berries as much as possible. You should end up with half a jar of blackberries and juice. Fill the jar with sugar and mash again. You'll now have three-quarters of a jar of purple syrup. Fill the jar with sugar again and stir, and repeat once more. Don't add any water unless you want dipping jam. You can eat it straight away but it'll be a little crunchy, or leave it for a while to allow all the sugar to dissolve. Lovely!

We continued clocking up the miles. Stopping for lunch, Joe was reluctant to continue so quickly and wanted to snooze. Dave and I left him, agreeing to meet later. We wanted to get that third and final pass out of the way. At the top of Alto da Fontaneira, we felt happy that today's work was over but, unknown to us, our map hadn't bothered to mention the fourth pass.

Today had been a very tiring 60 miles and more metres of ascent than we wanted to calculate. We'd no idea how far away Joe was and so at five o'clock, and with rain imminent, we started to look for somewhere. I quickly found a large field, surrounded by hedges. Joe arrived half an hour later.

Although we'd only been on the road for seven weeks, I felt like I'd been doing this my entire life. It was genuinely hard to imagine a time when I could spend my money freely and buy what I wanted. The discomfort of camping, of sleeping on the ground and waking up whenever it started to rain or with every strong gust of wind, had become entirely normal. I didn't think I'd ever be able to sleep on a real bed again, unless I first filled it with stones. I liked the routine we'd developed. What I missed most was having the sort of laugh you only have with your best friends. Dave and Joe were great but they both seemed to be introverts, preferring silence to noisy banter.

I made another curried toad-in-the-hole, a filling meal for less than 60 cents. Horror of all horrors, Dave and Joe had run out of lentils. Their meal consisted of tomato sauce and *fideos*, the two centimetre-long noodles not much thicker than a needle, designed to add bulk to soup rather than as the star of a pasta dish. It was the cheapest pasta available and made for a dense and sloppy sauce that looked particularly unappetising. Dave said it was his favourite pasta yet. Dave's odd.

I had a clear out of my fishing tackle. All the metal parts of my telescopic rod had rusted, causing a horrible grinding noise whenever I tried to extend it. I decided to bin it, along with all the tackle that'd also rusted up. I kept a few lures and my pen rod.

"I like this little rod," I said. "It's dinky. It's the sort of rod James Bond would use."

"Yes, I can just see him in his next film," said Joe, "standing around for four hours, catching nothing."

It was getting dark. Tonight's campsite was a working field but Joe seemed to be slowing down, despite his extra meals, and needed more sleep.

"What time should we get up?" I asked.

"I know what time I'd like to get up," said Joe.

"Midday?"

"Very funny."

"Nine?"

"OK."

The next morning we set off and quickly reached Castroverde. Every Spanish town with even the slightest ambition of attracting a tourist displays a large, brown sign at its entrance featuring its name and an illustration of the town's key feature, whether a castle, a cathedral or an aqueduct. Castroverde's large brown sign displayed its name but, instead of the illustration, there was an empty, brown void. We weren't expecting much of this place.

Castroverde might have had little to offer but we'd high hopes for Lugo. It's apparently the only city in the world completely surrounded by an intact Roman wall. The wall was impressive enough, but what lay inside was less so, with a collection of mostly modern shops and knackered apartment buildings. The great wall only served to make the newer buildings look uglier.

One building that outshone the more recent ones was the city's cathedral. Inside, it had a moody feel, full of shadows, the air thick with incense. Around the walls were chapels dedicated to various saints. Each one had an electronic candle machine outside. If I wanted the conjuring skills of, say, Saint Kevin to help me in my hour of need, I could drop a coin into his machine and a little bulb would light up.

Joe looked at the machine and pulled his face.

"I know the expression 'light a candle for me'. It's not really the same to ask someone to 'light an LED for me', is it?"

I suppose it was refreshing that the church was embracing modernity, even if that modernity was only electricity and cheap bulbs, but what's the point of lighting an LED for an hour or two? Does the saint in question have an equivalent switchboard in Heaven just waiting for a light to come on before springing into action like a superhero?

Our plan was to stay about ten miles shy of Santiago and then make an assault of the city in the morning. We still had a long way to go today if we were going to achieve this. We cycled a long, tedious road towards Ourense. I realised my back tyre wasn't as well-filled as it should've been. I stopped to inflate it only to realise my old bicycle pump wasn't working. It'd done well to last twenty years. Neither of Dave's or Joe's had the right sort of fitting for my Schrader valve. Luckily, just over the next hill was a petrol station that dispensed free air with a nozzle to match my bike. It was quickly inflated and was soon as hard as Danny Dyer thinks he is, but I now had to worry that if I suffered a puncture on my back tyre before I could buy a new pump, I wouldn't be able to fix it.

We stopped for lunch under the shade of some plum trees.

"What do you reckon your first meal will be when you get home?" asked Dave.

"I don't know," I replied. "But I bet I'll be eating a lot less meat in future."

"I know what mine will be," he continued.

"What?"

"Lentils, sausage, pasta and egg."

"The same thing you've eaten nearly every day for the last month?"

"Yes."

He grinned widely.

After a long search, up and down some steep lanes, I finally found a patch of forest in which we could sleep. We pushed our bikes inside and set up our tents. Dave then picked up his toilet roll and his sanitary trowel and disappeared out of sight.

"That's his third time today," I said. "Why so often?"

"It's a ruse. He's gone to buy a burger," joked Joe.

He was silent for a minute.

"You know, I suspected you were both cheating."

"Doing what?"

"Well, you cycle ahead, and you can go much further than I do without getting tired. I suspected you were stopping and buying food. It'd be easy for you."

I couldn't really explain why I didn't feel more tired, but I certainly wasn't sneakily cramming more calories.

"I once cycled from Edinburgh to London," he continued. "We did 130 miles a day for five days. I could cope with that because I could eat what I wanted. This is different."

Suddenly a herd of cows passed through the woods followed by a farmer. If he saw us, he wasn't bothered by our presence.

We ate our dinner and climbed inside our tents. A little later, from inside my little home, I heard a stilted conversation between a woman and Joe. She'd say something and he'd repeat *"No entiendo"*. I could've left the tent and translated but then she might've told us to sod off and so Joe was better off languishing in his linguistic ignorance.

This afternoon I had, perhaps foolishly, splurged a full day's budget on a bottle of soy sauce, so important was it for reviving dinner time morale. I'd now need to limit myself to a jam-and-baguette-only-diet for a couple of days or else risk going over budget. Which was rubbish really because who wants soy sauce on a jam butty?

Today our eleven day pilgrimage from the French border to Santiago would be complete. Well, if we could work out how to get into the city, that was. As is the case with a lot of the larger Spanish towns, the main road into Santiago had been upgraded to a motorway, meaning there was now no A-road for use by farmers, horse riders, mopeds, less confident drivers or cyclists. Signs told us on two wheels to follow the Camino's footpath instead. Less confident drivers just had to use the motorway and hope they didn't kill anyone.

Today was the first time we could see with our own eyes just how popular the Camino was. The path was heaving with walkers all shuffling along in our direction. As we passed by, a lot of them wished us *"Bon Camino!"*, which was nice if a bit tiresome after the twentieth one. Do they do this every time they see a new walker? If so, they'd have no time to do anything else.

The path was rough in parts and went constantly up and down. I picked my way carefully through the crowd, ringing my tinkly bell to warn walkers when I was behind them. Lacking his own bell and not wanting to say "Excuse me" in Spanish, Joe employed a more aggressive approach. He would ride as quickly as he could down a hill and then when he got close to a group of walkers blocking his path he'd slam on his brakes and skid his back wheel. Alarmed at the squeal of rubber and fearing they'd just luckily escaped an accident, the pilgrims span around suddenly before leaping out of the way like startled cats. I can't imagine this won over to our side anyone who was currently ambivalent towards cyclists.

It wasn't only Joe's behaviour that was making today's pilgrimage a less than spiritual undertaking. Walker numbers were so high nowadays that stalls selling pilgrim-inspired tourist tat lined the path. If you want a walk with time and space to reflect, then this one, especially this stage of it, isn't the one for you. Unless, that is, you're Alan Sugar and the thing you want to reflect upon is how best to milk a bunch of pilgrims.

We eventually reached the summit of the 370 metre Monte de Gozo, or the Hill of Joy, where pilgrims get their first view of the cathedral towards which they've been aiming all this time. It was all downhill from here.

We cycled through the ugly suburbs of modern Santiago and headed to the cathedral. Given the numbers we'd seen on the path we were surprised how few people were here, maybe 50 or 60 people dotted about. And the cathedral wasn't all that.

Another cyclist, Henry, showed up. He was a Belgian,

whose own pilgrimage had begun in Marrakesh for some reason. He was one of those fact-finding cyclists who wants to know all the tiny details of your ride, like daily distance and number of punctures. He was most surprised we'd been doing the same distance as he had on our tiny budget and resulting calorific intake. I asked him to take a group photo in front of the cathedral, which he very kindly did, but in each of his three attempts he managed to chop off a limb of at least one of us. Ansel Adams he wasn't.

Joe went to see how we could get into the cathedral and that's when he realised we were standing at the exit rather than the entrance. We wheeled our bikes through the fifteenth century streets and into an enormous square and then, for the first time, we saw the magnificent cathedral in all its splendour and the thousands of people who'd just finished their pilgrimage. A group of blue t-shirt-wearing teenagers with godly slogans whooped and sang and banged on tambourines.

"Friends of yours?" I said to Dave.

"Those sort of Christians annoy me," he replied.

Other groups, young and old, were equally vociferous. I imagine if you've spent five or six weeks walking every day on blistered feet then the euphoria you feel upon reaching here would put you in a party mood. It was a lot easier by bike, although perhaps Joe might tell you otherwise.

Now at the proper entrance, Joe went off again to see if we could get into the cathedral. While I waited outside with the bikes, I was pounced upon by a happy young fella from the Spanish postal service who offered to ship my bike back to the UK for 90 euros. I was impressed by the proactive approach from a normally staid organisation but couldn't see how I'd get to Gibraltar if I took him up on his offer.

Joe returned with the unfortunate news that we'd have to pay to enter the cathedral. It would've been free if we'd bothered to get a Pilgrim Passport before we'd started and had it stamped at places along the way. That said, I'm not sure who stamps it when you live in the woods. Regardless, funds were getting tight and so we ended our pilgrimage outside, rather than inside, the cathedral. It would seem we were too poor to receive a blessing from Dave's God.

Days Completed: 53
Ride and Seek: **Total spend £47.56, per day £0.90**
Live below the Line: **Total spend £50.36, per day £0.95**

Chapter 13: The Valley of Fruit

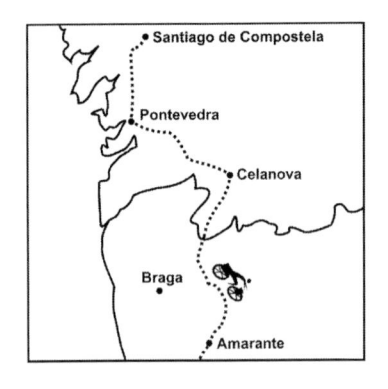

Escaping Santiago was even more difficult than entering. Close to town, my map showed only motorways and dual carriageways, and we were banned from these. I used my compass to navigate us in the direction we needed to go but local electromagnetics messed with my pointer and made it spin like Alistair Campbell.

We inched our way out of the centre, asking directions and acting upon often conflicting instructions. Eventually, after two hours, we were pointed down the path we believed would free us from the shackles of Santiago. But later, fearing we'd made a wrong turn, I stopped to confirm with a young woman that we were still heading in the right direction. It felt slightly pervy to tell her I was looking for Cuntis.

We found ourselves tipped on to a busy road heading to Pontevedra. We passed through Padrón, a town famous for its peppers. Really though, it should be more famous for clever marketing. In many Spanish restaurants you'll find *Pimientos de Padrón*, a dish of inch-long, green peppers. I was told that, although the peppers are usually mild, one in ten has a fiery kick. You're supposed to sit around a table with your friends, taking one pepper at a time, playing a sort of blistered tongue version of *Russian Roulette*. What a great way to sell more peppers! Except that whenever I've eaten them, every single one of them has been boringly mild.

Perhaps inspired by the marketing genius of being unexpectedly burnt, *Doritos Roulette* were introduced recently to the UK. Most of the crisps inside the bag are mildly spiced but a few are coated in a chilli powder twenty times hotter than a jalapeño. The crisps were banned by a Scarborough school after a pupil ate a spicy one and suffered an asthma attack. The most worrying aspect of this story is the attack occurred, according to the *Belfast Telegraph* at least, a full seven days after she'd eaten the hot snack. This means not only are *Doritos Roulettes* the spiciest crisps around but they can also hang around your system and bugger you up when you least expect it, like syphilis. Either that or, I dunno, the asthma attack was totally unrelated.

The day turned grey and Joe was getting tired. Dave and I waited for him at one point and it took him 50 minutes to catch up. Clearly, his supplementary meals weren't making enough of a difference.

Once past Pontevedra, we turned inland to look for a field. After all my promises to Dave, the rain came down, a sort of determined drizzle. The hot tarmac steamed, filling the road with ghosts. The route suddenly steepened and the rain came harder but houses still lined the road. We knew we'd have to escape civilisation before we'd find anywhere to stop. Eventually, already soaked, we saw a picnic spot, a couple of benches beneath a few trees. It was visible from the road but only a complete bastard of a policeman would move us on in this weather. Knowing how averse the Spanish are to rain – they basically have the same molecular structure as the witch from *The Wizard of Oz* – I doubted a copper would've left the warmth of his car in these conditions.

It was too wet to cook. The ceiling of my tent was too low to fire up a stove inside it. Joe's tent had a larger porch and so he rustled up something for himself and Dave. I'm guessing it was lentils, pasta and egg. I just dipped the remains of my baguette into the sloppy blackberry and apple jam I'd made. That might not sound like much of a dinner, and you're right, but it still tasted great.

The drizzle crackled on my tent with the occasional plop of a larger drop dripping from the branches above. It wasn't late – probably seven o'clock – but the minging weather had put an early end to another day. I lay inside thinking about Gibraltar. I was looking forward to it in the way my six year-old self used to look forward to Christmas.

The morning, with its bright blue sky, came as a pleasant surprise. What was less pleasant for Joe was when I said that, now I'd checked the map a little more carefully, today's ride would be around 80 miles.

"What's the rush?" he said.

We now, however, had a real deadline. Unwilling to pay through the nose for the long trip from Gibraltar to Santander, Dave had decided to book a relatively inexpensive flight out of Gibraltar, and there were only two flights a week. To give him enough time to find a cardboard box for his bike, we needed to reach Gibraltar by the 21st of September.

"If we're too slow," I said to Dave later, "you could always speed up and get there before us."

"No," he replied. "I don't want to cycle into Gibraltar without you and Joe."

Perhaps energised by this deadline, Dave set off like Usain Bolt, racing ahead of us and only stopping when he came to a junction. We trundled along behind, occasionally stopping to pick fruit, the usual share of blackberries and apples, but we also plundered an abandoned vineyard that Joe found. I wasn't bitter that he'd been the one to discover it, but they were definitely sour grapes.

We climbed a large hill. Once on top, the surface disintegrated and became something reminiscent of Ukraine.

"This is the worst road I've ever cycled," said Joe.

Nevertheless, he and Dave screamed down, crashing through the potholes. This was no worry for Dave. Between his thick mountain bike tyres and the huge load he was carrying, he probably did more damage to the road than to his bike.

We passed through obscure, little villages built of grey stone that felt more Yorkshire than Spain. One even had a hulking hilltop building with the flavour of Royston Vasey's local shop. The climbing continued. Long and steep, on a hot afternoon, we thought we'd reached the top only to discover a false summit and see another hour of ascent ahead of us. Eventually though, we got there and we tore down a five mile-long hill, losing four hours of ascent in fifteen minutes. Unfortunately, upon meeting the river at the bottom, the road started to climb again.

In Celanova, at six in the evening and still 30 miles short of our target, we had a decision to make. Joe didn't want to go any further and, if I'm being honest, I'd had enough too. We decided to spread the remaining distance over the next few days and hope the terrain wasn't as knackering as today's. We were slipping behind our new schedule and needed to speed up if we were going to get Dave to the airport on time.

We started looking for somewhere immediately, but we still had to climb to escape Celanova's residential outer shell. Soon though, the houses were replaced by dense forest. We sneaked inside but it was hardly ideal. We had to spend half an hour removing brambles before there was sufficient room for three tents. Even Dave wasn't thick-skinned enough to survive a mat-less night sleeping on their thorns.

The closer we got to Gibraltar, the more the conversation focussed on the amazing culinary experiences we were going to have there. The place was taking on a magical quality. Gibraltar was the Land of Oz and *Morrisons* the Emerald City. It was becoming a place of fantasy, like a myth we tell our children, possibly because our reality was getting a little too much for us.

We woke up to grey clouds. What had gone wrong with the weather?

The hill we'd started to climb yesterday had to be completed before breakfast. We topped the pass of 850 metres at Alto do Vieiro and trundled into the small town of Bande to look for a supermarket. Old Spanish women shuffled around in big coats, miming to each other how cold they were and saying '*frio*' every other word. The Iberian August was broken.

In the supermarket, Joe went for a change of strategy. Rather than buying a baguette, he did a cost-benefit analysis and plumped for a multipack of cheap biscuits.

"More calories per euro," he said proudly. "And I'm also a bit of a biscuit fiend."

We rolled south, heading for Portugal, and the sun came out. At the side of the road, we found a huge, over-productive apple tree and started to pick a few fruits. An old woman appeared, a tiny, shrunken elf in black, carrying a small scythe. She waved it about a bit and yabbered something with a mouthful of cavities. From her expression, we understood her dance to imply "Go on, lads, help yourselves!" Although I suppose she could equally have been yelling, "Touch my apples and I'll cut your fuckin' feet off!"

She asked where we were going and where we'd been in an accent I could barely understand. Around here, the magic word seemed to be 'Santiago'. As soon as we mentioned it, in this and other conversations, we earned the highly desirable status of pilgrims, which seemed to permit us to do anything. We'd remember this if Dave was ever caught in flagrante with a goat.

A little later we discovered a plum tree. I tasted one and they seemed blander than normal, barely worth taking. It didn't stop Dave from stripping the entire tree. He was the foraging equivalent of *Agent Orange*.

We headed through Lobios and into the Serra do Xurés National Park with its granite hills covered in Pyrenean oak and birch. This reserve straddles the Spanish-Portuguese border. The international crossing lay on top of a hill. We snaked up the hillside as a team, Joe's previously weary legs powered by biscuits.

Crossing this way by car you'll pay a €1.50 tax for the privilege of driving over the most pockmarked road in western Europe. We'd no idea what happened to the money. It certainly wasn't being used to maintain the road. We steered around the holes, past dozens of semi-clad tourists on their way to the pools and fountains a few metres from the roadside. The apparent summit at the border turned out merely to have been a stopping point. In a stifling heat, the road continued to climb, shaded by tall trees. Then came a splendid, four-mile descent, twisting and turning on switchbacks, overlooking the silver-blue water of the dammed Rio Cávado, now acting as a leisure lake, full of splashing tourists. At the bottom of the hill, Joe was lacking motivation.

"This weather makes me feel sleepy," he said.

I think he preferred the cold.

Looking at the map, it was only three miles to our next turning. Unfortunately, what the map didn't say was this distance was straight up the other side of the river's steep valley. Sweat leaked down our faces as we huffed our way to the top in the mid-30s heat. Once there, we looked out across the mountains to see the lake far below and a forest fire marching across the horizon. Fire-fighting planes dipped into the water, scooping liquid and hopefully avoiding the more adventurous holidaymakers who'd liloed too far across the lake.

The rest of the afternoon took us through dormant villages. Another team of costumed motorcyclists phut-phutted their way past us on small, underpowered bikes. One wore a huge pair of cow horns on his helmet. They waved at us madly, like they'd just escaped from somewhere.

"So, have you noticed any differences between Spain and Portugal yet?" I asked.

"It's scruffier," said Dave.

"But at least there are some larger supermarkets," said Joe.

A car came around the corner, seemingly out of control, and narrowly missed us.

"And the drivers are worse."

Just before Cabeceiras, we decided it was time to stop. We passed a large field, lined by trees on its far side, with a track disappearing between them. We pushed our bikes across the grass, followed the track over the world's tiniest, most rickety bridge one at a time and discovered a lovely meadow hidden from the road.

Immediately after setting up our tents, Dave disappeared off into the woods with toilet roll and trowel.

"If I had to go as often as Dave," I said, "I think I'd seal up my arse."

"Hmm," replid Joe. "I'm not sure that'd solve your problem."

Joe started to cook up some lentils and passed me the bottle of meths we'd only bought two days earlier. It felt a quarter full. Meths was the last food-related item we were sharing. Mr Pettiness was back in town.

"How can this be so empty? I've only cooked one meal with it."

"I don't know," said Joe.

It was hard to explain. Joe had bought his own personal bottle of meths to cook his supplementary meals. But, as we now made separate dinners, our fuel use had increased. Still, their two-pan pasta, lentil and egg dishes took about twenty minutes of cooking while my omelettes or toad-in-the-holes took five. Rightly or wrongly, I felt diddled.

"It's irrelevant really," I said. "If this weather stays like this I won't want to eat hot food. So I won't need any more meths."

I didn't want to spend my tight budget to fund their fuel-heavy dinners. I don't think Joe liked my decision. If I wasn't paying for meths, he and Dave would have to share the cost of the entire bottle, and the last one we'd bought was €2.60, nearly a day's budget for each of them. Who knew how much it would cost in Portugal?

"How do you feel about just having uncooked dinners, Dave?" asked Joe a little grudgingly.

"Yeah, I'm happy to have uncooked dinners," he replied brightly.

I wondered how much torture Dave would have to endure before you managed to wipe the smile from his face.

Despite the blistering afternoon, the evening froze. I'd been expecting balmy nights this far south but I slept wearing my fleece. In the middle of the night something large and snorty came a-snuffling around my tent. Was it Dave arsing about? Probably not. I slapped the side of my nylon house and it scampered away into the trees.

We stood outside a small *Coviran* supermarket in Cabeceiras trying to pool our knowledge of Portuguese. It was a very shallow pool indeed. I could only offer 'hello', which was basically the same as in Spanish, and 'thank you', but even with this paltry amount of knowledge I was still well ahead. We decided to google a few choice phrases. At least we now knew how to ask 'how much?', although we'd have no idea what number lay concealed in the shopkeeper's answer. I was glad we'd only be here a few days. I didn't like this feeling of impotence, but we had no money to buy the linguistic *Viagra* of a phrasebook.

Dave went into the supermarket while a wedding party milled around outside, the women dressed immaculately, the men like gangsters. Dave came out with a small bag of shopping. He'd blown €3.48, nearly two and half days' worth of budget. *Coviran* is a Spanish and Portuguese supermarket chain whose USP appears to be small and dingy shops selling a tiny range of goods at high prices. We'd already learnt this in Spain. We wondered why Dave had chosen to spend so much there, especially when we rolled to the next junction and saw a *Continente* supermarket the size of a football stadium. Baguettes there were less than half the price Dave had paid. We sat on the steps outside, eating bread overloaded with blackberry jam. On a trip like this, the taste of cheap food was always sweeter.

The morning was a beautiful ride, warm but not too hot, on a quiet, tree-lined B-road, parallel to the river Támega. We curved through countryside that was becoming more parched the further south we cycled. We dubbed this place The Valley of Fruit. A woman pulled two swollen lemons from her tree and offered them to Joe. Apples, oranges, peaches and fat, juicy plums were everywhere. As always, Dave struggled with the concept of taking only what he needed. He ended up filling two carrier bags.

Near one village we could hear the distorted music from overburdened loudspeakers as the place enjoyed its summer fiesta. Firecrackers exploded, seemingly oblivious to the nearby tinderbox forest. We hoped the party wasn't going to heat up too much later.

In order to continue, we had to cross the river we'd shadowed near Amarante. Our map said we needed a road called the N210. In a moment of road-building idiocy, there were two N210s, entirely unconnected and one of them took you on to a motorway and the other was the one we wanted. Guess which one we found.

With the help of my phone, we corrected ourselves and I hit the edge of Amarante first. I came to a petrol station and tried its toilet to get some water. The door was locked and so I helped myself to a tap on the forecourt.

Dave rolled up behind me.

"Oh, a petrol station," he said. "I wonder if it has a toilet."

"It does. But the door's locked."

"Ah."

"Just go into the shop and do a 'I need the key for the toilet' mime."

He looked hesitant.

"No, it doesn't matter. I'm not desperate."

Dave cycled off while I finished filling my bottle and Joe appeared.

"Toilet?" he said.

"Yep. But it's locked. You'll need to do a mime."

He wasn't prepared to humiliate himself either.

"It doesn't matter. It can wait."

We cycled into the lovely centre of the old town, crossing an ancient stone bridge. Our mission was to find a sign to the next town, St Marco de Canaveses, a few millimetres away on my map. The sign was nowhere to be seen. At a junction I asked if anyone spoke Spanish, or French, or English.

Suddenly, we were the most interesting thing to happen in town all day. A crowd gathered around. I told them where we wanted to go. A street discussion ensued about where this mysterious place could be.

"I know!" said a woman. "It's about 80 kilometres north-east."

"Er, no, it isn't," I said.

I had map-based evidence.

"It's east of here," said a young fella.

"No, it's not. It's south. Look at my map."

After ten minutes of toing and froing, a local expert pointed us down one of only three routes out of town. St Marco was farther away than we'd expected – about twelve miles – but how was it possible that an entire townful of people didn't know where the next village was? It's not like it was an obscure little place. Ten thousand people lived there, for Christ's sake!

Despite being surrounded by hills, the road to St Marco was flat and through lush trees that shaded us from the intensifying sun. On the other side of St Marco, I suggested a left that turned out to be a massive navigational balls-up. I took us up a huge, steep hill, its gradient Devonesque. I'd added an unnecessary 300 metres of ascent and several miles to an already long day. Dave and Joe heaved themselves up the hill behind me, sweating like furnacemen, and, I assumed, justifiably cursing me.

Eventually we found a tiny track and tumbled down the hill, ending up a little way further along from where we'd started about two hours earlier. On the way, we passed a peach tree. If there'd once been low-hanging fruit, they'd long since gone. Joe extended his telescopic rod and fished a fat peach from near the top of the tree. At last he'd caught something worth eating.

From our elevated position we could see a bridge across

the wide Douro river. Our target was on the other side. We barrelled down the hill, crossed the water and started to look for somewhere to stop. Joe was struggling. His magic biscuits weren't capable of compensating for my navigational clumsiness.

We hit the wall that was the opposite bank of the river. The road snaked up it, too steep on either side to offer a place to sleep. Joe was miles behind. We kept climbing and eventually found a knobbly field with deep, scraggy grass. We pitched our tents and cooked some food. With no wind shield on his stove, Joe set fire to the grass, another event that was the worst thing in the world. He stamped it out quickly. He would have struggled to pay the fine out of his one pound for starting a forest fire.

Now we were in Portugal, a country in the same time zone as Britain, the evenings became darker an hour earlier than in Spain. It was nearly pitch black by nine. The heat of the day lingered. Crickets chirped on the first balmy night of the entire trip. Finally, our summer had begun just 55 days after we'd started.

The next morning we had to continue up the steep hill through the town of Cinfães. On the way, we came to a garage and filled up with water. The young guy behind the counter was keen to try out his English on us. I looked at a large map of the area on his wall. I pointed to this morning's objective.

"How high is this pass?" I asked.

"Mmm. A thousand metres and something."

"Something?"

That something was quite important. A woman came out of the back office. He asked her.

"A thousand, fifteen hundred, two thousand," she replied, wobbling an outstretched hand to indicate her uncertainty.

"What I know," said the man, "is that it's very difficult."

We cycled through the village, its cobbles rattling my teeth, and then I made another navigational blunder and took us up another needless hill again. I'd taken the wrong turning back in town. Dave and Joe must've hated the fact I was the only one with a map of Portugal.

We rolled back down the hill and into the village. There, we had a minor dispute. The morning air was cool and refreshing, but it wouldn't stay like that for long. I wanted to climb as high as I could as early as possible to take advantage of the lower temperatures. Joe wanted his breakfast right now. He'd already mentioned this to Dave, who had of course agreed with him. Still, we didn't all need to agree. They had their breakfast and I'd grab a few apples on the way up the hill. We arranged to meet at the top.

It was a long but gentle climb up the mountainside. From a distant hill, the voices of a church choir drifted across the valley. I was in a movie with its own score. Looking across to the source of the music, it was lovely to see the ancient terraces, still maintained, covering the slopes but with modern wind turbines on top, generating clean, renewable energy, the old and the new working together.

Towards the top, I overtook a couple of local fellas, stripped to the waist and shiny with sweat. On the summit they came over to me and in a strange mixture of English, Portuguese, Spanish and French we managed to communicate. They recommended a few places to visit but we already had a date for this evening.

The wind on the other side of the mountain acted as a natural brake and extended a perfect descent in glorious sunshine. Realising we were ahead of schedule, we took a long lunch break on the town hall steps of Calde. Dave managed to drop and smash his Tigger bowl. I was surprised the 83 individual layers of food in its centre hadn't held it together.

Today we were heading to Anne's, an ex-Open University student, who I'd first met on my 22,000 mile ride through Europe. She and husband James had a beautiful, old cottage in a village near Milton Keynes, which they'd managed to sell the day I turned up. Since then they'd packed up and moved to a village near Viseu here in Portugal and had once again invited me to stay.

Anne had given me directions. We were looking for two particular numbered roads. Unfortunately, very few of the signs in Portugal bothered to use these numbers. We were also told it was near Igreja Matriz, a church.

As we approached the ring road around Viseu, I took out my phone to get a more detailed map than my paper one, as neither of Anne's roads appeared on it. Since the last time I'd used my phone – about half an hour ago – my phone company *Three* had suspended my service despite having plenty of credit. My phone was useless. Joe's phone was also out of commission, having his own problems with *Three*.

"We'll just have to use the rough map I have," I said. I'd made a little sketch of where we needed to go in case of an emergency. I'd hoped not to have to use it. "The road we want should be a right turn off this one. I just don't know how far it is."

We cycled for a couple of minutes and then we had an amazing stroke of good fortune.

"Look! Igreja Matriz!" I said.

A sign pointed us to the place we were looking for. We followed the sign but it didn't help. It was only later that we learned that 'Igreja Matriz' translates as 'Parish Church'. There are thousands of them in Portugal.

We circled around. I asked directions several times, hoping Spanish was close enough to Portuguese, but we were getting nowhere. No one seemed to know where we needed to be and advice was contradictory. We were sent up and down the same road.

"I've an idea," said Joe. "The last time I bought credit for this phone, it all disappeared. Maybe if I buy some more, it'll work."

And it did. We managed to find our location and Anne's house and piece together a route through Viseu's suburbs. When we arrived, Anne's big, black gates were open. We walked inside, down a gravel driveway, and stood surrounded by an enormous vineyard, acres of vines sloping towards us, the gravel track lined with fruit trees. We walked towards an old, stone house, past what appeared to be a chapel.

"I don't think this is right," I said. "It seems too big."

The grounds of their English home had been huge too, but Anne and James were hardly teenagers and I'd assumed, or perhaps remembered being told, they were downsizing. This place felt like the home of a well-to-do, retired Mafia boss. It was stunningly beautiful.

I knocked on the front door but there was no answer. I saw a second-floor, open window and shouted a hello. I hoped this didn't really belong to the Mafia. The last thing I needed lobbing at me from that window was a horse's head.

Anne's face appeared. We were ushered inside, up the stone steps to their terrace. Beers were produced and quickly necked. We each had our first shower in five weeks. It felt wonderful.

Anne threw on the washing machine and did our laundry. I feared the worst when I learnt that the batch involving the majority of my clothes also included the pair of socks Dave had worn every day since we'd landed in France and, worryingly, had never washed. Perhaps his feet were more fragrant than mine. If I'd worn a single pair of socks for a month, my toes would've dissolved. I was glad I'd stuck to sockless sandals, even if the sun had caused my bare feet to resemble a tiger's.

Anne didn't eat much meat and James didn't eat any but that didn't matter. She put together a feast of various tasty salads, eggs, bread and cheese and tuna mayonnaise. This was followed by coffee and ice cream. We were in heaven.

I felt like I was talking endlessly, but I'd a lot of words to get out, ones locked inside without a willing recipient for weeks on end. Joe and Dave sat there mostly in silence although Anne did try to draw them in.

"Did you ever feel like giving up?" she asked.

"I didn't feel like giving up," said Joe. "But I seriously considered going slower and telling Dave and Steven to go on without me."

Dave's answer was more of a surprise.

"There was one particular day for me," he said. "Remember when we went to that supermarket in France on a Sunday and it closed at twelve-fifteen? I'd had enough. I wanted to leave. But I thought I'll just stick it out until Santander and then jump on a ferry home."

"It's just as well we didn't go to Santander then," I said.

After dinner, we went into the garden. Beside a walnut tree that'd produced a hundred kilos of nuts the previous year, there was a tunnel of wisteria with some comfortable chairs inside. We sat there and talked.

"The vines weren't in very good condition when we arrived," said Anne. "But they're improving each year. This year we're hoping for 70 tonnes of grapes. At their best, they could produce 90."

Anne and James didn't know how many bottles of wine that equated to. They sell the grapes to a cooperative who make the wine themselves. It turns out 90 tonnes of grapes produces 70,000 bottles of wine. That'd be one hell of a party.

They had big plans for the site. They wanted to restore the old chapel and perform weddings there. James had a large, Alan Moore-style beard and would've made a great priest but he'd leave that job to someone else. There were also four derelict cottages near the entrance that could be converted into holiday homes. It'd be an inspiring place for any wedding photographer.

The next morning Anne and James helped us to forage some fruit from their trees, oranges, lemons, plums and nectarines. She also gave us a handful of her home-grown onions.

After a breakfast of muesli and scrambled eggs on toast – the scrambled eggs were on the toast, the muesli wasn't – it was time to say goodbye. We set off again having been thoroughly spoilt, now with clean bodies and clothes that smelled of soap. I felt energised and ready to tackle the last ten days of this hungry adventure.

We cycled through Viseu and, on the edge of town, discovered another huge shopping centre, which included a supermarket. Once through the sliding doors, I was transported into the future. From the lobby, I could see six storeys of pure white joined by gleaming escalators. It looked like an artist's impression of how they wanted it to be in reality. And despite this being a workday morning, it was full of people, loaded with multi-coloured carrier bags, doing what was expected of them in this cathedral of consumerism. We, on the other hand, popped to the supermarket and each bought a small packet of bread rolls for 48 cents. If everyone lived like we had over these last two months, the economy would collapse. With a little tweaking – like the addition of a loving partner, a couple of witty best friends, a tiny pile of books and the occasional pint – I think there'd be more meaningful satisfaction in our current lifestyle with its exercise, fresh air and healthy eating than could be generated by attempting to buy happiness with an already overburdened credit card in a massive, sparkly mall.

My mind was off in the clouds. I was brought down to Earth as I left the shop when an English woman walked past.

"Oh my, that beard!" she said in a shocked voice.

I'd seen my reflection in Anne's bathroom mirror – it was the first time in several weeks – and I was taking on the appearance of a pale-faced Osama bin Laden. My facial hair was doing that weird thing that only seems to happen to the religious, where that part on the edge of the jaw flares up and thickens. It made me look like a Hajj was imminent.

The direct route towards Seville should've been due southeast but the huge Estrela mountain range obstructed our way. We'd therefore head south and hang a left later. This laziness had perhaps saved us other pains. An enormous fire raged across the distant mountains close to the road that a more direct route would've taken. On a windless day, the smoke climbed high and billowed outwards at altitude. It looked worryingly like a nuclear explosion.

We passed a restaurant offering a similar deal to the one ubiquitous in Spain, a daily three-course menu. However, in Portugal, the name of this offer was a *diaria*. The stressed syllable of that word would determine how appealing it sounded.

I'd asked Anne if she had an old paperback she no longer wanted, the weirder the better. In a layby I was reading an old, unwanted gift of hers, a book called *The Magic of Precious Stones*. It was completely bonkers.

Where the hell was Joe? I'd been there for half an hour. Now we were down to one functioning phone, no one could contact anyone else when we were separated. I'd give him another ten minutes and then go back and look for him.

I returned to my book. The first page included nonsense

about cosmic forces, planetary spirits and archangels. It was clear this paperback would at least provide some comedy for the remainder of the trip. By page three, I'd been told the ordinary sense organs are shaped by the ordinary planets, like Venus and Jupiter, but the clairvoyant senses by "mystery" planets. Which was half true, given that neither clairvoyant senses nor mystery planets actually exist, but not what the author meant. It was like rifling through Derek Acorah's underpants, full of spiritual bollocks.

Joe didn't appear and so I cycled back to find him. A mere half mile down the road, I saw him coming towards me. He'd suffered yet another double puncture. It was another blow on what hadn't been his favourite day so far. The sun had been shining strongly since morning and it was now properly Mediterranean in its summer heat. I much preferred it to the rain but Joe looked like he was melting.

At 45 miles, today had been our shortest day since arriving on the continent but it was that time again. We cycled down a road that disappeared into a forest and found a large clearing. In the distance, another forest fire had created a second mushroom cloud. It was the end of the world.

We set ourselves up and, using the last of the communal meths and my remaining eggs, we had our final cooked meal. From now on, it'd be raw food all the way.

The next morning, the sun had disappeared again, something Joe seemed happier about. Despite having altitude to attain, the hills at the beginning of the day were the perfect gradient to power up and I quickly ticked off the miles. I stopped to pick some roadside mint for my evening meal.

At a *Lidl* in Arganil, Joe decided just what type of raw food he'd be eating for the remainder of his journey. Once again, his decision was based entirely on calories rather than gustatory considerations. He bought a box of instant mashed potato. Without fuel to fire up his stove, he intended to reconstitute this astronaut food using cold water. He was already used to having certain meals taste-free and unheated. Dave and I had already donated what was left of the porridge. I'd have baulked at cold porridge, especially with nothing to jazz it up. The warm stuff was bad enough. Just because we had the tiniest of budgets, it didn't mean we couldn't *try* to eat well.

As we sneaked over the southern edge of the Estrela Mountains, we climbed high and once through the trees we popped out on one of Europe's most magnificent bits of tarmac. The word 'skyroad' was spray-painted on the ground. The name was apt. We stayed high and the road hugged the contours of the mountainside, remaining almost flat. The sun had since come out again but the altitude kept us cool. We could see for miles on a road that snaked gloriously through the mountains for twelve miles. This was a special road. The views were staggering.

We arrived in the town of Pampilhosa da Serra and sprawled out near its fountains for a rest and something to eat. I read my book for a bit and learnt that crystals are always found with their points facing upwards because they are tugged by a 'star force', which is definitely something the author should tell scientists about because it'll be news to them. Maybe if I could fill my pockets with sparkly rocks, this mystical energy would help me over the hills later this afternoon. I'd have a look in Dave's magpie collection. Perhaps he'd found something already.

"Last night," said Joe, "I dreamt of figs." Dave and I looked at him wordlessly. "Those are the kind of dreams I have these days."

That was probably my fault. I'd been extolling the virtues of the humble fig and hoping we'd find some ripe ones before the trip was over. So far we'd found none.

Although the afternoon was hilly, the gradients once again allowed us to keep moving. By the time we stopped and found a place in a hillside forest, we'd cycled nearly 80 miles, the longest day of the trip. From the road outside the forest, we could look down to a distant city sitting on an infinite dusty plain.

Foodwise, it was now every man for himself. How would Dave cope with the removal of his lentil, pasta and egg staple, the meal he'd enjoyed a variation of every day for a month?

Chickpeas are a useful cold ingredient on a budget, a large cooked jar of them costing only 55 cents (39p). We'd all opted for them in a variety of recipes. Joe had an instant mash and chickpea salad, which looked as dull as it sounds, and Dave had chickpeas and mystery-meat sausage. I decided to fancy mine up a bit. After I'd complimented Anne on one of her salad dressings, she pre-mixed me a small bottle of olive oil and balsamic vinegar to take on the road. I built a salad of chickpeas, orange segments, finely chopped onion, torn mint leaves and bready croûtons, and drizzled it with a combination of Anne's dressing mixed with a drop of my own chilli sauce. It was wonderful. Well, it was better than instant bloody mash.

I was waiting on the road when Joe pushed his bike out of the forest. He stopped walking and looked down at his bike.

"Oh my God! Why?" he wailed.

He'd suffered another puncture. His inner tubes had more holes than the wall around Oliver Reed's dartboard. He was out of spare inners, which meant we'd once again have to sit patiently while he fixed it.

At least I had my book. I learnt how to use crystals to make wishes. Each request has to be repeated three times in exactly the same words. Apparently, the angels merely notice you the first time, give serious consideration the second time and it's only the third time they get to work. Angels are obviously paid by the hour. I picked up a pebble and wished Joe wouldn't have any more punctures. It didn't work.

We finally set off. A little ahead, I discovered a thing of beauty and was really glad I hadn't wished for it or else I might've had to accept angels and magic stones really do exist. It was a small tree dripping with purple figs. I ate one or two of the plump, fat ones, so soft and sweet, the interior blood red. Even better were the ugly, shrivelled ones, those that looked like they'd be better left on the branch. They were wonderfully chewy, their sweetness intensified. I filled a bag and continued.

I was approaching Salgueiro de Campo. On the hill into town, I stamped down a little awkwardly on my pedal and heard a crack. My chain had snapped. Salgueiro was only small and seemed unlikely to have a bike repair place. I'd have to push to the next big town twelve miles away.

Luckily, our team had someone who knew more about mending bikes. Two minutes after Joe had started, my chain was as good as new. It was the first time I'd watched someone fix one. It looked embarrassingly easy, something I should obviously know but didn't. I shared my haul of figs as some sort of half-arsed thank you. Joe popped one into his mouth with fingers black with chain oil.

We arrived in Castilo Branco and had a choice of two large supermarkets. We picked one at random. As though psychically knowing our mission, a bloke approached us.

"The other supermarket is cheaper," he said.

Or maybe we just looked desperate. But, anyhow, if the other one was cheaper, why did our advisor go into this one? We were suspicious. I went inside, bought a baguette, some more chickpeas and a couple of tomatoes and then made a dick of myself trying to use the Portuguese-only self-service checkout. I wasn't the only one struggling. We would all have got out of there a lot more quickly if the shop assistant helping us duffers had just sat at a till and swiped the products herself.

I was a long way ahead. I discovered two more fig trees – the first one hadn't been an anomaly – and filled another bag. I sat at a bus shelter waiting for Dave and Joe to come past. I ate the figs like sweets, forgetting about their laxative effect. When the party in my stomach kicked off, I decided to go easy on them for a while.

Dave and Joe found some figs of their own. The combination of Dave and figs didn't sit well. He was already overly fond of the porcelain throne. If he also filled up with figs, he was condemning himself to a lifetime on the toilet.

Five miles down the road was the town of Segura, with its lovely hilltop church. Out the other side, the Roman de Segura bridge straddled the Erges river that acted as a natural border between Spain and Portugal. A sign on the bridge showed exactly where the border was. Dave posed for a photo with a foot in each country, a game that's lost most of its meaning in these post-Schengen times.

There was only Spain left now. It was time to put this thing to bed.

Days Completed: 58
Ride and Seek: **Total spend £53.08, per day £0.92**
Live below the Line: **Total spend £55.34, per day £0.95**

Chapter 14: Led Astray by Teens

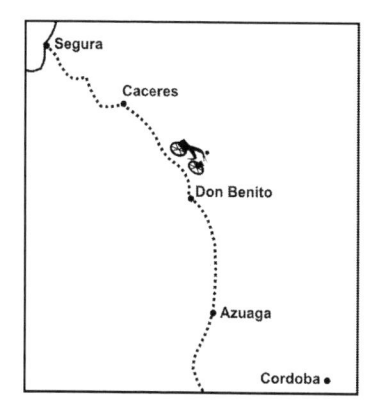

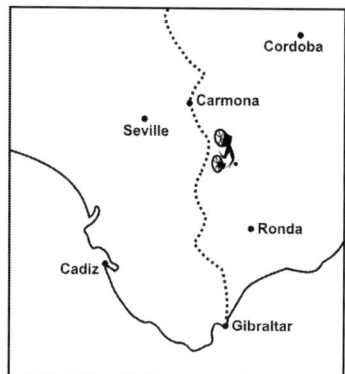

The Spanish roads were quiet. This was Extremadura, one of the wildest, least populated regions of Spain. The few cars that did come in the opposite direction often tooted and waved as though they hadn't seen a human for weeks.

We crossed the impressive six-arched, second century bridge near a modern hydroelectric station and climbed into Alcántara and out to the lonely countryside beyond. Near a lake were some orange fields surrounded by a fence but with an open gate. A sign hanging upon it seemed to suggest the area was open to public hunting – that is, hunting *by* the public rather than hunting *of* the public – although that could've been selective translation on my part. A track disappeared over a little hill.

"There doesn't seem to be anyone around," said Joe, ready to stop.

"I'll have a look over that hill." I wheeled my bike up the rough, stone track and could see a farmhouse a quarter of a mile away and then reported back. "As long as we go down by that wall, I doubt anyone will see us."

We set up our tents and knocked some food together. Then a bull turned up. I hadn't noticed livestock on this arid land. The cattle must have been on the other side of the hill. The bull and two cow-friends watched us for a while, waited for us to move but then got bored and wandered off.

"That was close," said Joe.

"At least no human's gonna find us."

"*Buenas!*" said a gruff Spanish voice.

We swivelled our heads. The farmer came walking past with a barking sheepdog. We said hello. He clearly didn't give a sod. The more we wild-camped in Spain, the less anyone seemed to care.

Today we discovered a new malady. All three of us were suffering from 'fig tongue', a sort of mild, slightly uncomfortable burning sensation in the mouth. Apparently, it's caused by the fig's abrasive skin. We didn't need to worry though. I'd done my own research and I knew the perfect crystal to cure us.

We sat under the trees, near the wall by the lake.

"Wow," said Joe. "Look at that!"

"What?"

"That there. It's a hoopoe."

"A what?"

"A bird. I've never seen one before," he said.

I only relate this brief, seemingly unremarkable tale because Joe would later describe this incident as the highlight of his entire trip. He said it made him realise he was somewhere a bit exotic. Apparently, you don't get these orange-crested, black-and-white birds in the UK and it was, for him at least, a bit special. Maybe if you're a keen twitcher yourself, you can appreciate the value of Joe's sighting, or maybe everything else about Joe's trip had been so thoroughly miserable that this was the only joy he could wring from his 58 days so far.

The situation with Nina took a sudden kicking. I'd been planning to spend winter in Andalusia. Unfortunately, money was tighter than normal and I could no longer afford to live in the coastal resort I had in the past. I needed to move inland where property was cheaper, but I also wanted to live somewhere I knew people. Nina's village was ideal. For reasons not entirely clear, she said she'd prefer I didn't live there.

After a breakfast baguette smeared with home-made fig jam in the attractive old centre of Brozas, we climbed back on to the bikes and heard a familiar wail. Upon closer inspection, Joe discovered last night's campsite had kindly donated six tyre-piercing thorns. Dave and I sat on a wall in the sun, waiting for the repair.

I read some more of my book and learned that a precious stone doesn't even have to be a real stone to weave its magic. If your office has an environment of rivalry and dispute – and whose doesn't? – then you can eradicate this negativity by simply drawing a picture of a crystal and putting it inside one of your drawers. Amazing. I drew a sketch of a hamburger, but it didn't make me feel any less hungry.

Eventually, we got going again. We came to a petrol station and needed the toilets. The doors were locked and so I asked for the key.

"For the gents'?" asked the woman behind the counter.

That question took me by surprise. I hadn't realised that, with my huge beard, I was looking so androgynous. Conchita Wurst might be able to pull it off but I'd make one ugly woman.

After yesterday's fig overload and resulting 'fig tongue',

we were going a little easier on the purple fruit. In any case, we weren't all sure how much we liked them. Joe was particularly unimpressed with the large jar of fig jam he'd made and, sensing an opportunity, he tried to sell it to Dave. Dave, however, was shrewd enough to know it was a buyer's market and refused the offer. In the end, knowing he was never going to eat it himself, Joe simply gave Dave the jar so he wouldn't have to carry it any longer.

We made our way towards our last city of the trip, Cáceres. As we approached town, the traffic thickened and the roads grew angrier. By the side of the road was a *McDonald's*. Nothing surprising there, but attached to it was the *Ronald Gym Club*. How great to think you could spend three hours pumping iron and then replace those calories next door with two fries and a quarter of a *Big Mac*. We could see through the window of the gym. It was completely empty. No *McFlurries* were being burnt off today.

We continued to fight the traffic until we found the pedestrianised centre. A huge restaurant poster advertised grilled pork chops. I rarely eat chops but I felt a sudden craving. My mouth filled with saliva and my brain with disappointment. We pushed the bikes into the sloping main square and lazed on the steps of the town hall, people-watching. I had to console myself with fig jam butties instead.

As always the topic of conversation was food. We had become slightly obsessed by our pancake-like omelette thing. At an inch and half, it was too thick to be a pancake and, by including flour, it wasn't an omelette, but it was the perfect carrier for other ingredients. We'd already made the plain version served with jam or soaking up soy sauce while served with lentils and pasta, and the caramelised apple variety as well as the sausage one. Joe wondered if it could be converted into something more pizza-like with the addition of tomatoes and melted cheese. I'd been fantasising about one that included peanut butter, bananas and crushed ginger biscuits drizzled with honey. Talking about food seemed to fill the hole left behind by not eating enough of it.

We also discussed the concept of a *Ride and Seek Cookbook*, a series of daily menus that came to less than a pound. But would people really want to eat what we'd been eating for these last weeks? Weren't we enjoying our food merely because we were starving? Would we even want to recreate any of these dishes once we were home? Dave clearly wanted to live on lentils, pasta and egg forever but I had no idea.

Leaving Cáceres was a lot easier than entering. I followed the south-east point on my compass to escape the warren of streets and eventually hit a long, dusty road out of town. We stopped at a garage to refill our bottles only to discover they had no water. Fortunately, the next one was better equipped. It also had a vine snaking around its exterior. We each picked a bunch or two of grapes.

The road was wonderfully quiet. We came to an old chapel sitting in a picnic ground. We wheeled the bikes inside for a rest and realised what a great place it'd be to camp, the church hiding us from the road, even though there was no one to hide from.

Tonight's meals made me realise a *Ride and Seek Cookbook* was almost certainly a bad idea. As a cost-reducing exercise, I simply had some more tasty fig jam baguette. Joe made a foul-looking dish of cold instant mash, onions and chickpeas. Dave experimented with a salad of chickpeas and orange. In itself this would've been alright, except he didn't drain the peas and poured their salty, preserving liquid on to his salad, and then added soy sauce to make a gloopy, dishwater grey concoction.

I went to sleep dreaming of a Full English Breakfast version of our omelettey-pancakey thing, with bacon, sausage, black pudding and mushrooms. And I realised that constantly calling it an omelettey-pancakey thing was a bit rubbish and we needed a proper name for it, something short and snappy. I had it! Your typical omelette is a bit insubstantial. Even its name suggests it's a diminutive version, an -ette, of something else. And it is. It is the smaller version of our omelettey-pancakey thing, our robust Om, spelt with a capital O so as not to get lost in its host sentence. I toyed with the idea of following its name with an exclamation mark – the Om! – but that was probably overselling it. It was, after all, nothing more than egg, flour and water.

It was long, sober nights lying in a tent and trying to go asleep while feeling hungry that filled my head with this sort of crap.

We cycled into Valdefuentes to discover it was market day. Everyone had come into town. The supermarket was rammed with old dears and their tartan, wheely shopping bags blocking the aisles. At the outdoor market, cheesy Spanish pop floated up from the CD stall. I bought 30 cents' worth of plump, ripe tomatoes from a veg stand, which doesn't sound like much until you realise they were an extremely reasonable one euro for two kilos. We sat in the town's little square, watching people mill about. For breakfast I had a baguette with sliced tomatoes dressed with salt, pepper and the dregs of the olive oil that'd accompanied us from the beginning, almost the archetypal Spanish breakfast.

We had overcome our fig overdose from a couple of days ago and were ready for more. We found a nice, overloaded tree and collected a bagful, but soon we'd find something we wouldn't have expected to forage.

As we cycled along, we saw a tomato lying at the side of the road, and then another. Every 100 metres another tomato would appear, ripe but split. The farther we cycled, the more tomatoes appeared and their frequency increased.

"It's like a Hansel and Gretel trail," I said.

"But where's it leading?" asked Joe.

"There!"

At the side of the road, just as we approached Miajadas, was a huge, red statue of a tomato on a ten metre pole. We had arrived in *La Capital Europea de Tomate*, Tomato City. Tomatoes are grown all around here and brought into town for processing, falling off the backs of lorries as they do. Dave and Joe started to scrabble around on the ground.

"Seriously?" I said.

"Some of these are pristine," said Joe, stuffing tomatoes into a bag.

Maybe I was just peeved that I'd had to pay for mine. At the next garage they washed their haul under its outside tap and sat admiring them smugly.

The road continued, now free of tomatoes, running parallel to a large motorway. There was no traffic on either. This part of Spain sometimes felt post-apocalyptic.

We had lunch in Don Benito, a scruffy, charmless sort of place. Joe popped into *Lidl* to buy more instant mash. He hadn't managed to convince anyone else it was the way to go but he clearly liked it, the freak.

Don Benito had originally been our proposed end point for today but it wasn't too late and so we continued onwards another twenty miles to Quintana, blown by a strong tailwind down a dusty road, and I'm really glad we did. We stopped at a garage on the edge of town and noticed a large fig tree. I got a small bagful while Dave stripped the rest of the tree.

Once through the painfully cobbled main street, we found another picnic site on the other edge of this tiny town and thought its well-shaded grass would be as good a place as any to stay the night. We were wrong. It turned out to be better than that.

We plonked ourselves down on a picnic bench and ate some baguette. Joe made a list of all the things Dave needed to do before checking in his bike. We weren't the only ones on the site. In the distance, fifteen teenage girls, somewhere between fourteen and sixteen years old, were shrieking and whooping. They seemed not to have noticed us.

Joe continued to make his list when suddenly the girls, and a handful of lads, gathered around our table and assaulted us in Spanish.

"There's no beach here," one of them said.

It was a strange opening statement.

"What?"

"There's no beach here," said three of them in unison.

"Yes, I know."

"But there's no beach."

"Yes. I know there's no beach."

Which part of my reply weren't they understanding?

"There's no beach," someone repeated.

"Yes. I know!"

"Oh."

Why the hell might we think there'd be a beach nearby? We were 200 miles from the nearest coastline.

"Do you want a drink?" one of the girls asked.

I wasn't expecting that.

"What kind of drink?"

"Gin."

Now I know the legal and moral issues involved if you *provide* alcohol to teenage girls and so surely the most ethical approach in a situation like this was to relieve the youngster of her alcohol.

"OK then."

"Lemon and ice?"

Ice? Oh my God! Ice!

"Yes, please."

Suddenly from nowhere three improvised cups appeared, the sawn-off bottoms of old *Fanta* bottles, full of lovely gin, lemon pop and ice. And they hadn't gone easy on the gin.

Sitting in the evening sunshine, the chilled drink tasted wonderful. The alcohol slowly seeped into our bloodstreams. The girls wandered off, but when they saw we were getting low on booze they returned.

"You want another one? We've got rum too."

"Why do you have all these drinks?" I asked.

"It's a party. Rum?"

"Yes, please. Whose party?"

It was the seventeenth birthday of Lidia, who appeared to be the leader and the only one of them who could speak any English. She was from Madrid but almost everyone else hailed from the Basque Country. I asked but never truly understood why they'd all travelled hundreds of miles to party in a small village in remote Extremadura.

But there was a problem. One of the girls had taken Lidia to one side and seemed to be lecturing her. I assumed she was annoyed that the party drinks were being so generously gifted to the foreigners, but it turned out to be far sweeter than that. She was worried we'd get too drunk and be ill. Clearly, she hadn't heard the stereotypes about the English.

Another drink arrived and the girls gathered around our table. Questions went back and forth. Lidia and I acted as interpreters, a job made easier for me with the addition of gin and rum.

"Here, have this," said Lidia.

She dropped a sixteen litre bucket on to our table. Dave, Joe and I peered inside. It was half full of a dark reddish liquid. Ice cubes and half a watermelon floated on the surface.

"What is it?" I asked.

"Wine and cola."

Wow. That was a lot of liquid.

"How much wine?"

"Half and half. Have it. We don't want it."

So we'd now received about four litres of free wine. I feared mixing it with cola might have buggered it up, but it tasted great.

The girls disappeared for a bit before returning.

"Sorry," said Lidia. "We just had to take someone to the hospital."

"Why, what happened?"

"A girl broke her nose. She fell over." She quickly changed the subject. "Why are you here?"

We explained what we were doing and mentioned foraging. A young lad had been listening. He left our table for ten minutes and then returned with a gift.

"For you," he said.

He presented us with a watermelon and a honeydew melon.

"You foraged these?"

"He took them from that field over there. It's alright. The farmer won't miss them."

The wine was making us giddy. I convinced one of the girls to give flamenco lessons to Dave. He pranced around, giving it his best, a huge, beaming grin painted across his chops.

"Are you going to write a book about your trip?" Lidia asked.

"I hope so."

Everyone suddenly went mental. It was as though I'd just told them I was Simon Cowell and that right here, right now, I was going to make one of them a star.

"Can we be in your book?" one of the girls asked.

"If you give me your names."

A pen appeared from somewhere and the huddle around the table started to write on the inside cover of *The Magic of*

Precious Stones. So here's a big shout out to Cabo, Carolina, Chema, Francisco, Juan Antonio, Juan Sierra, Leire, Leonor, Libe, Mari, Maria, Mariangeles, Naiara, Noe, Paqui, Paula and Ruben.

Around ten o'clock, some older lads, in their early 20s, turned up in cars with angry engines. Being more dangerous than we were, the girls' attention drifted in their direction. We didn't mind. By then we'd finished the bucket. I bet the youths were pissed off we'd necked all the strong stuff. I'd have no trouble sleeping tonight.

The next morning, alone at the picnic area, we surveyed the detritus from the night before. Despite there being dozens of orange and *Coke* bottles scattered around, I could only see one empty bottle of rum and another of gin, and they'd given a lot of those to us. If the teenagers had gone to the not inconsiderable trouble of accessing so much booze, it was odd they were so reluctant to drink it. Kids today, eh?

We decided on two breakfasts. The first was yesterday's honeydew melon. It was deliciously sweet but not filling enough and so we cycled into town, back over the annoying cobbles. This pueblo appeared to have only a crappy little supermarket and the only fresh bread on offer turned out not to be. Rather than a stale baguette, I opted for a laboratory-made sliced loaf.

We had our second breakfast in the town's main square. It was a strange place, with a few large, stone benches and then, beside each of them, a half-metre square piece of astroturf, like the world's smallest putting green.

I remembered back to the days when we shared a communal loaf. We'd sometimes have only two or three slices for breakfast. Here I was scoffing six slices and it still wasn't enough. My body had become used to starting the day with a substantial baguette rather than this sliced rubbish that felt like 95% fresh air.

I wasn't altogether enjoying my breakfast and it wasn't just the bread. I was sick of eating parts of my own beard every time I took a mouthful of food. How the hell does Brian Blessed cope? With no razor on board and no willingness to waste precious funds on a new one, the beard would have to stay until Gibraltar.

In lots of countries, the sight of a man on a bike full of luggage will win you a lot of attention, in some places too much. Spain isn't like that. I reckon we could've been dressed as Barney the Dinosaur and still been ignored. Don't get me wrong. Spanish people are perfectly friendly and will return or even initiate a hello, but it's a rare occasion when they stop you in the street and ask you why you're sitting in their obscure, little village. And so it was a surprise when a bloke came up to us and asked to take our photo. We stood beside our bikes but the fella struggled to get his flash to work. He asked us to move into the sun, which we did. Now in the spotlight, we'd become professional models. This gave the green light to two other photographers, who started snapping away. It was like a mini press conference, except no one asked us anything.

With the photo-call over, we pushed our bikes out of town led by the original photographer. He lived in Barcelona but was here for a three-week holiday. Maybe he just liked peace and quiet. Or maybe this backwater was Spain's new Benidorm.

The morning's ride was flat and uneventful, and a strong headwind made it unpleasant. By lunchtime we'd reached Azuaga and found a park for lunch. A party was going on. It was the 15th of August. The Azuagueños were celebrating Mary's admittance to Heaven, as was most of Catholic Europe. I bet Jesus was glad to see his old mum again. At least now he had someone to do the ironing.

My stomach didn't feel like partying. I repeatedly loaded two more slices of bread with fig jam, ate them and then waited until I felt some relief from today's gnawing hunger. I got through twelve slices before I was anywhere close.

We continued out of town, back through the dusty, orange landscape with few villages and only the odd, lonely house. Hoping to spark another gin-fuelled event like yesterday, we found a picnic site on the edge of a town. I'd worked out how many miles we needed to do each day to get to Gibraltar in time for Dave's flight. It meant a daily average of less than 50. This wasn't enough to fill the day. We had arrived at the picnic site too early. Dave and I sat around, reading. Joe just looked bored. It was just as well we hadn't stuck to the original daily mileage. We would've had an extra two hours of this every day since we arrived in France and there'd still be six more weeks to go.

Mild relief came at dinner time. Joe had instant mash, raw onion and roadkill tomatoes. Low on cash, Dave just had a sandwich. I made a chickpea and fig salad with a lemon and olive oil dressing. It wasn't enough.

As it started to get dark at half past nine, we put our tents up but sleep was difficult. We might not have found a party but someone else had. Although distant, the music and compère were loud, but it was nice to know at least someone was having a good time in this town.

The music continued until six in the morning. Mary must have been one hell of a woman. We got up and had breakfast. I finished off the useless loaf I'd bought the day before and vowed never to buy such insubstantial shite again. The music started up again and continued until we left around ten.

We rolled through a village called Malcocinado, bizarrely meaning 'undercooked'. Maybe it wasn't the best place to order chicken. We needed to find a town called Alanis and, beyond it, the gateway to Andalusia. I asked an old fella if we were going in the right direction. He gave a five minute answer, most of which I didn't understand.

"Is that a yes or a no?" I asked.

Again, his response flowed in paragraphs.

"Yes or no?"

"Yes."

"Thanks."

Maybe he just wanted someone to talk to.

Today we decided on a new eating strategy. To make our food feel like it was going further without actually increasing the volume, we'd have two half-lunches, one around midday and the other a couple of hours later. Ours was in the shade of a petrol station. Joe took austerity off the scale by manufacturing both a sugar sandwich and a salt-n-pepper sandwich. We were living the dream!

Later on, we passed the day's only fruit tree, a type of plum, purple-skinned with yellow flesh and a saliva-sucking dry aftertaste. We saw lots of brambles loaded with fruit but no one could be arsed to pick them any more. The figs had made us lazy. Half an hour of fruit-picking from a blackberry bush would generate the same quantity of fruit as two minutes with a fig tree. Unfortunately we couldn't find any fig trees.

Our second lunch was taken in Constantina, a lively town that was chilling with a cold beer in the afternoon sun before its fiesta kicked off again in the evening. We sat on a bench on the town's main pedestrian thoroughfare and watched people walk past with their dogs. The hounds would squat and do what nature intended. One owner even picked up after her pet. When it came to civic responsibility, Spain was finally moving into the 1970s.

The town was surrounded by forest. We looked for a place to stay but we'd become hooked on picnic sites for our evening accommodation. We could hang about there inconspicuously, and sitting on benches was more comfortable than the ground. And then, as darkness fell, we'd quickly set up our tents. There was also the false hope of another bucket of wine. Unfortunately, this area was devoid of picnic sites.

We screamed down a hill and realised we were nearing the larger town of Lora del Rio. We found a grassy spot not even slightly hidden from the road and, more through lack of imagination than anything else, decided to stay. We'd become less and less bothered about being concealed from view. Nobody cared.

Before dinner we chatted. I asked Dave and Joe what, if anything, they'd miss about the trip.

"I'll miss the camping," said Dave. "Especially camping in farmer's fields. I enjoyed that." He paused for a moment. "And I'll miss you and Joe."

"Aww," Joe and I said in unison.

"Yeah, I know. It's a bit gay, isn't it?"

I'd never been able to work out how Joe really felt about things. Unless he was tired or setting fire to himself with his stove, he kept his feelings unexpressed. I suspect he merely tolerated me. I know he was up for the challenge and would've tried to reach Gibraltar even if Dave and I had given up, but I'd no idea if he'd actually enjoyed it.

"I'll miss the lack of responsibility," said Joe. "Whenever I'm at home, I always feel like there's something I should be doing. Like finding a job. I haven't felt like that on this trip. What about you?"

He still wasn't giving much away.

"I'll miss the fruit," I said. It was true. I love fruit but when you're on a tight budget, as I'd been before the trip, it's the first thing cut from it. Here, on this ride, I'd eaten more fruit than I'd done in my entire life. I wasn't getting five a day, more like 35 a day. And I was feeling and looking healthier. "I'll also miss the freedom, being permanently outside, breathing fresh air all day long."

It was probably telling that neither Joe nor I had echoed Dave's sentiments about missing the other team members. I liked them both but this felt more like a professional arrangement to me, and I suspect also for Joe. We had a job to do and we would work together to get it done. It wasn't the beginning of a life-long friendship. My real-life friends, the ones I prefer to spend time with, tend to be a lot gobbier than Dave and Joe.

We had dinner. After this afternoon's rash purchase of a one euro pack of salami, there was no money for anything more than sticking it on a baguette with some fig jam. Dave also had fig jam sandwiches and, when the bread ran out, he took to tipping huge spoonfuls of the fruity preserve into his face. Joe went for instant mash, chickpeas and tomatoes.

"Hasn't your food become less interesting since we stopped cooking?" I asked Joe.

"No. This mash is great."

After three years of low-budget student meals, it seemed he could enjoy anything.

We lost the light and set up our tents. And that was when we noticed we'd camped near a kennels or a dog pound or some other form of canine penitentiary. One dog would bark and then 200 others joined in, most of them little, yappy ones. Then a larger, deep-voiced German Shepherd-type would tell them all to shut up. After a few minutes they'd start up again. I don't think Dave would miss this sort of camping.

After a sleepless night, we reached the centre of Lora del Rio. It seemed an oddball sort of town. Every village I've ever visited in this country has one or more small supermarkets, the popular Spanish chains like *Coviran*, *Komo Komo* or *Dia*.

Lora del Rio had two supermarkets with no names at all. The insides of both were similarly Communist-Russian in their product choice and quantities for sale. A huge shelf would display a single bottle of shampoo or a small bag of peanuts. It was as though my mum had used the contents of her kitchen cupboards to open a shop.

The day was warm. Although the rain had held back since we crossed into Portugal, many of our daily rides had been under an overcast sky. Even when the sun was out, the days rarely got as hot as they should've done for this time of year. Maybe Dave's God was giving us an easy ride.

The morning took us through a mostly flat landscape of orange soil and orange trees. At the side of a typically quiet main road, we passed a giant fig tree and restocked. I'd run out of sugar and didn't have enough money to buy any more. I'd still be able to make sugar-less jam with the figs. They were sweet enough by themselves. They'd have to be.

We stopped for our first lunch in the lovely old city of Carmona, built on a hill overlooking a vast plain. Old folk milled around, filling the benches in the main square. We found a spot and sat down. I placed my solar panel against a lamppost a few metres away to angle it towards the sun and then spent the rest of my time paranoid that a dog was going to sneak up on it and take a crafty piss.

It had taken Joe quite some time to catch us up in Carmona. He was falling further and further behind, even with his extra biscuits and instant mash. I too had started to feel a bit weary in the last few days. It wasn't much of a surprise. Restricted calorie intake aside, today was our 63rd day in a row – nine weeks – that we'd been on the bikes and the daily average for the last four weeks was over 60 miles. The cumulative impact was taking its toll. I think we were all ready to finish.

Maybe we should've had some rest days, but what would

we have done with them when we had no money to spend? I love books but I really don't want to spend an entire day reading. Any other sort of activity – going for a walk or exploring a city – wouldn't really be a day off. I was used to this. The only time I'd ever truly had a rest day on my 472-day ride around the capital cities of Europe was when I had an exam to revise for or an assignment to write. Presumably Joe's body needed more days off.

We left Carmona with a urine-free solar panel. Near a roundabout, an awkwardly positioned signpost took us down a steep hill it shouldn't have. Joe wasn't happy to have to regain the height to get back on the right road. If Dave was annoyed, he didn't show it.

We continued along the flat plain and stopped for a second lunch in the nothing town of El Arahal and a further rest in the equally uninspiring El Coronil. It was only fourteen miles between these two dusty pueblos, little more than an hour's ride, but Joe rolled in half an hour after Dave. He was seriously running out of juice, but an emergency rest day was out of the question. We had to get Dave to Gibraltar in time for his flight.

We decided to stop for the night. On the other side of town, we found a small, dilapidated picnic site. Its concrete benches had been partially destroyed. The ground was hard and would be difficult to penetrate with a tent peg but nobody could be arsed to look for somewhere better.

"I'm knackered," said Joe.

"We only have three days left," I said. "And if we can get close enough to Gibraltar on Wednesday, the last day is merely a short, flat trundle."

"Good."

"We shouldn't have any problems from now on."

I don't know where this prophecy came from. If I had a crystal ball, then it wasn't working properly.

"Have you decided what you're doing once we get to Gib?" I asked Joe.

Dave had decided to spend the time ahead of his flight in an inexpensive hotel in La Linea, the ramshackle Spanish town next door to Gibraltar. I'd do the same. Joe didn't have the necessary funds to stay in a hotel, even a cheap one.

"The campsite in La Linea is too expensive. I'll find somewhere nice and laze about for a few days, eating myself back to my starting weight."

It was hard to tell how much weight Joe had lost. He was skinny to begin with, but he'd mentioned his clothes were too big for him now. The small pot belly Dave had started with had also vanished.

The topic of *Morrisons* reappeared. Dave was now fixated on a peanut butter and *Nutella* baguette as well as a ham salad baguette. Our fixations were odd. Joe craved a packet of bourbons.

Joe had been particularly disappointed to learn the *Morrisons* in Gibraltar didn't stock their budget range, the food that had eased our passage through Britain. Even once the ride was over, Joe would be living on a tight budget until the end of his stay in Spain. He'd been banking on *Morrisons* to provide his staples.

Morrisons was less important to me. I just wanted a huge pizza and a gallon or two of cold beer. And I wanted to buy an English newspaper and sit alone outside a café in the shade reading it, drinking coffee and expending about seven calories all day long.

With Joe hiding away in the woods somewhere, the team in or near Gibraltar would be reduced to just Dave and me. I've never had kids but there was something about Dave that made me feel I was responsible for him while in Gibraltar. At times he was so innocently child-like. I worried if I didn't look after him he'd toddle in front of a truck or stick a knitting needle into an electrical socket.

At three in the morning my tent lit up. A car had pulled into the picnic area. With its engine purring it hung around for five minutes and then drove away. I quickly fell back asleep.

"Did you see that car last night?" said Joe as soon as I got up.
"I saw its headlights."
"It was a police car."
What would've been the point in moving us on? Where would we have gone? They could have tried to force us into the town's only hotel but I doubt its owners would've thanked them for the late night intrusion. The police simply took the Spanish approach. *No pasa nada*. Life's a lot less hassle if you let the little things slide.

We pushed our bikes out of the picnic area.
"Not again!"
There was a weary acceptance in Joe's voice. He mended his puncture while Dave and I hung about.

We reached Montellano in time for breakfast. It was shortly after this that everything went wrong. The plan had been simple. We'd pass through three towns – Puerto Serrano, Villamartin and El Bosque – and finish in or near Ubrique. As usual, I was out in front. We were only a few miles from Montellano when I saw a vague road sign suggesting I turn right. To begin with, it felt wrong, but then bingo! I saw a sign saying El Bosque was only fourteen miles away. I'd somehow managed to miss out two entire towns by taking a road not on my map and would save myself ten or fifteen miles in the process.

I couldn't guarantee Dave and Joe would take the same

turning as I'd done and so I texted Dave to tell him I'd meet them both in El Bosque.

Despite a long hill in hot sunshine through the trees that gave El Bosque its name, I reached the village about two hours earlier than originally planned. I found a shady spot on a bench beneath a tree and waited.

Now that we were back in Spain, *Three* had kindly enabled our phones again, which was just as well. I received a panicked text from both Dave and Joe. They'd become separated. Joe didn't worry me. He had a map. Dave didn't though. Not only that, Dave didn't even know where he was. It's difficult to send directions when you don't know where someone's starting from. I messaged Dave and told him to find El Bosque. I wasn't sure how he was going to do this. Along with no map, he had no Spanish either.

Things got worse. Joe was not far from Montellano, the town we'd stopped for breakfast, and had loads of punctures. He'd tried to fix them but there's only so many times you can patch an inner tube. He was stuck. He was going to push the bike to Puerto Serrano. If he couldn't find a bike shop, he'd have to hitch-hike to the bigger town of Ronda over 30 miles away. The team was in pieces.

After half an hour of waiting, Dave's gingery head appeared.

"I went into a petrol station and asked directions," he said.

"Good."

"Yeah, I would never have had the confidence to do that before this trip."

He didn't explain the mechanics of the exchange. I've yet to meet a petrol station worker in rural Spain who could speak English. I'd have paid money to see how he managed it. Not much though. I still needed to eat.

Dave and I waited for news from Joe. I lay on a stone bench and tried to snooze. A small group of Spaniards walked past and, seeing our bikes, tried to engage Dave in conversation. When they realised this wasn't possible, they started to ask other passers-by if they could speak English. I shook myself from my slumber and tried to interpret.

I told them where we'd been, what we were doing and why we were stuck here. They were impressed with our distance. One of the women looked at me sheepishly.

"But how is your, er, bottom?" she asked.

If I had a pound for every time a non-cyclist asked about the effects long-distance touring had on my arse, I could afford to rebuild it in titanium.

"Beautiful," I replied.

Joe texted again to say his battery was low and he'd now only use his phone in an emergency, but we should carry on to Ubrique and find somewhere to stay. If he didn't make it there tonight, we should set off in the morning and he'd try to catch us up the next day. If Joe couldn't get to Ronda today, we'd be forced to leave him behind or risk missing the flight altogether.

Unsure about what the next few hours would bring, Dave and I continued to Ubrique. Through its twisty and convoluted one-way system, we popped out the other side and started to look for somewhere that wouldn't attract the attention of the police but which we could easily describe to Joe. A couple of miles outside of town, we found the world's largest picnic site. It was huge, covering two entire fields. If we camped in its middle, we'd be unseen from the road. And surely Joe wouldn't have a problem finding something of this size. It was probably visible from space.

It was only around five in the afternoon. We sat around in the sun. I ate a couple of bread rolls with fig jam and Dave had a chickpea and fig salad. And we talked.

I discovered Dave had four sisters and he was the youngest in his family. The amateur psychologist in me wondered if this was why he lacked confidence. Perhaps he'd always been treated as the baby. That might also explain his fondness for *Sherbet Dib Dabs*.

And rather than being attracted to dead goats, Dave told of Cynthia. Apparently, a few texts had been flying backwards and forwards during the last weeks.

"I have met a beautiful Kenyan lady," he said. "And she has stolen my heart."

I felt like I was listening to a Victorian gentlemen.

"Oh, Dave. You old romantic!"

He had met Cynthia via a Christian website and was looking forward to getting home so he could see her again. He hoped to marry one day and have kids.

"If you got married, would you only consider a Christian?"

"Yeah. It's important to me."

He described his work history in more detail. He'd done various jobs but the only one he'd ever enjoyed was as a train conductor. Unfortunately, he'd been made redundant but longed to return. In the meantime, he'd done various unskilled jobs and ended up as a pot washer, stuck in a low-paid job going nowhere. Quitting the job to come on this ride hadn't been very difficult.

"So what will you do when you get back?" I asked.

"I don't know."

"Have you got any goals? Anything you want to do?"

"I don't really have goals."

He was quiet for a minute.

"What about you?" he asked.

"What, goals? I've got too many. I always feel I have to be doing something, moving forward. I can't switch it off. That's why I end up organising stupid shit like this."

"Well, I've enjoyed it," he said.

It started to get dark and so we set up our tents. We still had no idea where Joe was. He could be stuck in Puerto Serrano, or in Ronda, or anywhere in-between. As the light failed, my phone bleeped. Joe was approaching Ubrique and wanted to know where we were.

Our clever plan to place ourselves in the world's largest picnic area was for nothing now that it was this dark. Joe wouldn't have been able to differentiate our picnic site from a precipice. We waited by the road with our head torches. Cars occasionally rolled by. We must have looked very suspicious. After ten minutes, a tiny white light appeared. It moved slowly up the hill towards us. We shone our torches in its direction. My torch picked out a face.

"What a day!" said Joe.

He'd found Puerto Serrano's only bike shop but he'd had to wait two hours for it to re-open after lunch. The man there sold him two new inner tubes and a puncture repair kit. After surviving all this time on a pound a day, Joe had spent five day's budget in one bike shop transaction.

"Something weird happened tonight," I said to Joe.

"Yeah, what?"

"I talked to Dave."

"Eh?"

"We talked. Did you know he has four sisters?"

"No."

"Why didn't we know that? We've been doing this for over nine weeks."

"Well, men don't talk about things like that, do they?"

Don't they? I bloody do. But why hadn't I?

The next morning we began the long, often steep climb to Cortes. There was a sense of excitement in the air. Tomorrow this would all be over. We could stop pedalling. For now though, we had hills to negotiate.

The road, almost entirely free of cars, wound upwards, cork trees shading the tarmac. It was about fifteen twisty miles to Cortes de la Frontera, a bustling, white-washed village in the middle of its annual fiesta. It seemed like a friendly town. While filling up my water bottle at a fountain, an old, grey-haired English gent, who looked simultaneously intelligent and slightly wild, collected water in large jars. We exchanged hellos. I got the smell of turps off him.

"Are you a painter?" I asked. I could imagine him knocking out thoughtful but explicit nudes.

"No, I'm a journalist."

I didn't mention the turps. Maybe it was gin. We had a chat. He'd lived there a long time. He gave Joe a tip about a pretty spot to camp further along the road to Gibraltar. It wasn't always so friendly around here. I read a journal of a female cyclist who came this way in 2006. She was stoned by some kids who tried to wrestle her bike from her, poor sod.

I'd been looking at our numbers. Running two accounting systems side by side – the *Ride and Seek* rules and the *Live Below The Line* rules – had introduced some confusion. *Ride and Seek* allowed us to start with food that didn't need to be counted towards the budget. It also allowed us to receive free food along the way. *Live Below The Line* allowed neither. Under *Ride and Seek*'s rules we were well within the pound-a-day budget. By *Live Below The Line*'s rules, once we calculated how much we'd started with and factored in a realistic amount for the free meals we'd received, we were dangerously close to failing. But then I thought a little harder about it and realised we'd included quite a lot of things in the *Live Below The Line* account that shouldn't have been there. After all, you don't pay for cooking fuel with *Live Below The Line*, and you don't shell out for toilet paper, inner tubes and bicycle pumps. Taking this into account, we'd each a couple of extra quid in the bank. For our last day, we could get a little decadent. As Prince once said, tonight we're gonna party like we'd one pound ninety-nine.

We hit Cortes's largest supermarket, which, given this was a Spanish village, still wasn't very large. We bought potato tortillas, sausages, tomatoes and paté. Joe also got a bar of chocolate. We each also bought a one-litre tetrapack of 59 cent red wine. Don't say you're not jealous.

We had breakfast in Cortes outside the supermarket. My paté and fig jam baguette was amazing but I could hear the sound of a man approaching orgasm. I turned to look. Joe had constructed something he'd frequently talked about, a chocolate bar sandwich. No butter, no marg, you simply split your baguette, place a chocolate bar – the thicker the better – between the two halves and eat. It had to be tastier than *Smash*. Joe was in his happy place.

We trundled out of the centre of Cortes. Just as we'd left the masses behind, we saw a very special fig tree, the best yet. The plump fruits were the size of tennis balls. They could've won first prize at a horticultural show.

We were heading for the road joining Ronda to Gibraltar. The narrow tarmac took us down and down. After three miles of descent, we came to the bottom of the valley. Here we found Cortes's tiny railway station. It must be a right pain in the arse for the unaware to turn up here late at night with heavy suitcases and no taxis hanging about.

We could see where we were heading, to the top of the opposite side of the huge, lush, tree-covered valley. It looked high. Despite a temperature in the mid-30s, we sailed up the hill. Powered by his chocolate bar sandwich, Joe steamed to the top. This was the last serious hill before the Spain-Gibraltar border.

We had lunch in Gaucín at 600 metres above sea level and then began to roll down the hill towards Gibraltar. Looking back across the valley, Cortes was a thin, white streak splashed against the greenery. In the other direction, we could see The Rock in the far distance, standing proudly in a silver sea. Our work was almost done.

We didn't want to arrive in Gibraltar too late in the day – there was something we had to do there before the challenge was over – and so we'd already decided to get within a few miles of the place and find somewhere to camp. We passed through Los Angeles, a village as far removed from its American namesake as could be, and found a comfortable spot by a track in the woods.

We had our decadent meal. Only after what we'd been through over the past 65 days would a meal of processed tortilla, unspecified paté and tramp's wine feel decadent. But it did, and it was wonderful.

We discussed the past weeks, our highs and lows.

"I've never felt despair like I did after my seventh puncture yesterday and knowing I couldn't fix it properly," said Joe. "But when I had the eighth and ninth, I just laughed." He thought for a moment. "I think I went slightly mad."

"Do you reckon there's anything you'll do differently now, y'know, afterwards?" I asked.

"My diet's definitely going to change," said Dave. "Less meat, and more cost-conscious."

"I know what I'm going to do differently," said Joe.

"What?"

"I won't go on stupid adventures with people I've met on the internet."

He was joking but many a true word and all that.

"My only other tour was alone," said Dave. "I prefer cycling in a group."

"Maybe we can do another one of these," I said. "In eastern Europe. *Ride and Seek 2: The Baltic Challenge*."

"Yeah, I'd do that," said Dave.

My rose-tinted glasses were on. I took them off and remembered the hunger and frustrations.

"Nah, probably not."

"I hope I don't stop appreciating food," said Joe. "We did this as a challenge, an adventure, a bit of fun. We could've stopped at any time. But just imagine how awful it'd be to really only have a pound to live on."

While we were in such a talkative mood, there was something I had to ask Dave.

"You are, Dave, possibly the least decisive person I have ever met in my entire life." Dave gave a big grin. "How the hell did you decide to come on a trip like this?"

"Crumpets!" he said. "Well, I saw your thread on the cycling forum and thought I might enjoy it. Then you got all those negative comments from people saying you couldn't do it, or people would die and stuff. I wanted to give it a go and succeed. And then turn around and say ya-boo sucks to the naysayers!"

So, thank you, naysayers. Thank you for saying nay.

It was getting dark. Dave and Joe put their tents up. I tried an experiment instead. It was warm and so I tried to sleep outside my tent. It wasn't as idyllic as I'd imagined. Insects squeaked and landed on my face, and tree rats scurried along the branches over my head. I got about an hour's sleep.

Dave emerged from his tent singing *So This Is Christmas*. It was. It was Christmas morning and we were also off to meet The Wizard, the Wonderful Wizard of Gibraltar. We still had twenty miles to go, but it was all flat or downhill.

The further we got, the gnarlier the route became. On our road's crash barrier, graffiti told us Gibraltar belonged to Spain, and the English pirates should sod off. Spain's moral claim to Gibraltar could be taken a little more seriously if they handed back the two similar-sized enclaves they govern over in Morocco.

And then the road popped out of the trees and we suddenly saw Algeciras, the town across the bay from Gib, in all its horror. It is, possibly, the ugliest town in the world. It makes Port Talbot look like the sort of place cartoon animals might frolic. Algeciras is twinned with the Western Saharan town of Dakhla, which I'm reliably informed is a shithole, and the Death Star.

Eventually, we reached Petrochemical City and had a problem. According to the signposts, the only way to get to Gib from here was via the motorway. A Spanish guy in a little van was parked up. I cycled off to speak to him. He said he'd show me the way.

"Follow that van!" I shouted to Dave and Joe.

Like the *BMX Bandits* chasing a baddie, we followed him down a small side road, where he pulled over.

"Now just go straight on," he said. "All the way. If you come to a roundabout, just go straight across it."

The weather had started off promising. Since then it'd clouded over and was now getting seriously grey.

"Don't worry, Dave. The weather will get better when we get a bit further south."

We hit the coast and could see Gibraltar or, rather, about a quarter of it. The rest was smothered by dense cloud. We weren't really going to get rain on our very last day, were we?

We followed the coast through La Linea, opting for the cycle path. I felt a spot of rain on my forehead. We made our way to the border crossing, excited at the thought of an imminent meeting with relative financial freedom and a ton of shit from *Morrisons*. And then, in seconds, we were on the other side.

Across the airport runway we pedalled and hit the centre of town and Casemates Square. The place was rammed. Despite the weather hardly feeling like it, we were at the height of the tourist season. There were too many people about. We got off our bikes and pushed. For three scruffy tramps, we got a lot of smiles. But not everyone was happy.

"Bicycles on Main Street! Whatever next?" moaned a miserable old git on a mobility scooter, apparently annoyed by the space we were taking up, and without any irony whatsoever.

"Hey!" said a young fella. "Where've you been?"

We told him about the distance, the countries.

"And we've done it on a pound a day," I said.

He could have looked a little impressed.

"Yeah, you can live on a handful of rice a day, can't you?"

He wandered off. I looked at Joe.

"Could you live on a handful of rice?"

"No."

"Dave?"

"No."

"No, me neither. Silly bastard."

We pushed through the masses to the end of Main Street and got back on our bikes.

"Ready?" I said.

Joe looked up at the mountain, a little concerned.

"How far do we have to go up?"

"Just until we meet a monkey."

"How far is that?"

"About two thirds of the way up."

"Really?" said Joe, unable to hide the disappointment in his voice. "I thought it was going to be a lot smaller."

The roads were steep, not Porlock Hill steep, but still stupidly so. No one else was cycling up here. We came to the ticket office. There was no tariff listed for cyclists. The last time I'd come this way, the man on the desk had simply waved me through. This time it wasn't going to be so easy.

"How many of you are there? That'll be three pounds

please."

"What? No."

I couldn't pay him. That would've taken us over budget. I'd assumed we'd get through for free again.

"It's the same price for walkers," he explained.

This was a new pricing detail added since last time. It was the first time I'd had to adopt salesman mode since that farmer's field in northern Spain.

"Hang on a minute," he said. He left his booth and went into an office. Come on, I thought. Let us through. Two minutes later, he reappeared. "Since there are special circumstances, you can go through. But you can't visit any of the attractions."

"Thank you," we said in unison.

Upwards we went and to the point where I'd seen apes last time. There weren't any about. I'd heard some of them had been culled recently. They'd been getting above themselves and raiding the town. One had sneaked into a local hotel and caused mischief, the cheeky monkey.

And then, at last, we saw one, an adolescent ape, sitting alone, being photographed by a Japanese couple.

"Go on, Dave," I said.

He posed while I took a snap of him with his not too distant relative.

We'd done it! We'd cycled 3,359 miles in 66 days and by the rules I'd set, as well as *Live Below The Line*'s, we'd spent £66 pounds or less each on the road. The naysayers had been told ya-boo sucks. Yes, to travel a sizeable distance on one pound a day is possible, very, very possible.

I just really, really, really wouldn't recommend it.

Days Completed: 66
Ride and Seek: **Total spend £64.17, per day £0.97**
Live below the Line: **Total spend £65.89, per day £1.00**

Chapter 15: Filling a Void

Our first taste of frivolous spending happened two minutes after the monkey shot. On the hill back down into town, there sat an ice cream van, not a high quality purveyor of artisanal ices, but an old-fashioned *Mr Whippy* type. Y'know, the sort selling ice cream with the texture of shaving foam and a slight chemical aftertaste. We got a *99* each. Do you know how difficult it is to eat an ice cream while sporting a huge, unkempt beard, the majority of which dangles over your lips? I managed to get a mouthful or two, but in the end I looked like I'd just gone down on Frosty the Snowman's girlfriend.

It was very odd to spend money again, especially on something as unnecessary as this. After so long keeping a tight hold of the purse strings, it felt like cheating, like participating in something grubby.

While Dave and Joe ate their ice creams and I smeared mine all over my face, we looked down on to the town.

"I can see it!" said Joe in the voice of a man who'd crawled across a desert and spied an oasis. "*Morrisons*!"

"Yeah, but there's something I need to do before we go there," I said.

"What?" asked Joe.

"Beer."

Five minutes later, we were sitting outside a busy bar in Irish Town, which isn't a town at all, just a single street, with a pint in front of each of us. I had a cold glass of *Old Speckled Hen*. I don't remember what Dave and Joe had to drink. I was too focussed on my own.

Apart from a few small bottles of lager at Anne's in Portugal, our previous pint had been back in England over six weeks earlier. We'd had to be polite at Anne's. We couldn't sit there chugging one beer after another and yelling, "More, woman! Bring more!" But now we could.

That said, we still had to visit our Mecca to discover what we'd most missed during our ten weeks of deprivation and we didn't want to be sloshed for that. There was plenty of time for that later. We had a second pint and then hit the supermarket.

It was the first time I'd properly looked around a supermarket since we'd started. It was quite horrifying to see how far from nature humans have been removed. Everything, absolutely everything, is processed and packaged to death. Part of me wanted to get back on the bike and head for the woods. A slightly larger part though wanted to see if that shit tasted as good as I remembered. I bought *Haribo*, a bag of caramels, a packet of *Frazzles*, dry roasted peanuts, ginger biscuits, two steak bakes and, to quell my disturbing meths fixation, a bottle of *Jim Beam* whiskey. (Yes, I appreciate *Jim Beam* isn't like schnapps, but it was on offer and old habits die hard.) I also bought the necessary equipment to remove this sodding beard. When I included some plastic tubs and a tiny frying pan to make my onward journey easier, the whole lot came to over 30 quid. I'd spent more in one fifteen-minute shopping spree than I'd done in the entire previous month and, steak bakes aside, there were no meals to show for it.

"Me and Dave need to sort our hotels," I said to Joe. "Do you know where you're staying?"

"Yeah. We passed a place on the way in. Lots of trees. Seemed like it'll be alright."

We agreed to meet up the following lunchtime. Joe was going to stay near Gibraltar for the weekend.

In La Linea, I found Dave a cheap place but, aside from tonight, the hotel only had one room available. I'd have to find somewhere else tomorrow.

It was early evening. In my room I blasted through the *Haribo* and the peanuts and made a start on the *Jim Beam* while having my first shower in nearly two weeks. There was something immensely unsatisfying about everything.

I attacked my face with the razor I'd bought and within a few minutes had reduced my visible age by a couple of decades. It was nice to feel my chin again.

I put on my cleanest clothes – a t-shirt and pair of shorts that'd remained in my bag since Anne's washing machine – and hit the town. Well, I walked around the corner, found a bar, ordered a beer and then messaged Dave to tell him where I was. He came bumbling down the street a few minutes later.

"Crumpets!" he said. "You look weird without a beard."

"Cheers."

Around eleven, after an alarmingly small number of beers, we were tiddly and went hunting for food. We found a pizzeria and ordered two sixteen-inch pizzas.

"No," said the woman on the till. "That size is for two people. You should share one."

"You reckon you could eat a whole one yourself, Dave?"

"Definitely."

"Me too. Two pizzas please."

We took the food back to our respective rooms. My pizza fell down my cakehole in seconds. I was still hungry. I ate my caramels. I felt like I had a hole in the core of my being that begged to be fed but couldn't be sated.

I switched off my light and tried to go asleep. Joe popped into my head, all alone in the dark woods. It suddenly seemed scary, like something only a nutter would do. Just a few hours ago it felt like the most natural thing in the world.

The next morning, the hole was still there. I went out for breakfast, ordering an espresso and a *tostada con tomate*, the typically Spanish self-assembly snack. I rubbed the toast with garlic, loaded it with chopped tomatoes, liberally applied olive oil, added lots of salt and pepper and scoffed the lot. Despite costing two days' budget, it wasn't enough. I ordered another coffee and toast. I told Dave where I was. By the time he arrived, I was ordering my third breakfast. I feared I was John Hurt in *Alien* and, any minute now, something evil with big teeth was going to burst from my stomach. This hunger was untameable.

I marched off and found someone who would relieve me of my wild locks. She even trimmed my eyebrows unasked, a sign my body hair had probably gone a bit too caveman.

Making my way back to Gibraltar to meet Joe, I realised I'd overdone it on the coffee. My head was pounding and I felt sick. The blood pressure-reducing effect of weeks without alcohol and caffeine, on a restricted, fruit-heavy diet with loads of exercise – I'd lost three stone (20 kg) in 66 days – had been undone in one evening and morning session. I found a bench and lay down for a while, hoping the nausea would pass.

Twenty minutes later, I arrived at the same pub as yesterday. Dave was already there. Joe laughed when he saw the short-haired, beardless version of me.

"That's just strange. It's like the same voice and personality but an entirely different person."

"How was last night?" I asked.

"Yeah, alright. I might have somewhere else to stay tonight."

"How come?"

"I just got speaking to a bloke. He was asking about the trip. He said I could stay at his place. He said he didn't know if I was a dick or not, but at least I'd be an interesting dick."

I was feeling a bit better by now. I ordered another *Old Speckled Hen* and a lasagne, eleven days' food budget. Now I knew how little I could live off, it felt wrong to be spending as much as I was doing on very average pub food. By most people's standards, this would've been a cheap meal. To me now, it felt painfully expensive.

I wasn't able to find a room for tonight in one of the cheap but clean hovels in the centre of La Linea and so I booked a more expensive place a mile or so away. If you're used to the ridiculous prices paid for hotel rooms in Britain, then 50 quid for this hotel probably won't seem like much. But I was now working on a different scale. All prices were considered in terms of how many days I could've survived on that amount. It was a nice hotel but it was hard to accept that one night in its admittedly comfy bed was equal to a month and half's existence.

Nina had been back in touch. She repeated that she didn't want me to move to her village. It was, apparently, asking for too much commitment. It didn't seem like commitment to me. Living in the same town as someone is usually where a relationship starts, not something it builds up to over several years. She said she wanted her space, but I wanted to move into her village, not her house. She wanted me to live in Nerja as I'd done in the past, but I still couldn't afford it. And I didn't want to live somewhere I didn't know anyone. After the lack of conversation on this trip, I needed community. I asked her what she'd prefer, me in her village or me back in the UK. She said she didn't want me in her village.

Dave and I had been fantasising about a Chinese during the latter stages of the ride. Perhaps the All-You-Can-Eat buffet at the restaurant near my hotel would provide a more emotionally satisfying experience than everything else since I'd reopened my wallet. And perhaps it'd fill the void that still howled from my stomach.

The place was huge and the selection impressive but I made a fundamental schoolboy error and loaded my first plate with a mountain of deep-fried starters. It certainly filled the hole in me, albeit temporarily, but didn't leave room for the more interesting later dishes. Once again, the things I'd craved were not living up to their billing.

After the meal, Dave and I said goodbye to Joe for the last time. He got on his bike and cycled back into the woods. After 66 days of being trapped together every morning, lunchtime and night, he was gone forever.

Looking back, I feel I owe Joe an apology. There were many times, as he lingered in his tent craving a longer lie-in, or trundled along miles behind, or wanted to finish early, that I called him a wuss, if only inside my own head. I'd judged him unfairly. I'd assumed because he was young and slim, he should have been able to outgun Dave and me. But it was stamina that was missing, and you only build stamina over time. It's not by accident the best marathon runners are usually in their mid-30s. They certainly aren't 21. Our adventure was a marathon, both a mental and physical one. I should've cut him more slack, and for that I apologise. On *The Jam Issue* and his daily misappropriation of an extra tablespoon, however, he should've been sliced into small pieces and fed to piranhas.

The next day I drifted. I got a newspaper and drank some beer. I had a lot of spare pound coins in my pocket and so I headed back to *Morrisons* to see if there was anything I'd missed last time around. I bought a pork pie. It was rubbish.

It was our final night. Dave had organised a bike box from a local cycle shop and was ready to leave in the morning. We went out for a few beers and wandered around La Linea. We talked about his lack of confidence.

"In future, Dave, whenever you're feeling low in

confidence, you should remember this trip."

He smiled.

"You did it, Dave. Some people said it couldn't be done and you wanted to prove them wrong. You did it."

"I did."

"The other day you said you didn't have any goals. You did. You had this goal. Not only that. You did it on the shittest bike known to man."

He laughed.

"And you know what's more amazing? You never once complained."

"No."

"Not once. Joe complained. I complained. You didn't. You're amazing."

A big grin grew across his face.

"You are. You're amazing."

I gave him a moment.

"I am. I'm amazing," he said gently, like he'd finally absorbed it.

"Don't forget it."

It was all over, the ride and the three-day after-party. As far as rides went, it'd been an odd one. With no money to spend on hotels or in bars or restaurants, we hadn't met as many people as I had on previous trips and I'd missed that. But in its place was a more profound connection with nature, with paring down life to its simplest elements, finding food, moving along the road and seeking out a place to rest your head. But I needed people, different people, talkative people, funny people. I needed community. It was good to know that, should my finances fall even further, I could actually live like Ken, that rocket-eating mountain man, but I didn't want to. It was more comforting to know that, in future, no matter how poor I was, I could afford to travel, on one pound a day if necessary, but hopefully on three, five, ten or twenty.

The only time I didn't want community in future was while actually cycling along. I realised now that I preferred to cycle alone, except for a day or two here and there with close friends. Don't get me wrong. It was great to cycle with people who brought skills to the group. Sabby was a wonderful cook, Joe knew his stuff about bike maintenance and was a great navigator and patient teacher, and Dave was, well, Dave. But I like to move at my own speed and cycle for as long or as little as I want. I didn't like waiting around for people. I'd thought I was a lot more patient than I actually turned out to be. Maybe the lack of calories affected my mood. Or maybe I'm just becoming a grumpy, old man.

I'd been quite disappointed by the support from *Action Against Hunger*, the charity we were raising money for. After all, the more they promoted us, the more people would hear about the ride and the more donations they'd receive. They'd tweeted about us a few times and even said ours was the most gruelling challenge ever undertaken for their charity, but we never appeared on their website. We still don't. I have a theory why this is.

Perhaps the *Live Below The Line* campaigners, with whom the charity works closely, had told *Action Against Hunger* not to push our project too much. I'd written to the *Live Below The Line* people before I started planning the trip. I thought they'd be excited about what I was proposing to do. They didn't even respond. Perhaps they thought we were belittling the whole *Live Below The Line* concept. After all, if we could live on a pound a day for 66 days, pay for all our cooking fuel and travel from Liverpool to Gibraltar in the process, then their normal challenge – a mere five days of stationary deprivation – might not seem like much. But you should try it. It's an eye-opener. To last the five days is harder than you think. You'll probably obsess about food for the whole period. That obsession will make you hungrier than normal. You won't die but you'll begin to get a hint, but only a hint, of what it might be like to live with such poverty, just as a billion people on our planet do every day.

The next morning I was back on my bike. I climbed the huge hill to Ronda, an ascent of more than 1,000 metres, and under a hot sun reached the historic pueblo with a deep chasm running through its centre, a town cleft in two. My thinking was similarly divided. I had a choice. From here I could cycle 100 miles south and head to the eastern Costa del Sol, find a cheap apartment I could afford in an undesirable village where I knew no one and appease the woman I loved but who wanted to keep me very much at arm's length. Or realising that a relationship in which both parties couldn't inhabit the same town wasn't much of a relationship at all, I could retain some semblance of self-respect and pedal another 2,000 miles north to a different future.

I still miss her every day.

Appendix 1: Gear

Some readers are interested in a list of gear used by cyclists on rides like mine. Most aren't. That's why the list is tucked here at the back. This is what I took.

The Bike

My bike is a *KTM*, a manufacturer more famous for motorbikes, but I think they've started to sell their bicycles in the UK now. I bought mine in Austria fifteen years ago. I don't remember the name of the model and all the transfers that might have given me a clue have been rubbed off over time. It's a great, light, strong bike that is very comfortable to ride and cost me somewhere around £800. It has 700C wheels and is made of aluminium. Everything except the frame, handlebars and mudguards has been replaced at least once. I can't remember how many cassettes and chains I've gone through. It has now done in excess of 30,000 miles despite living in a garage unused for eight years of its life.

The Bags

The panniers are made by *Carradice*, two on the front and two on the back, and a handy bar bag for valuables. Despite being made of thick canvas and water-resistant, I always line them with plastic rubble sacks to keep the water out. They're very strong and durable.

The Home

The tent is a *Decathlon Quickhiker*. It is supposed to be a two-man tent but I wouldn't want to share it with anyone except an emaciated lover. In truth, it's a roomy one-man tent. The sleeping bag, whose stuff sack doubles as my pillow, is some obscure German make I bought twenty years ago. My ground mat is one of those five quid foam jobbies. While cycling, the sleeping bag lived in a front pannier but the tent and ground mat were encased in a rubble sack and bungeed to the back rack.

The Kitchen

This was my first time using a *Trangia 27* meths-burning stove. It was great and came with a nice selection of pans although the frying pan isn't really tall enough and, with flat sides, it made extracting Oms more difficult than it needed to be. I also took a chopping board, a rolling pin (never used) and a decent kitchen knife. I had a plastic bowl for mixing Om batter and eating food, a small, plastic cup, a fork, a spoon and a penknife.

The Wardrobe

I took two t-shirts and two pairs of cycling shorts, a donated cycling shirt from *Action Against Hunger*, a pair of walking-around-town shorts, a pair of sloppy shorts for the camp, a fleece and a rainproof jacket. On my feet was a great pair of super-durable *Keen* adventure sandals. Importantly, I took no socks or underwear. The sandals' ventilation reduced sweaty feet. Had it been colder, they may not have been so useful. I washed the shorts whenever I could. Because I was foolishly expecting hot weather, I took no hat or gloves.

The Bathroom

I took shower gel (used to wash clothes too), deodorant, a toothbrush, toothpaste, *Vaseline*, sun cream and a toilet roll. A sanitary trowel dug toilet holes. I also carried a first aid kit.

Foraging Gear

I had a telescopic rod that slowly rusted up and a box of

hooks, lures, spinners and weights that did the same. I also had a net with a telescopic handle and a backup pen rod.

I carried a cheap catapult but it was never used. When I took it out of the bag for the first time, I discovered the rubber was already splitting, and that was after only about ten practice shots.

I had a five-book library of *Collins Gems*, on foraging in general, mushrooms, fish, trees and the seashore. It's painfully slow to use them in the field and so we seldom did.

I also had some gardening gloves for tackling thorns and loads of resealable plastic bags for gathering and storing food.

Tech

A *Canon* digital SLR lived in my bar bag. If my *Kindle* had done the same, it wouldn't have broken after a few days. I also had a phone and a solar panel to recharge it.

Bike-related

I carried various tools, a puncture repair kit, two spare inner tubes and a folding tyre, none of which was needed. My front and rear lights were also never used. I had two 750 ml water bottles and occasionally filled an additional 1.5 litre pop bottle for extra water.

Everything Else

I had a passport, lots of blood pressure medication, maps of the UK, France, Spain and Portugal, a sewing kit, my diary and a few pens, a head torch and a wallet that saw less action than any other journey in my lifetime.

Appendix 2: Costs

In these costings, I only provide details for Dave, Joe and myself. The cost of all communal food that we bought is shared between however many of us were present at the time. When we were given meals, I have valued them at the average we were paying per meal on that particular leg of the trip. Although we all brought a different amount of food to begin with, it was shared communally and so everyone's initial food costs are the same. The *Ride and Seek* total is Purchased Food (which also includes drinks) plus Purchased Other, such as fuel, toiletries, inner tubes, etc. The *Live Below The Line* total is Initial Food plus Donated Food plus Purchased Food. With a total of 66 days of travel, our total budget in both cases was £66.

The exchange rate was €1.40 to the pound.

DAVE

Initial Food: £3.80
Donated Food UK: £4.32
Donated Food Europe: €1.40 (£1)
Purchased Food UK: £11.73
Purchased Food Europe: €62.70 (£44.79)
Purchased Other UK: £0.00
Purchased Other Europe: €2.91 (£2.08)
Ride and Seek **Total: £58.60**
Live Below The Line **Total: £65.64**

JOE

Initial Food: £3.80
Donated Food UK: £3.60
Donated Food Europe: €1.40 (£1)
Purchased Food UK: £11.73
Purchased Food Europe: €61.12 (£43.66)
Purchased Other UK: £0.00
Purchased Other Europe: €13.05 (£9.32)
Ride and Seek **Total: £64.71**
Live Below The Line **Total: £63.79**

STEVEN

Initial Food: £3.80
Donated Food UK: £4.32
Donated Food Europe: €1.40 (£1)
Purchased Food UK: £11.73
Purchased Food Europe: €63.06 (£45.04)
Purchased Other UK: £0.00
Purchased Other Europe: €10.36 (£7.40)
Ride and Seek **Total: £64.17**
Live Below The Line **Total: £65.89**

Also from Steven Primrose-Smith

NO PLACE LIKE HOME, THANK GOD
The No. 1 Amazon Bestseller

After a near fatal illness, Steven Primrose-Smith decides that life is too short to hang around. Inspired, he jumps on his bicycle to travel a road that stretches 22,000 miles across the whole of Europe.

During his ride through 53 countries, climbing the equivalent of 20 Everests, he dodges forest fires, packs of wild dogs and stray bulls, is twice mistaken for a tramp, meets a man in Bulgaria who lives under a table, discovers if ambassadors really do dish out pyramids of Ferrero Rocher at parties, transforms into a superhero after being savaged by radioactive mosquitoes near Chernobyl and comes close to death in France, Norway, Ukraine and Russia.

Such a massive challenge requires calories and Steven gets his from the more unsavoury elements of European savouries: brains, testicles, lung and spleen stew, intestine sandwiches, sausages famous for smelling of poo, a handful of maggots and even a marmot. Nobody eats marmots.

But the distance and his culinary adventures are only a part of the mission. His real objective is much more difficult. Will he be able to confirm something he has long suspected or will he, after all his searching, eventually find somewhere in Europe worse than his home town of Blackburn?

"There are many books about cycle touring but few are as entertaining, informative and engaging as this one...The result is a funny and informative account of his travels to some of the Continent's well-known and more undiscovered corners. The writing is excellent..." - **CYCLE *Magazine***

Also from Steven Primrose-Smith

GEORGE PEARLY IS A MISERABLE OLD SOD

Seventy year-old British ex-pat miserymonger George Pearly lives on the Costa del Sol, all alone except for his ancient, three-legged dog, Ambrose. George hates his life and everybody in it. These feelings are mutual. Everyone hates George too.

From this unhappy equilibrium the situation quickly deteriorates. First, George discovers he is dying of a mystery illness. Then his 35 year-old ape-child nephew, Kevin, moves into George's tiny and once tranquil home with a passion for Vimto, Coco Pops and slobbing around in his greying underpants. Worst of all, George's neighbours start to disappear and all accusing fingers point towards George.

Pull up a sun lounger, grab yourself a piña colada and enjoy a murder-mystery romp on Spain's sunny southern coast.

Printed in Great Britain
by Amazon